☆ ☆ ☆

# PARTY
# LEADERS

*in the House of Representatives*

☆ ☆ ☆

RANDALL B. RIPLEY

☆ ☆ ☆

# PARTY LEADERS

*in the House of Representatives*

☆ ☆ ☆

THE BROOKINGS INSTITUTION
*Washington, D.C.*

© 1967 by
THE BROOKINGS INSTITUTION
*1775 Massachusetts Avenue, N.W.*
*Washington, D.C. 20036*


Published December 1967


Library of Congress Catalogue Card Number 67-30601

☆

TO VIVIAN

☆

THE BROOKINGS INSTITUTION is an independent organization devoted to nonpartisan research, education, and publication in economics, government, foreign policy, and the social sciences generally. Its principal purposes are to aid in the development of sound public policies and to promote public understanding of issues of national importance.

The Institution was founded December 8, 1927, to merge the activities of the Institute for Government Research, founded in 1916, the Institute of Economics, founded in 1922, and the Robert Brookings Graduate School of Economics and Government, founded in 1924.

The general administration of the Institution is the responsibility of a self-perpetuating Board of Trustees. The trustees are likewise charged with maintaining the independence of the staff and fostering the most favorable conditions for creative research and education. The immediate direction of the policies, program, and staff of the Institution is vested in the President, assisted by an advisory council chosen from the staff of the Institution.

In publishing a study, the Institution presents it as a competent treatment of a subject worthy of public consideration. The interpretations and conclusions in such publications are those of the author or authors and do not purport to represent the views of the other staff members, officers, or trustees of the Brookings Institution.

# Foreword

This study of party leadership in the House of Representatives is part of a broader effort by the Brookings Institution to improve understanding of that complex and fascinating organ of government, the Congress of the United States. Numerous members of the House and Senate have generously assisted in these studies by giving information and opinions, participating in Brookings round table conferences and seminars, and acting as advisers to projects and critics of manuscripts.

The last book-length studies of party leadership in Congress were written in the 1920's, and articles of a more recent date are scarce. A 1963 Brookings study, *The Congressman,* by Charles L. Clapp, raised a number of interesting questions about the structure and importance of party leadership. In the present book the author has sought to answer these questions and to fill a gap in the literature by examining the development of party leadership in the House since 1861, emphasizing its present effect on the legislative business.

The Institution and the author are grateful to the Advisory Committee (Congressman Ed Edmondson of Oklahoma, Congressman Charles A. Mosher of Ohio, and Richard F. Fenno, Jr., Professor of Political Science, University of Rochester) whose members discussed the research with the author at several stages and read and commented on the manuscript.

A number of other persons also read and commented on the

manuscript. The Institution and the author are indebted to George A. Graham, Director of Governmental Studies, James L. Sundquist and Franklin P. Kilpatrick of the Institution staff, Professor Frederic N. Cleaveland of the University of North Carolina, Professor Charles O. Jones of the University of Arizona, Professor Joseph Cooper of Rice University, Professor Lewis A. Froman, Jr., of the University of California—Irvine, Professor Robert L. Peabody of The Johns Hopkins University, Professor Nelson W. Polsby of the University of California—Berkeley, Professor John F. Manley of the University of Wisconsin, and Vivian Usher Ripley, the author's wife.

Randall B. Ripley, a member of the Governmental Studies staff at Brookings from 1963 to 1967, now teaches political science at Ohio State University. The general outlines of his study took shape during a period of service in 1963 as an intern in the office of the Democratic Whip in the House, Hale Boggs of Louisiana. He wishes to thank Congressman Boggs and his administrative assistant at that time, D. B. Hardeman, for their extensive help.

The opinions, interpretations, and conclusions of this study are those of the author, and do not necessarily represent the views of the Advisory Committee, other persons who commented on the manuscript, or the trustees, officers, or staff members of the Brookings Institution.

KERMIT GORDON
*President*

*August 1967*
*Washington, D.C.*

# Contents

Text Tables

Appendix Tables

# ☆ 1 ☆

# Introduction

The American Congress has two broad responsibilities to the public. First, the legislation shaped by the Senate and the House of Representatives should be responsive to the needs of the country. Second, the legislative process should be conducted so that potentially disruptive conflict over fundamental social issues is avoided, or at least contained. Since the time of the Civil War, which saw the emergence of two-party politics, leaders in Congress have consistently exerted great influence in meeting these responsibilities.

Parties have organized the two houses of the American Congress since the beginning of the Republic. Only since 1861, however, has there been a clear majority party (in both a numerical and organizational sense) and a clear minority party in the House.[1] The goals of the majority and minority parties during

[1] On the change in internal House politics wrought by the Civil War see Neil MacNeil, *Forge of Democracy* (McKay, 1963), pp. 28-29, 72-73; and Mary P. Follett, *The Speaker of the House of Representatives* (Longmans, Green, and Co., 1896), p. 97. See also Appendix C in Follett, pp. 336-41. The figures on the election of Speakers in this appendix indicate that before the Civil War the votes for Speaker often did not range one united party against another. After the War each of the two candidates for Speaker had an almost completely united party voting for him. Only once since the Civil War, in 1923, has a factional fight endangered the chances of election of the majority party's candidate for Speaker. A compromise on some rules changes allowed him to be elected after several ballots. After the 1916 and 1930 elections the control of the House was in doubt. But in both cases a clear majority had emerged for the winning candidate by the

1

this period have changed, both in substance and in clarity. Their institutional arrangements also have varied greatly, as have the styles and personalities of individual leaders. Unlike the period before the Civil War, however, leaders of a majority party and a single minority party have occupied an unquestionably central place in the legislative workings of the House.

The party leaders, for purposes of this study, are the Speaker, the Majority Leader, the Minority Leader, the Majority Whip, and the Minority Whip. These are the most important formal positions of leadership, attained either through election by the parties or through appointment by elected leaders. The corporate concept of "the leadership" also includes officials of various party caucuses, committees, and organizations that are, from time to time, important in relation to legislation.

## Context of Party Leadership

Because this study focuses on the party leaders in their House setting, they may at times appear to make decisions solely on the basis of internal considerations. Thus it is necessary to keep in mind that other factors also influence the patterns of activity of the party leaders and members.

The President is an important influence on the role of party leaders. Over the last hundred years the President has become increasingly active in the legislative arena. Lincoln acted on his own and then sought some form of congressional ratification for his actions. Cleveland asked Congress for specific actions, particularly for substantial tariff reform. McKinley was more active than many of his predecessors in asking for congressional actions in both the domestic and foreign fields. Theodore Roosevelt presented the first full-blown presidential legislative program. Woodrow Wilson went further, presenting a broader program and laboring harder to make Congress enact it. Since 1933 every

---

time of the balloting. By contrast, four times (1839, 1849, 1855, and 1859) before the Civil War the House was almost unable to pick a Speaker.

President has assumed the necessity of presenting a comprehensive legislative program to Congress.[2]

From the Civil War until the end of the nineteenth century, the House leaders of the President's party maintained an attitude of independence toward the White House. As presidential initiative in the legislative sphere increased during the first three decades of the present century, they began to look to him for major legislative recommendations. They were willing to work for passage of many of these proposals, although they still reserved the right to object to individual bills.

Recent Presidents have enlarged and formalized White House ties with Congress. In 1937 Franklin Roosevelt began meeting weekly with Democratic congressional leaders, and his successors have continued the practice.[3] Presidents Truman, Eisenhower, Kennedy, and Johnson all appointed close advisers responsible for congressional liaison.[4]

Since the beginning of Franklin Roosevelt's administration, the House leaders of the President's party have, in effect, acted as lieutenants of the President, accepting virtually his whole legislative package and working for its adoption.[5] They have concentrated more on the volume of business handled by the House than on the content of legislation. It is now assumed that if the President proposes a bill, they will support it.

Leaders of the non-presidential party generally can define their party's legislative goals themselves. Thus, from 1955 through 1960 Speaker Sam Rayburn and Senate Majority Leader Lyndon Johnson announced party positions for Democrats in Congress without feeling the necessity of consulting noncongressional leaders. They refused to join the Democratic Advisory Council, which sought to coordinate congressional and noncongressional leaders and views. In 1965, Republican congres-

---

[2] See MacNeil, *Forge of Democracy*, pp. 237-39.

[3] Paul T. David, in "The Changing Political Parties," in Marian D. Irish (ed.), *Continuing Crisis in American Politics* (Prentice-Hall, 1963), pp. 55-56, fixes the date of the first regular meeting as November 15, 1937.

[4] MacNeil, *Forge of Democracy*, pp. 36-37. See pp. 255-69 for a good description of President Kennedy's liaison operation.

[5] On the change in 1933 see *ibid.*, pp. 33-35.

sional leaders helped initiate and participated in the Republican Coordinating Committee, but they dominated its proceedings and thus, like Rayburn and Johnson, remained the chief spokesmen for the party out of power.[6]

Within the House itself, the party leaders are influenced by the wishes and behavior of the standing committees, particularly the chairmen and the ranking minority members.

The changing nature of the governmental mandate has also influenced the way the House parties have organized themselves and the way in which their leaders have behaved. From the Civil War until 1929, the prevailing presumption and sentiment was that the government should intervene in the economy only in cases of gross mismanagement by private interests, and the market was presumed to be adequately self-correcting. The depression shattered this illusion. Since then the government has progressively assumed responsibility for preventing business recessions, attaining full employment, and fostering economic growth. The judiciary has affirmed the constitutional power of Congress to enact the legislation necessary to attain these ends, and the public has gradually accepted vast new areas of federal activity. Major responsibilities in fields almost devoid of federal participation three or four decades ago—education, health, welfare, housing and other urban problems, economic development, and research—have been assumed by the national government.

Assumption of international responsibilities and the necessities of the Cold War have also had dramatic consequences for the country and for Congress. The government has embarked on foreign ventures different in character from the conventional pre-World War II diplomacy: foreign aid, limited wars in an

[6] A simple comparison of membership lists indicates the alternative routes chosen by the Democratic congressional leaders in 1957-1961 and the Republicans in 1965. In May, 1960, the Democratic Advisory Council had thirty-one members. Only four of these were from Congress—all Senators. Two of them had joined only because they were trying to win the 1960 Democratic nomination for President. None of the four was a leader in the Senate. In early 1966 the Republican Coordinating Committee had twenty-nine members. Twelve of these members were from Congress, five from the Senate, and seven from the House. All of the central Republican leaders in the two houses were members.

atomic age, and participation in multi-national peacekeeping operations through the United Nations.

The changing nature of the American economy and society, and new international requirements, have altered the size, scope, and expertise of the American government. The executive branch has changed more rapidly and visibly, but the changes in Congress are also great. The problems with which it must deal have made it necessary for Congress to meet from 17 to 20 months out of 24, instead of 10 or 12 months as in pre-depression years.[7]

Longer daily sessions, more days in session, more bills, more new statutes, and a broader scope of activity have characterized congressional life for the last three decades. Some members still

[7] The average (mean) length of Congresses in months was computed for six different ten-year periods. The results: 1861-71, 14 months; 1881-91, 12 months; 1901-11, 10 months; 1921-31, 13 months; 1941-51, 22 months; and 1955-65, 17 months. The figure for 1941-51 is considerably inflated by long recesses for Easter, conventions, and election campaigns. The figure for 1955-65 is only slightly inflated by short recesses for Easter and one pair of national conventions. Before the adoption of the 20th Amendment to the Constitution in early 1933, the first session of a Congress typically lasted from December of an odd-numbered year (thirteen months after the election) until July or August of the following summer. The second session (called "lame duck" session because the members defeated in November still sat in Congress) lasted from December of the even-numbered year until March third of the odd-numbered year. This schedule—with substantial variations and some special sessions—was followed until the Seventy-third Congress (1933-35). Since that time the first session of a Congress meets in January of the odd-numbered year (two months after the election) and now typically adjourns sometime the following fall. The second session meets in January of the even-numbered year and now typically adjourns sometime late summer or early fall. Members defeated in November do not again sit unless there is a session during the two months between the election and the following January.

Throughout this volume a Congress will be referred to both by number and by the years during which it first met and during which the terms of its members expired. For example, the Thirty-seventh Congress (1861-63)—the first with which this volume is concerned—met in special session from July 4 to August 6, 1861; met again from December 2, 1861, to July 17, 1862; and met in lame duck session from December 1, 1862, until March 3, 1863. The Eighty-eighth Congress (1963-65) met from January 9, 1963, until December 30, 1963, and from January 7, 1964, until October 3, 1964. It did not actually meet in 1965, but the terms of its members did not expire until the new members were sworn in on January 4, 1965.

retain their private legal practices and business interests, but fifty years ago this was the norm and not the exception. Most members now are primarily full-time legislators.

All of these changes have altered the party leaders' duties by increasing their volume of work. In this sense they have become more important. But the legislative initiative has, at the same time, shifted from Congress to the executive branch. Thus the party of the President has become more reliant on him and on the executive establishment, and this has changed the character of the leaders' task. They are now concerned with the flow of legislation rather than its detailed contents.[8] Seldom do they take a direct part in framing legislative language and in initiating legislation. They assume that either the executive branch or the relevant congressional committees will do these jobs.

## Leaders' Resources

As they pursue their goal of influencing legislative results, the leaders have four important resources upon which they can draw.

*First.* Leaders are in a particularly advantageous spot to use the rules of the House for party ends. They, more than any other members, know how to make use of the intricacies of these rules.[9]

*Second.* Party leaders control or influence a good deal of the tangible rewards or preferment for individual members of the House. They have a large voice in appointing members to standing committees. They have even more influence in appointing members to select committees and commissions and to delegations for international meetings. With the cooperation of committee chairmen, they can halt or expedite the progress of

---

[8] For an indication that three important Speakers since the 1920's did not pay much attention to the details contained in bills see MacNeil, *Forge of Democracy,* p. 89.

[9] See Lewis A. Froman, Jr., *The Congressional Process: Strategies, Rules and Procedures* (Little, Brown, and Co., 1967).

specific bills and projects. They help distribute the limited patronage available to members. Assignment of office space is also partly under their control.

The leaders can also be of tangible help to members in their pursuit of re-election, and sometimes personally campaign for particular members in their districts. They may also send letters or telegrams for use in a campaign, or they may aid fund-raising by contacting wealthy constituents. Republican leaders have had more money to spend through their Congressional Committee than Democratic leaders, and they have also been freer to discriminate between more loyal and less loyal incumbents in apportioning the funds.[10]

*Third.* Party leaders control much of the psychological rewards or preferment available to party members. Some members attempt to gain reputation and influence by appealing to persons outside the House, but those who rise to the top in terms of both position and reputation do so through appealing to the judgment of their colleagues.[11] The party leaders are in a good position to influence the attitude of the House toward a member early in his career by telling other members what they think of him. There are also visible ways, such as the Speaker's selection of members to preside over the House or over the Committee of the Whole, by which party leaders indicate the younger members whom they regard highly.[12]

Members and students of Congress alike have testified that iso-

[10] See *One Hundred Years: A History of the National Republican Congressional Committee,* published by the Committee in 1966.

[11] See, for example, Nelson W. Polsby, "Two Strategies of Influence: Choosing a Majority Leader, 1962," in Robert L. Peabody and Nelson W. Polsby, *New Perspectives on the House of Representatives* (Rand-McNally, 1963), pp. 237-70. For evidence that internal considerations were not always the most important in choosing House leaders see Albert V. House, "The Speakership Contest of 1875: Democratic Response to Power," *The Journal of American History,* Vol. 52 (September 1965), pp. 252-74.

[12] See MacNeil, *Forge of Democracy,* pp. 111-12, concerning the significance of these visible actions. Speaking specifically of the choice by the Speaker of chairmen of the Committee of the Whole, he says, "Such assignments, denoting the Speaker's approval of a member, have always been carefully watched by members of the House. The men receiving them have acquired immediately, in the inner life of the House, recognition by their fellows as friends of the Speaker with the added influence and prestige that such friendship has always meant."

lation is likely to be the fate of a maverick, and this fact gives party leaders a powerful tool in seeking support for legislation. As one scholar has put it, "The desire to 'belong' is not merely a passive but also an active instrument in the hands of the leadership. . . . 'Independence' can be lonely and uncomfortable if one feels that one's colleagues and 'natural' allies are increasingly cold."[13]

Leaders can also give a general boost to members' morale and make life more enjoyable by providing long recesses, daily adjournment in time for dinner, or new restaurants and gymnasiums. The resulting good will can help solidify their influence.

*Fourth.* Party leaders dominate the House's internal communications process that is crucial to the operations of individual members. In any struggle to obtain the support of the members, for example, those who supply the largest number of Congressmen most consistently with useful and reliable information about the schedule, the substance of proposals, the use of the House rules, and the intentions and positions of the President, administration, and members or committees of Congress, have a large advantage.[14] Also, if the leaders can demonstrate that they accord substantial weight to the wishes of individual members, they create important good will among those members.

## Basic Characteristics of Party Behavior

Previous research and commentary on the House have yielded only a few general statements that are useful as background for this study. (Appendix A contains an analysis of the existing scholarly literature, which does not provide a complete picture of the role of party leaders in the House. Three especially impor-

---

[13] Robert Dahl, *Congress and Foreign Policy* (Harcourt, Brace, 1950), p. 50.

[14] Concerning the importance of information, see Randall B. Ripley, "The Party Whip Organizations in the United States House of Representatives," *American Political Science Review*, Vol. 58 (September 1964), pp. 561-76; Lewis Anthony Dexter, "Congressmen and the Making of Military Policy," in Peabody and Polsby, *New Perspectives*, pp. 321 ff.; and Charles L. Clapp, *The Congressman* (Brookings Institution, 1963), p. 302.

tant gaps remain: almost no systematic historical analysis is available, although interest in this aspect of Congress is increasing;[15] there is only fragmentary analysis of the activities of contemporary leaders as they use the resources available to them to increase their legislative influence; there is almost no material on the members' perceptions of the leaders, their activities, and the meaning of party loyalty.)

The following generalizations are widely accepted as valid by students of the House and are further examined and developed in this volume:

Members of the House tend to know the members of their own party better than members of the opposition, and close friendships with other Representatives tend to be limited to members of their own party. Requests from fellow party members are likely to have substantial weight for this reason.

There seem to be significant psychological pressures attached to floor action that push an individual member to act in accord with the majority of his party.

There are other loyalties that motivate members. The most important competitor of the party is the constituency: the wishes, real or imagined, of the individual member's district.

Judged by roll call votes, party is the most important single factor in the internal operations of the House and in influencing the behavior of individual members. Party leaders are particularly important as cue-givers on roll calls.

Party machinery seems to have an impact in persuading members to support the party leaders.

\* \* \* \* \* \*

The purpose of this volume is to analyze the legislative role of the party leaders by investigating the degree and nature of their influence on the legislative behavior of the members of the

[15] See, for example, Charles O. Jones, "Policy-Making Functions of the Minority Party in Congress" (paper prepared for delivery at the 1966 meeting of the American Political Science Association); Nelson W. Polsby, "The Institutionalization of the U.S. House of Representatives" (paper prepared for delivery at the 1966 meeting of the American Political Science Association); and H. Douglas Price, "The Congressional Career—Risks and Rewards" (unpublished paper).

House. Better understanding of how party leaders perform their duties, and what difference their performance makes, should ultimately provide a clearer picture of the capacities of Congress for meeting its legislative responsibilities.

This study depends on a variety of data. Much of the existing research on the House has been based on roll call analysis, which is valuable and will be used where appropriate. But propositions thus grounded describe the *results* of leadership activity, not the *activity* itself.

Three additional kinds of data have been used: personal observation in the years between 1963 and 1967; formal interviews with House members and staff personnel and informal discussions with other knowledgeable persons; and historical material, including biographies, memoirs, newspapers, periodicals, and commentary.

Historical comparisons can be highly useful in testing or generating hypotheses, although much of the previous research on Congress has neglected history. Political scientists who use history must not only recite details; they must also be willing to generalize and indicate trends. On some points of this study the evidence is abundant and in agreement; on other points it is abundant but conflicting; and sometimes it is slim. Thus, some of the specific historical judgments made here may be found in error by subsequent research. But the disadvantages of using historical material that is uneven in quality and quantity are outweighed by the advantages of viewing the House in broad historical perspective and of developing categories for understanding changes that have occurred in it.

# ☆ 2 ☆

# Development of Party Offices, Caucuses, and Committees

In the Eighty-ninth Congress (1965-67) the Democratic majority was led by a Speaker, a Majority Leader, and a Whip. The Whip had an organization of nineteen members. There was also a Steering Committee of eighteen and a seventeen-member Committee on Committees. The Republicans were led by a Minority Leader, a Whip with an organization of fifteen members, a conference chairman, a chairman of a Research and Planning Committee of eight, and a chairman of a Policy Committee of twenty-eight. Thirty-eight more Republicans also performed an important task for their party as members of the Committee on Committees. More than a century earlier, in the Thirty-seventh Congress (1861-63), the Republican majority in the House was led in name by a Speaker and in reality by the chairman of the Ways and Means Committee. The Democrats did not have a readily identifiable leader.

This chapter will examine the developments between 1861 and 1967 that brought all of these leadership positions into existence, the innovations that changed loosely structured entities into highly structured party organizations, and the leaders' use of some of the resources available to them. These developments, innovations, and uses of resources will be assessed to see if there are trends in the past that help explain the present and predict the future.

## The Speaker

The Speaker is the one political officer of the House who has been functioning since 1789, but little has been written about the office. The last studies of the Speakership (and of the House leadership in general) were written in the 1920's, and the best single volume was written in the late nineteenth century by Mary Parker Follett.[1]

Before the Civil War most Speakers were party leaders, although some were merely pawns for the real leaders and others were purposely apolitical. The Civil War years saw the transformation of the Speakership into a consistently partisan political office.[2] Since then all Speakers, except one (Frederick H. Gillett, 1919-25), have been among the important leaders of the majority party. The Speakers since 1861 are listed in Table I.

Speakers are nominated by a caucus (a meeting of the entire membership of a party) of the majority party, and formally elected by the whole House.[3] With the exception of Sam Rayburn (1940-47, 1949-53, 1955-61), their length of service as Speaker has varied little; but their seniority, age, and prior leadership positions in the party have all changed dramatically. Between 1861

[1] See Paul D. Hasbrouck, *Party Government in the House of Representatives* (Macmillan, 1927); Hubert B. Fuller, *The Speakers of the House* (Little, Brown, and Co., 1909); Chang-wei Chiu, *The Speaker of the House of Representatives Since 1896* (Columbia University Press, 1928); George R. Brown, *The Leadership of Congress* (Bobbs-Merrill, 1922); and Mary P. Follett, *The Speaker of the House of Representatives* (Longmans, Green, and Co., 1896).

[2] Follett, *Speaker*, pp. 96-97.

[3] Men outside the House have sometimes influenced the caucus action. In 1875, national party figures, especially editors, intervened in support of Michael Kerr. See Albert V. House, "The Speakership Contest of 1875: Democratic Response to Power," *The Journal of American History*, Vol. 52 (September 1965), pp. 252-74. Senators in 1899 were instrumental in the Republican decision to nominate David Henderson for the Speakership. They opposed the nomination of Joseph Cannon in 1903 but could not prevent it. See Nathaniel W. Stephenson, *Nelson W. Aldrich* (Scribner's, 1930), pp. 163, 212. In 1919 leading Republican Senators were important in engineering the nomination of Frederick Gillett, as was the Republican National Chairman. See the *New York Times*, January 16, 19, and 27, 1919.

and 1899 they had, on the average, been in the House for only four terms (eight years) before being elected Speaker—generally not long enough to have held other leadership positions in their party. They were young, averaging forty-four when elected. Since 1899, however, when elected the Speaker has served in the House an average of three times as long and has been twenty years older. All but two have held other major leadership posts.

Neither party has deposed a sitting Speaker while it remained in the majority. Only two former Speakers, Samuel J. Randall (1876-81) and J. Warren Keifer (1881-83), were refused renomination for the Speakership when their party regained control of the House after a period in the minority. Only two, Keifer and Joseph W. Martin (1947-49, 1953-55), were denied or removed from leadership positions when their party was in the minority. In general, the Speaker retains leadership status in his party as long as he remains in the House.[4]

MODE OF LEADERSHIP

Table II presents a simple classification scheme to describe the changing mode of leadership exercised by the Speaker. The table shows that his role is not limited; he can, to some extent, choose its dimensions.

The column headed "style of leadership" indicates whether

[4] Randall was Speaker from 1876 to 1881. He was almost denied renomination by his party in 1879. See Adlai E. Stevenson, *Something of Men I Have Known* (McClurg, 1909), p. 36. The Democrats were in the minority from 1881 to 1883. When they returned to the majority in 1883 they did not renominate Randall, although he continued to serve in the House until 1890. His position in favor of high tariffs was the principal reason for his failure to be renominated.

Keifer was the Republican Speaker from 1881 to 1883. When the Republicans became the minority party in 1883 they renominated Keifer for Speaker, knowing he would lose, but specifically made another man Minority Leader. Keifer remained in the House until 1885 and served again from 1905 to 1911, but was never again given leadership responsibilities. His lack of ability to make the majority party effective legislatively was the reason for his ouster. See Samuel W. McCall, *The Life of Thomas Brackett Reed* (Houghton Mifflin, 1914), p. 117.

Martin served for four years as Minority Leader after he had completed the second of two terms as Speaker. He was then replaced by another man, although he served in the House for eight more years. His defeat was not because of his performance as Speaker but because of his performance as Minority Leader and his advancing age.

TABLE I

## Speakers of the House of Representatives, 1861–1967

| Name and State[a] | Party | Dates of Service as Speaker | Years of Service | Years in House Before Election as Speaker[b] | Age at Election as Speaker[c] | Leadership Positions Before Election as Speaker | Reason for Leaving Office |
|---|---|---|---|---|---|---|---|
| Galusha Grow, Pennsylvania | R | 1861–63 | 2 | 10 | 37 | none | Retired from Congress |
| Schuyler Colfax, Indiana | R | 1863–69 | 6 | 8 | 39 | none | Became Vice President |
| James G. Blaine, Maine | R | 1869–75 | 6 | 6 | 39 | none | Party became minority |
| Michael C. Kerr, Indiana | D | 1875–76 | 1 | 8 | 47 | Min. leader 1869–71 | Died |
| Samuel J. Randall, Pennsylvania | D | 1876–81 | 5 | 13 | 47 | Chm., Approp. Comm, 1875–76 | Party became minority; not renominated when party became majority again |
| J. Warren Keifer, Ohio | R | 1881–83 | 2 | 4 | 45 | none | Party became minority; not retained as minority leader |
| John G. Carlisle, Kentucky | D | 1883–89 | 6 | 6 | 47 | none | Party became minority |
| Thomas B. Reed, Maine | R | 1889–91, 1895–99 | 6 | 12 | 49 | Min. leader 1883–89, 1891–95 | Party became minority (1891); Retired (1899) |
| Charles F. Crisp, Georgia | D | 1891–95 | 4 | 8 | 46 | Min. leader 1890–91 | Party became minority |
| David B. Henderson, Iowa | R | 1899–1903 | 4 | 16 | 59 | none | Retired |
| Joseph G. Cannon, Illinois | R | 1903–11 | 8 | 28 | 67 | Chm., Approp. Comm., 1889–91, 1895–1903 | Party became minority |

| | | | | | | | |
|---|---|---|---|---|---|---|---|
| Champ Clark, Missouri | D | 1911–19 | 8 | 16 | 60 | Min. leader 1908–11 | Party became minority |
| Frederick H. Gillett, Massachusetts | R | 1919–25 | 6 | 26 | 71 | none | Elected to Senate |
| Nicholas Longworth, Ohio | R | 1925–31 | 6 | 20 | 55 | Maj. leader 1923–25 | Died |
| John N. Garner, Texas | D | 1931–33 | 2 | 28 | 62 | Min. leader 1929–31 | Became Vice President |
| Henry T. Rainey, Illinois | D | 1933–34 | 2 | 28 | 72 | Maj. leader 1931–33 | Died |
| Joseph W. Byrns, Tennessee | D | 1935–36 | 2 | 26 | 65 | Chm., Approp. Comm., 1931–33, Maj. leader 1933–35 | Died |
| William B. Bankhead, Alabama | D | 1936–40 | 4 | 20 | 62 | Chm., Rules Comm., 1934–35, Maj. leader 1935–36 | Died |
| Sam Rayburn, Texas | D | 1940–47, 1949–53, 1955–61 | 18 | 28 | 58 | Maj. leader 1937–40 | Party became minority (1947, 1953); Died (1961) |
| Joseph W. Martin, Massachusetts | R | 1947–49, 1953–55 | 4 | 22 | 62 | Min. leader 1939–47 | Party became minority |
| John W. McCormack, Massachusetts | D | 1962– | | 33 | 70 | Maj. leader 1940–47, 1949–53, 1955–61; Min. Whip, 1947–49, 1953–55 | |

a Omitted from this table (and from all discussion of the Speakership in this volume) is Republican Theodore M. Pomeroy of New York, who served as Speaker for one day between Colfax and Blaine. b Averages are as follows: entire period, 17 years; 1861–99, 8 years; 1899–1967, 24 years. c Except in cases of mid-Congress elections, this was the man's age on the expiration date of the Congress previous to election as Speaker. Averages are as follows: entire period, 55 years; 1861–99, 44 years; 1899–1967, 64 years.

TABLE II

## Mode of Leadership by the Speaker, 1861–1967[a]

| Name | Style of Leadership | | | Use of Powers | | |
|---|---|---|---|---|---|---|
| | Personal | Collective | Figurehead | Innovative | Conservative | Retrogressive |
| Grow | – | – | X | – | X | – |
| Colfax | – | – | X | – | X | – |
| Blaine | X | – | – | X | – | – |
| Randall | X | – | – | X | – | – |
| Keifer | X | – | – | – | – | X |
| Carlisle | – | X | – | X | – | – |
| Reed | X | – | – | X | – | – |
| Crisp | X | – | – | X | – | – |
| Henderson | – | – | X | – | – | X |
| Cannon | – | X | – | X (1903–10) | – | X (1910–11) |
| Clark | – | X | – | – | – | X |
| Gillett | – | – | X | – | – | X |
| Longworth | – | X | – | X | – | – |
| Garner | X | – | – | – | X | – |
| Rainey | – | – | X | – | X | – |
| Byrns | – | – | X | – | X | – |
| Bankhead | – | X | – | – | X | – |
| Rayburn | X | – | – | X | – | – |
| Martin | X | – | – | – | X | – |
| McCormack | – | X | – | – | X | – |

[a] Speaker Kerr, who came between Blaine and Randall, is omitted because he served less than a year. Available evidence on Kerr suggests he would not have been innovative. See Albert V. House, "The Speakership Contest of 1875: Democratic Response to Power," *The Journal of American History*, Vol. 52 (September 1965), pp. 272–74.

the Speaker made major legislative decisions essentially by himself, or perhaps working with the President ("personal"); jointly with other major figures of his party in the House ("collective"); or did not participate in major legislative decisions, either by choice or because a President or other House leaders were able to operate without his concurrence ("figurehead"). Eight of the twenty Speakers since 1861 have demonstrated the personal style of leadership, six the collective style, and six have been figureheads.

The column headed "use of powers" indicates the Speaker's impact on the office. If he was able to expand the powers he inherited—either through use of the rules or through greater personal activity in persuading the members—he is labeled "innovative." If he did not expand his powers, he is labeled "conservative." If he willingly or unwillingly gave away some of the Speaker's powers—formal or informal—he is labeled "retrogressive." Again the Speakers since 1861 show a wide distribution: eight are judged innovative, eight conservative, and five retrogressive. Five of the innovators who had a major impact on the growth of the Speaker's powers exercised a personal leadership; three had a collective style.

From 1861 to 1869 the Speakers were figureheads and conservative. For the next thirty years most of them had a personal style and were innovative. From 1899 to 1925 the Speakers lost or gave away powers, but showed no characteristic style of leadership. No dominant style of leadership has emerged from 1925 to 1967, but all except one of the Speakers were content to conserve their powers.

Thus 1869-99 was the era of growing power for the Speaker. From 1899 to 1925 some of these powers were given or taken away. Since 1925 none have been taken away, and a few powers have been added. The current powers of the office, however, can hardly be said to be stable or defined for all time, nor can it be said that a dominant style of leadership will not again emerge.

Speakers' relations with Presidents have varied. Thomas B. Reed (1889-91, 1895-99), for example, had little respect for President William McKinley and viewed himself as the spokesman for the Republican party. He realized, however, that he did not have the political weight to challenge McKinley's power. Rather than endure the frustrations of working with a President he did not like or trust, he simply left the House.[5] In contrast, Joseph G. Cannon (1903-11) felt that when he met with President Theodore Roosevelt on legislative matters they were equals sharing the leadership of their party.

In recent years, Speakers of both parties have come to view themselves as working primarily for the success of the President's legislative program when he is of their party. This does not mean that they forget the "prerogatives of the House." But, unlike

[5] Neil MacNeil, *Forge of Democracy* (McKay, 1963), pp. 64, 78.

Reed and Cannon, they do not express legislative preferences that differ from those of the President. When the President is of the opposite party, the Speaker has a natural claim to national leadership of his own party. Thus, during the six years that Sam Rayburn was Speaker and Dwight Eisenhower was President, Rayburn was consistently consulted by the press for definition of national Democratic positions.

## THE SPEAKER AND THE RULES

Speakers Randall, John G. Carlisle (1883-89), Reed, and Charles F. Crisp (1891-95) made the chief innovations in developing rules as a means of furthering party purposes. Randall made the power of recognition absolute and not subject to appeal, obtained a general revision of the rules, and strengthened the Rules Committee, of which he was chairman.[6] Carlisle was particularly astute in using the power of recognition for legislative ends agreeable to him and most of the Democrats, and he further developed the Rules Committee as an instrument of party government.[7] Yet he still felt bound to tolerate dilatory procedural motions that kept the House tied up for days at a time.[8]

Reed was intolerant of delay or legislative failure. He successfully asserted the right to count all members in the chamber for the purpose of obtaining a quorum (a majority of the membership, without which the House cannot conduct business). He had the House pass what are known as the Reed rules, which effectively outlawed dilatory motions and filibustering in the House. He also continued to use the power of recognition for party ends by calling on those whose statements would support his views and would not upset his procedural plans.[9]

Crisp was much less successful legislatively than Reed, but

[6] Albert V. House, Jr., "The Contributions of Samuel J. Randall to the Rules of the National House of Representatives," *American Political Science Review*, Vol. 29 (October 1935), pp. 837-41.

[7] James A. Barnes, *John G. Carlisle* (Dodd, Mead, 1931), p. 153; see also Robert Luce, *Legislative Procedure* (Houghton Mifflin, 1922), p. 457.

[8] *Ibid.*, p. 154.

[9] Luce, *Legislative Procedure*, p. 154.

continued to use the power of recognition for party ends.[10] He also extended the jurisdiction of the Rules Committee to bills still pending in substantive committees, and he expected his appointees on the Rules Committee (with himself as chairman) to use this power for the benefit of the Democratic party. Under him, the Committee began to grant special orders or "rules" that would allow legislation to be brought to the floor more systematically.[11]

Speaker Cannon did not make changes in the formal rules, but used them to promote his own legislative preferences and to stifle the preferences of progressive Republicans and Democrats. As the progressive movement became larger and aroused more fervor, and as President Theodore Roosevelt became clearly identified with it, the attacks on "Uncle Joe" mounted. Because his position as chairman of the Rules Committee and his power to appoint members to committees were used against them, the progressive Republicans led the demand for rules changes to curb the Speaker's power. Most of the Democrats gleefully joined them, as much for political advantage as from any conviction that rules changes were needed.

Between 1909 and 1911 the House took away much of the Speaker's power over the rules. In 1909, it established a consent calendar (which provided for the orderly consideration of bills to which there was no important opposition) and agreed to call the standing committees every Wednesday for consideration of business on the Union or House calendars. These changes limited the Speaker's arbitrary power to control the flow of business. On March 19, 1910, after a fierce floor battle, the Speaker was removed from the Rules Committee, which was enlarged and made elective rather than appointive. Later that year, a method of discharging bills from standing committees was approved that gave the majority of the House the right to bring a bill to the floor even if it was opposed by a committee chairman and the Speaker. In 1911, the rules were changed to provide for the elec-

---

[10] *Ibid.*, p. 457.

[11] See Christopher Van Hollen, "The House Committee on Rules (1933-51): Agent of Party and Agent of Opposition" (Ph.D. thesis, Johns Hopkins University, 1951).

tion by the full House of all standing committees and their chairmen. In practice, this led to the establishment of Committees on Committees by both parties.[12]

In the last few years the rules have been changed to strengthen the position of the Speaker somewhat. In 1961 and 1963 the Rules Committee was enlarged and made a fairly reliable organ of party leadership responsive to the wishes of the Speaker. In 1965, the House gave the Speaker discretionary power to recognize a standing committee chairman or member of the committee to call up for floor consideration a rule that had been before the Rules Committee for twenty-one calendar days, even if the Rules Committee had acted adversely on it. This reduced even further the chances that the Rules Committee could thwart the Speaker.[13] The House dropped this rule in 1967, however.

### THE SPEAKER AND TANGIBLE PREFERMENT

The most potent reward that the Speaker has been able to offer is appointment to a choice standing committee. Before he lost some of his powers in 1910-11, the Speaker appointed all members of standing committees, including minority members (except for the 1903-08 period, when he exercised a veto over the choices made by the Minority Leader).

Before 1910, most Speakers used committee assignments, especially the designation of chairmen, to help produce specific legislative outcomes. James G. Blaine (1869-75) was particularly adept at shaping committees to report legislation he desired. Samuel Randall opposed general tariff reduction, and thus re-

---

[12] This summary is based on the discussion in Chapter 1 of a book manuscript by Joseph Cooper. The tentative title is *Reorganization and Reform in the House of Representatives.*

[13] If the House, by majority vote, acted favorably on the rule then the substantive matter itself would come to the floor under the conditions provided in the rule. This procedure was used eight times in the Eighty-ninth Congress (1965-67). The House in 1965 made two other rules changes, both designed to enhance the power of the majority party. First, it gave the Speaker discretionary power to recognize a member to offer a privileged motion to send a bill to conference by majority vote. This procedure was not used at all in the Eighty-ninth Congress and is, therefore, still subject to interpretation. Second, it eliminated the provision that allowed a single member to demand an engrossed (that is, printed with all amendments) copy of a bill before final action on it.

placed a low-tariff chairman of Ways and Means.[14] John Carlisle exercised great care in picking the Democratic members of all important committees so as to bury bills that would reduce the Treasury surplus and provide free coinage of silver.[15]

Charles Crisp promised the most important committee chairmanships, Ways and Means and Appropriations, as a lure to convince two of his three rivals for the Speakership nomination to withdraw in his favor. The tactic assured his election and also worked to his legislative advantage. The one rival who remained in the race against him, Roger Q. Mills of Texas, was a former chairman of Ways and Means and an ardent advocate of sweeping tariff reductions. Crisp, more interested in the silver issue, replaced Mills with one of those rivals who had thrown their support to him.[16]

A number of Speakers, including both Reed and Cannon, used the device of waiting until the important business of the session was finished before appointing most committees. Thus the Speaker could extract loyal behavior on the major issue before the Congress, and then distribute rewards accordingly.

Joseph Cannon was notorious for his use of committee assignments and chairmanships to gain his legislative ends.[17] Even his predecessor, David B. Henderson (1899-1903, in most ways a figurehead Speaker), had the Republican Whip removed from office temporarily because he defied the Speaker's wishes and led a band of insurgents on a tariff bill.[18]

From 1911 until the present, the Democrats have relied on a Committee on Committees (the Democratic members of the Committee on Ways and Means) to make assignments. The Republicans have used a specially constituted Committee on Committees since 1917. The Speaker's power to affect legislative out-

[14] On Blaine, see Follett, *Speaker,* p. 104; and MacNeil, *Forge of Democracy,* pp. 30, 71-72. On Randall, see Festus P. Summers, *William L. Wilson and Tariff Reform* (Rutgers University Press, 1953), p. 56; and Samuel A. Pleasants, *Fernando Wood of New York* (Columbia University Press, 1948), pp. 178, 191-92.

[15] Barnes, *Carlisle,* pp. 137, 152-54; Luce, *Legislative Procedure,* p. 457.

[16] Summers, *Wilson,* pp. 124-25; Arthur Wallace Dunn, *From Harrison to Harding* (G. P. Putnam's Sons, 1922), Vol. I, pp. 77-78, 119.

[17] See George R. Mayhill, "Speaker Cannon Under the Roosevelt Administration: 1903-1907" (Ph.D. thesis, University of Illinois, 1942); Chiu, *The Speaker,* pp. 64-68; and Hasbrouck, *Party Government,* pp. 48-49.

[18] Mayhill, "Speaker Cannon," p. 26. See *New York Tribune,* April 17, 1902.

comes by giving or withholding committee assignments has been diminished but not eliminated by this change. Most members of the majority party still feel that the Speaker's good will is important to them in seeking assignments from the Committee on Committees. Speakers have regularly intervened in the case of assignments to the three most important committees: Ways and Means (Democratic members are elected by the caucus, but a Democratic Speaker usually controls whose name is put before the caucus), Appropriations, and Rules. In the case of other committees, intervention is far less frequent, but cannot be completely discounted by ambitious members.

Two post-1910 Speakers were particularly effective in exploiting their opportunities for influencing the composition of a number of committees. Nicholas Longworth (1925-31), in his first term, had four unreliable incumbent Republicans on the Rules Committee replaced with his own choices. The Committee on Committees, at Longworth's urging and backed by the conference (the Republican caucus) also punished the thirteen Republicans who had supported Robert La Follette and the Progressive party in the 1924 presidential election by removing them from their important committee assignments and stripping them of seniority on their minor committees by placing them at the bottom of the committee membership lists.[19]

Sam Rayburn made sure that the Democrats on the Ways and Means Committee were favorable to reciprocal trade and opposed to changes in the oil depletion allowance, and also intervened in specific instances to change the complexion of other committees. In the middle and late 1950's he liberalized the Education and Labor Committee by asking for the appointment of specific junior Democrats. In 1949, through the device of having the Committee on Committees pass resolutions governing its own behavior, he removed from the Un-American Activities Committee two Democrats who had supported a third-party candidate in the 1948 presidential election.[20]

[19] Hasbrouck, *Party Government,* p. 163; Clarence A. Berdahl, "Some Notes on Party Membership in Congress," *American Political Science Review,* Vol. 43 (1949), pp. 497-503.

[20] In the 1949 case, John Rankin of Mississippi was dropped from the Un-American Activities Committee because the Committee on Committees passed a

## THE SPEAKER'S OTHER RESOURCES

The Speaker's use of the resources of psychological preferment and communications is hard to document. His personal traits influence his ability to deal with members of his party. The one constant element is the importance of his showing trust in and respect for individual members of his party. A smile or nod of the head from the Speaker can bolster a member's ego and lead him to seek further evidences of favor. Being out of favor hurts the individual's pride, and may be noticed by his colleagues. Most Speakers have had an instinct for knowing their loyal followers on legislative matters. Others have either kept records themselves or made frequent use of whip polls and official records to inform themselves about the relative loyalty of their members.[21] Speakers have been able to convey critical information to members on a person-to-person basis, often with the help of the Parliamentarian.[22] They have also encouraged their floor leaders and whip organizations to become collectors and purvey-

resolution barring any chairman of other committees from serving on it. Rankin was chairman of Veterans' Affairs. F. Edward Hebert of Louisiana was dropped because of a resolution providing that "only experienced members of the bar" could be members. This also removed another member, J. Hardin Peterson of Florida, who apparently did not mind leaving. Rankin and Hebert were both unhappy about their fate. For details of the developments that led to this result see the *New York Times*, January 2, 9, 16, and 18, 1949.

[21] Henry Rainey, for example, kept extensive records of votes of Democrats so that he would know which mavericks needed branding. See Floyd M. Riddick, "The House of Representatives and the President," *South Atlantic Quarterly*, Vol. 34 (January 1935), p. 84. John McCormack constantly consults the polls taken by the Democratic whip organization and in this way keeps his "feel" for individual loyalties up to date. Others, such as Rayburn, relied on instinct and mental notes instead of written notes.

[22] A "Clerk at the Speaker's Table" had acted as a Parliamentarian since at least the late nineteenth century. A Parliamentarian was formally designated in 1927 and since 1929 the same man, Lewis Deschler, has held that position. Though an important arm of the Speakership, this office is bipartisan in advising members of both the majority and minority. When the Speaker wants to make a certain ruling, however, he can rely on the Parliamentarian to support him with precedent, aided by notebooks containing the precedents since 1936. These notebooks are not readily available to the members. The Parliamentarian is also included in some majority party strategy sessions so that he can advise the leaders what they can and cannot do.

ors of information on a larger scale. Particularly useful to a number of Speakers has been an informal gathering of intimates and friends of both parties to discuss the course of business in the House. Through such discussions, Speakers have been able to keep themselves informed of developments in the House and, at the same time, convey their desires to other members invited to attend.[23]

## The Majority Leader

The Majority Leadership did not become a separate and consistently identifiable party office until 1899.[24] Before then the chairman of the Ways and Means Committee was usually looked on as the majority floor leader, principally because the most important business before the House in most Congresses (the tariff) came from his committee. If he were not also able to lead on other matters, the Speaker would look to someone else for more general floor leadership.[25]

When Speaker Henderson appointed Sereno Payne Majority Leader, Payne was also named Chairman of Ways and Means. For the next twenty years, until 1919, the Ways and Means chairman was formally recognized as the Majority Leader. Since 1919 the two offices have been separate.[26]

The three most recent Majority Leaders have had about the same length of House service prior to their appointment as the

[23] Speakers Cannon, Longworth, Garner, Rayburn, and McCormack have all used variations of this type of informal gathering. See MacNeil, *Forge of Democracy*, pp. 80-84, 331-32.

[24] George B. Galloway, *History of the United States House of Representatives*, H. Doc. 246, 87 Cong. 1 sess. (1962), p. 211.

[25] DeAlva S. Alexander, *History and Procedure of the House of Representatives* (Houghton Mifflin, 1916), pp. 127, 108.

[26] Had the new Republican Majority Leader in 1919, Mondell, remained on a committee the now-hardened seniority rule would have prescribed that he would be second ranking on Appropriations. The "rule of seniority" is unwritten and simply means that the member of the majority party with the longest continuous service on a committee will be its chairman, the man with the next longest continuous service will be second ranking, and so on. The same "rule" applies to the minority side of committees too.

first three. The seven men in the middle period (1919-1940) had all been in the House much longer. They were also older. The earliest Majority Leaders held office for a relatively short period, partly because the average service of all members was far less than it is today. (Table III lists the Majority Leaders since 1899.)

The choice of Majority Leaders was affected as more members began to make a career in the House and the rule of seniority for committee rank hardened. The next seven incumbents were among the most senior men in their party, although the post had no formal seniority requirements. After the rapid turnover in the leadership ranks during the 1930's, caused in large part by the death of aged Speakers who had been promoted from Majority Leader, the Democrats in 1940 decided to elect a younger man with less seniority as their Majority Leader. They made the same decision again in 1962. The Republicans, who had a chance to elect their first Majority Leader in many years in 1947, made the same kind of choice.

Oscar Underwood, in 1911, was the first Majority Leader to be elected by the caucus of his party. Subsequent Democratic Majority Leaders have all been chosen this way. Payne was appointed by the Speaker and was never endorsed by the full Republican caucus, but when the party regained a majority in the House in 1919 its Committee on Committees nominated the Majority Leader. In 1923, the Republicans turned to election in the conference as the mode of choosing their Majority Leader.

The place and importance of the Majority Leader as a party leader varied from 1899 to 1925. Sereno Payne (1899-1911), as an appointee of the Speaker, had little independent weight in shaping party policy. He was regarded as a party wheel-horse who would perform faithfully the duties assigned to him, but neither the Speaker nor the other party leaders relied on him for advice before making decisions about legislation.[27] On the other hand, his successor, Oscar Underwood (1911-15), was the primary legislative leader of his party and overshadowed the Speaker.

Claude Kitchin (1915-19), Underwood's successor, was a relatively minor figure, overshadowed by the President instead of the Speaker. Because he disagreed with the war policies of Presi-

---

[27] Charles W. Thompson, *Party Leaders of the Time* (Dillingham, 1906), p. 149.

## TABLE III

### *Majority Leaders of the House of Representatives, 1899–1967*

| Name and State | Party | Dates of Service as Leader | Years of Service | Years in House Before Election as Leader | Age at Election as Leader[a] | Reason for Leaving Job as Leader |
|---|---|---|---|---|---|---|
| Sereno Payne, New York | R | 1899–1911 | 12 | 14 | 55 | Party became minority |
| Oscar Underwood, Alabama | D | 1911–15 | 4 | 16 | 48 | Elected to Senate |
| Claude Kitchin, North Carolina | D | 1915–19 | 4 | 14 | 45 | Party became minority |
| Frank Mondell, Wyoming | R | 1919–23 | 4 | 22 | 58 | Defeated for Senate |
| Nicholas Longworth, Ohio | R | 1923–25 | 2 | 18 | 53 | Became Speaker |
| John Tilson, Connecticut | R | 1925–31 | 6 | 14 | 58 | Party became minority; lost bid for Minority Leadership |
| Henry Rainey, Illinois | D | 1931–33 | 2 | 28 | 70 | Became Speaker |
| Joseph Byrns, Tennessee | D | 1933–35 | 2 | 24 | 63 | Became Speaker |
| William Bankhead, Alabama | D | 1935–36 | 2 | 18 | 60 | Became Speaker |
| Sam Rayburn, Texas | D | 1937–40 | 4 | 24 | 55 | Became Speaker |
| John McCormack, Massachusetts | D | 1940–47, 1949–53, 1955–62 | 18 | 12 | 48 | Party became minority; became Speaker |
| Charles Halleck, Indiana | R | 1947–49, 1953–55 | 4 | 12 | 46 | Party became minority |
| Carl Albert, Oklahoma | D | 1962– | | 15 | 53 | |

[a] Except in cases of mid-Congress elections, this was the man's age on the expiration of the Congress previous to his election as Leader.

dent Woodrow Wilson, his relations with the White House and with many Democratic members were strained. On the major bills with which he did not agree he would stand aside and take little or no part in floor debate, leaving the management of the bill to the committee chairman or another senior committee Democrat.[28]

Another change occurred in 1919, when the Republicans regained the majority of the House. The new Majority Leader, Frank Mondell (1919-23), was expected to head and work closely with a Steering Committee. Mondell's successor, Nicholas Longworth (1923-25), continued in this role, although taking more individual responsibility for promulgating Republican positions and strategy.

Since 1925, Majority Leaders of both parties have been the chief lieutenant of the Speaker. The Majority Leader and the Speaker together have been the chief House legislative aides for the President when he is of the same party. With the exception of Sam Rayburn (1937-40), who was Majority Leader during four years when the Speaker was ill much of the time, no Majority Leader since 1925 has been the principal leader of his party. He has been important, but less important than the Speaker and the President of the same party; consulted about party strategy, but not in command.[29]

## RESOURCES

Except through the Speaker, the Majority Leader does not have much power to use the rules in the drive to attain legislative ends—although a good Majority Leader must know the rules thoroughly. Neither can the Majority Leader be particularly effective in giving tangible rewards to members of his party except by advising the Speaker.

[28] Hasbrouck, *Party Government*, pp. 93-94; See also Alex M. Arnett, *Claude Kitchin and the Wilson War Policies* (Little, Brown, and Co., 1937).

[29] Unlike the Speaker, who is aided by the Parliamentarian, and unlike the Whip, who is aided by an extensive organization, the floor leaders operate primarily as individuals, although they have full access to and use of the whip organization and, when in the majority, the Parliamentarian. The staffs of the Majority and Minority Leaders are used more frequently for the business of their districts than for their floor duties.

Thus the main resources open directly to the Majority Leader are dominance over certain kinds of communications and psychological preferment. It was in the 1920's that the Majority Leader first sought to control centrifugal forces in his party by centralizing the informative power in himself and his chief lieutenants. In this period voting blocs frequently overshadowed the demands of party. To make their members less dependent on the blocs, the Republican leaders moved to make themselves the main source of information about the business of the House. The Majority Leader began the practice of announcing orally the following week's program at the end of each week. Later a tentative program for the coming week was put in writing and circulated to all Republican members. The Republican Steering Committee, chaired by the Majority Leader, took over this job. This information service was soon extended to listing the upcoming hearings of the various committees.[30] Because the Majority Leader's favor is eagerly sought by most members, he is also in a good position to stimulate desired behavior through manipulation of psychological preferment.

## The Minority Leader

Since 1883 the candidate for Speaker nominated by the minority party has clearly been the Minority Leader.[31] Like the Speaker, recent Minority Leaders have been older and have had longer previous service in the House than the earlier incumbents. The change is not so sudden and dramatic as in the case of the Speaker, but the turn of the century still presents a clear watershed. Table IV lists the Minority Leaders from 1883-1967.

[30] Hasbrouck, *Party Government*, pp. 110-11. In the 1930's the whip organization in both parties became responsible for circulating the program in advance and this piece of paper is now called the whip notice.

[31] Between 1861 and 1883, the identity of the minority floor leader is often unclear. The Democratic minority during the Thirty-seventh through Forty-third Congresses (1861-75) was completely disorganized. The Democrats did not nominate a candidate for Speaker in two of these seven Congresses and nominated no man more than once in the other five. The defeated candidates were not automatically looked to for leadership.

The conception of the office has changed through the years. For much of the time, the main job of the Minority Leader has been to obstruct the work of the majority. Only rarely has the minority tried to present its own major legislation. The goal of all Minority Leaders before 1911 (and many of them afterwards) was to wield a solid minority in an obstructive way and then, when the opportunity presented itself, to unite with enough dissidents from the majority party to defeat its proposals. Thomas Reed's notable success in implementing this conception was aided by his forceful personality, a minority essentially united on the great issues of the day, and the presence of a Republican President and Senate much of the time. Democratic Minority Leaders from 1895 to 1911 and from 1919 to 1931 were less fortunate. Eight different leaders labored for Democratic causes during these twenty-eight years. Their successes, with the exception of the rules changes adopted in 1909-11, were rare and not particularly important.

The Republicans from 1911 to 1919 and from 1931 to 1939 were largely ineffectual. Led by two men, their successes were few and their efforts were limited. The defeat of New Deal measures in the Seventy-fifth Congress (1937-39) was more because of Democratic defections than the activities of the Minority Leader.

In recent years a new facet has been added to the job of the Minority Leader. Now, at least for the Republicans (the minority party in all but four of the years from 1939 to 1967), he is expected to put forth legislative alternatives to Democratic proposals and to publicize these alternatives to the country.

RESOURCES AND THE IMPACT OF MINORITY STATUS

To keep his members united, the Minority Leader can use three of the four resources open to the Speaker—tangible preferment, psychological preferment, and communications. However, his resources (especially tangible preferment) are normally much smaller and less effective.

One of the Minority Leader's greatest problems is the generally demoralizing condition of minority party status. Minority

## TABLE IV

### Minority Leaders of the House of Representatives, 1883–1967

| Name and State | Party | Dates of Service as Leader | Years of Service | Years in House Before Election as Leader | Age at Election as Leader[a] | Reason for Leaving Job as Leader |
|---|---|---|---|---|---|---|
| Thomas Reed, Maine | R | 1883–89 1891–95 | 10 | 6 | 43 | Became Speaker |
| John Carlisle, Kentucky | D | 1889–90 | 1 | [b] | [b] | Elected to Senate |
| Charles Crisp, Georgia | D | 1890–91, 1895–96 | 2 | 7 | 45 | Nominated for Senate; Died |
| Joseph Bailey, Texas | D | 1897–99 | 2 | 6 | 34 | Elected to Senate |
| James Richardson, Tennessee | D | 1899–1903 | 4 | 14 | 55 | Retired |
| John Sharp Williams, Mississippi | D | 1903–08 | 5 | 10 | 48 | Elected to Senate |
| Champ Clark, Missouri | D | 1908–11 1919–21 | 5 | 13 | 58 | Became Speaker (1911) Defeated in District; Died |

| | | | | | | |
|---|---|---|---|---|---|---|
| James Mann, Illinois | R | 1911–19 | 8 | 14 | 54 | Defeated for Speakership nomination |
| Claude Kitchin, North Carolina | D | 1921–23 | 2 | 20 | 51 | Died |
| Finis Garrett, Tennessee | D | 1923–29 | 6 | 18 | 47 | Defeated for Senate |
| John Garner, Texas | D | 1929–31 | 2 | 26 | 60 | Became Speaker |
| Bertrand Snell, New York | R | 1931–39 | 8 | 16 | 60 | Retired |
| Joseph Martin, Massachusetts | R | 1939–47, 1949–53, 1955–59 | 16 | 14 | 54 | Became Speaker (1947, 1953); Defeated by Halleck |
| Sam Rayburn, Texas | D | 1947–49, 1953–55 | 4 | b | b | Became Speaker |
| Charles Halleck, Indiana | R | 1959–65 | 6 | 24 | 58 | Defeated by Ford |
| Gerald Ford, Michigan | R | 1965– | | 16 | 51 | |

a Except in cases of mid-Congress elections this was the man's age on the expiration date of the Congress previous to his election as Leader.
b Information omitted because the man had previously served as Speaker.

members—especially those in a long-standing minority—are less likely to be informed about what the House is doing. They are on the losing side much of the time both in committee and on the floor. They have little patronage inside the Capitol. Their smaller committee staffs make it difficult to prepare legislative positions, and they usually are unable to obtain such assistance from the executive branch. Yet they want to be informed, to win, and to have patronage, committee staffs, and executive branch cooperation. When they cannot gain these objectives, one target of their frustrations is the Minority Leader. A comparison of why twentieth century Majority and Minority Leaders have surrendered their positions is illuminating.[32] Of the twelve Majority Leaders, six became Speaker, four surrendered their positions when their party become the minority, one was elected to the Senate, and one was defeated for the Senate.

Of the thirteen Minority Leaders, three became Speaker, two died or were defeated in their districts, three were ousted by their party, two were elected to the Senate, one was defeated for the Senate, and two retired from the House.

This comparison shows that Minority Leaders are much more likely to leave the House (and their office) voluntarily than Majority Leaders, and are more likely to be ousted. Only two of the twelve Majority Leaders left the House voluntarily; five of thirteen Minority Leaders did so. No Majority Leader has been overthrown by his own party; three Minority Leaders have been.[33] Clearly, working in the majority is much more satisfying, and safer, than working in the minority. Upheavals take place in the minority party; the majority party members tend to remain more content with their lot.

[32] For a fuller discussion of various aspects of leadership change within a party see Robert L. Peabody, "Party Leadership Change in the United States House of Representatives," *American Political Science Review,* Vol. 61 (September 1967).

[33] One Majority Leader, John Tilson, was not elected as Minority Leader in 1931, even though the former Speaker had died and he was the highest ranking party official. Eight ballots in the conference were required before he was defeated. For some details of his defeat see the *New York Times,* December 1 and 8, 1931.

## *Whip Organizations*

The name Whip was not formally applied to a party official in the House until the end of the nineteenth century.[34] Before then, members functioned as whips—responsible for having their "fellow political members in the House when needed"—only in connection with important legislation, and when the division between the parties was close enough to require a high degree of party regularity.[35] Many of these unofficial whips were volunteers for a given floor fight only. Today, extensive whip organizations provide valuable assistance to the party leaders as they use psychological preferment and dominance of the communications process to achieve their goals. Table V lists the official Whips appointed by both parties and summarizes their House careers.

The first Whip was appointed by Speaker Reed in 1897 to help him keep track of the whereabouts of party members at the time of an important vote. Republican Speakers and Minority Leaders continued to appoint the Whip until 1919. From 1919 until 1965 the Republican Whip was elected by the Committee on Committees, although the party conference could, in theory, reject its choice. In 1965 the conference itself voted for the Whip and will presumably continue to do so. All Democratic Whips have been appointed by the floor leader (with the approval of the Speaker when the party is in the majority).

The creation of a formal party office of Whip was initially the product of the hard-fought party battles in the late nineteenth century. In both parties some of the early Whips were important assistants to the Speaker or floor leaders, and some began de-

[34] The name "whip" derives from the British fox-hunting term "whipper-in," used to describe the man responsible for keeping the hounds from leaving the pack. It was first applied to the British Parliament about 1770. See Luce, *Legislative Procedure,* pp. 501-02.

[35] The quotation is from Champ Clark, *My Quarter Century of American Politics* (Harper, 1920), Vol. 2, p. 337. On the informal whips before 1897 see MacNeil, *Forge of Democracy,* pp. 97-100; and Alexander, *History and Procedure of the House,* p. 104.

TABLE V

## Party Whips in the House

| Name and State | Years as Whip | House Career | | | Reason for Leaving Whip's Job |
|---|---|---|---|---|---|
| | | Years Before Becoming Whip | Years as Whip | Years After Being Whip | |
| *Democrats* | | | | | |
| Oscar Underwood, Alabama | 1900–01 | 5 | 1 | 14 | Not reappointed by Minority Leader |
| James Lloyd, Missouri | 1901–08 | 4 | 8 | 8 | Became Chm. of Campaign Committee |
| Thomas Bell, Georgia | 1913–15 (?) | ? | ? | ? | ? |
| William Oldfield, Arkansas | 1921–28 | 12 | 8 | — | Died |
| John McDuffie, Alabama | 1929–33 | 10 | 4 | 2 | Defeated for Speaker; not reappointed |
| Arthur Greenwood, Indiana | 1933–35 | 10 | 2 | 4 | Not reappointed |
| Patrick Boland, Pennsylvania | 1935–42 | 4 | 7 | — | Died |
| Robert Ramspeck, Georgia | 1942–45 | 12 | 3 | — | Resigned from House |
| John Sparkman, Alabama | 1946 | 9 | 1 | — | Elected to Senate |
| John McCormack, Massachusetts | 1947–49, 1953–55 | 18 | 4 | 18* | Elected Majority Leader |
| Percy Priest, Tennessee | 1949–53 | 8 | 4 | 4 | Party became minority (former Majority Leader made Whip) |
| Carl Albert, Oklahoma | 1955–62 | 8 | 7 | 5* | Elected Majority Leader |

## TABLE V *(Continued)*

| Name and State | Years as Whip | House Career | | | Reason for Leaving Whip's job |
|---|---|---|---|---|---|
| | | Years Before Becoming Whip | Years as Whip | Years After Being Whip | |
| Hale Boggs, Louisiana | 1962– | 17 | 5* | — | — |
| *Republicans* | | | | | |
| James Tawney, Minnesota | 1897–1905 | 4 | 8 | 6 | Appointed Approp. Comm. Chm. |
| James Watson, Indiana | 1905–09 | 8 | 4 | — | Retired to run for Governor |
| John Dwight, New York | 1909–13 | 6 | 4 | — | Retired from House |
| Charles Burke, South Dakota | 1913–15 | 12 | 2 | — | Defeated for the Senate |
| Charles Hamilton, New York | 1915–19 | 2 | 4 | — | Retired from House |
| Harold Knutson, Minnesota | 1919–23 | 2 | 4 | 26 | ? |
| Albert Vestal, Indiana | 1923–31 | 6 | 8 | 1 | ? |
| Carl Bachmann, West Virginia | 1931–33 | 6 | 2 | — | Defeated for House seat |
| Harry Englebright, California | 1933–43 | 6 | 11 | — | Died |
| Leslie Arends, Illinois | 1943– | 9 | 23* | — | — |

* As of the end of 1966.

veloping the rudiments of a larger organization. But it was not until the early 1930's that both parties possessed large whip organizations with constant importance to the leaders.[36]

## DEVELOPMENT OF THE REPUBLICAN ORGANIZATION

The second Republican Whip, James Watson (1905-09), was a close confidant of Speaker Cannon.[37] His successor, John Dwight (1909-13), was the first Republican Whip to appoint other members as assistants. He also began to use a systematic poll prior to an important vote.[38] But succeeding Republican Whips did not use assistants until 1931, when Carl Bachmann (1931-33) instituted a whip organization that is still in use. He divided the country in two, appointed an assistant whip for each division, and designated a "key man" in each state with Republican members. When a poll of the Republicans was necessary, Bachmann asked the two assistant whips to get reports about the state delegations from their key men.[39] Bachmann's successor, Harry Englebright (1933-43) retained the pattern of assistant whips (increasing them to three in number) and key men in state delegations.

The Republican Whip from 1943 to the present, Leslie Arends, formalized and expanded the key man system. In the Eighty-ninth Congress (1965-67) he personally appointed a deputy whip, three regional whips, and twelve assistant whips.

## DEVELOPMENT OF THE DEMOCRATIC ORGANIZATION

The first Democratic Whip, Oscar Underwood (1900-01), made his position strong enough to warrant having an assistant.

[36] See Randall B. Ripley, "The Party Whip Organizations in the United States House of Representatives," *American Political Science Review*, Vol. 58 (September 1964), pp. 561-76.

[37] Cannon thought so highly of Watson that he consulted him as a personal assistant in the 1910 rules fight, two years after Watson had left the House. Kenneth W. Hechler, *Insurgency* (Columbia University Press, 1940), p. 70.

[38] See MacNeil, *Forge of Democracy*, pp. 97-100; and Alexander, *History and Procedure of the House*, p. 104.

[39] Letter from Carl G. Bachmann to the author, August 15, 1963.

He and his immediate successor, James Lloyd (1901-08), were trusted and important lieutenants of the Minority Leaders who appointed them. From 1909 until 1921 the Democratic Whip was unimportant; during much of the time there may not have been a single, specifically designated Whip.[40] By 1929 the Democratic Whip had again become important enough to have several assistant whips.

The great expansion in the Democratic whip organization came under Arthur Greenwood (1933-35). He created an organization of fifteen assistant whips, each responsible for the Democrats in a specific zone. The zones were identical to those established for the Democratic Steering Committee, which was also created in 1933.[41] The Steering Committee withered quickly, but the whip organization prospered under Greenwood's successor, Patrick Boland (1935-42), who worked diligently to perfect its functioning. During his seven-year tenure, the press and the Democratic leaders began to take public notice of his operations.[42] No basic organizational changes have occurred

[40] In the 1900 Democratic caucus Underwood offered the resolution that created the offices of Whip and Assistant Whip. See the *Washington Post,* January 10, 1900; and the *New York Times,* January 10, 1900. Sydney P. Epes of Virginia, who died two months later, was named Assistant Whip.

It seems likely that there was a Democratic Whip during only two (or possibly four) of the twelve years from 1909 to 1921. The *Congressional Directory* floor plan of the Capitol for the Sixty-third Congress (1913-15) shows Thomas Bell as Whip. His obituary in the March 20, 1941, *Gainesville [Ga.] News* speaks of him as Democratic Whip "for a term or two." The floor plan for the Sixty-sixth Congress (1919-21) shows a Whip's office but does not indicate the name of the Whip. Champ Clark, as Minority Leader, did much of his own whipping in 1909-11. See Clark, *Quarter Century,* Vol. 2, p. 338. From 1911 to 1921, Underwood as Majority Leader (1911-15) used the binding caucus, and President Wilson dominated the legislative process after he left (at least until 1919). Under such conditions there was little need for a Whip. Bell was not an important part of the Democratic leadership during the one Congress he served as Whip.

[41] Letter from Clarence Cannon to the author, September 23, 1963; Cannon's *Precedents,* Vol. 8 (1936), pp. 961-62; and E. Pendleton Herring, "First Session of the Seventy-third Congress," *American Political Science Review,* Vol. 28 (February 1934), p. 69.

[42] See the statement by John McCormack after Boland's death, *Congressional Record,* Vol. 88, Pt. 3, 77 Cong. 2 Sess. (1942), p. 4318. See also the *Evening Star* (Washington), August 18, 1935; and June 4, 1936; and the *Washington Post,* August 25, 1935.

since the 1930's, except for an increase in the number of zones to eighteen and, in 1955, the addition of a deputy whip appointed by the Whip to help check floor attendance and voting.[43]

The Democratic assistant whips are either appointed by the dean (the most senior member) of the delegations for which they are responsible or elected by the members of those delgations.[44] In the Eighty-eighth Congress (1963-65) six assistant whips were appointed and twelve were elected.

The assistant whips are each responsible for a small number of Democrats, averaging about fifteen in recent Congresses. They, or staff members designated by them, make the regular contacts with all of the Democratic members' offices. This organization makes it possible for the leadership to alert all Democrats to come to the floor within fifteen to twenty minutes, and to ascertain the sentiments of virtually every Democrat in the House on a given bill within a day or two.[45] The Republican whip organization operates in the same fashion and with similar speed.

IMPORTANCE OF THE WHIPS

The House has, in tangible ways, recognized the importance of the individuals serving as Whips and their organizations. From 1911 until the present, the Republican Whip has had an office in the Capitol, unless he chose to operate from his congressional office. The Democratic Whip had an office in the Capitol in the Sixty-third Congress (1913-15) and has been quartered there continuously since 1919. Since 1913 the House has provided money to hire a messenger for each Whip. A clerk was added in 1947 and in 1953 the Whips were given administrative

[43] The post of Deputy Whip as a formal leadership position was created in 1955 for Hale Boggs of Louisiana. Boland had a "principal assistant" or "chief assistant" whip.

[44] In 1939 Boland threatened to "fire" some of them for disloyalty to the President's program. *New York Times*, August 22, 1939. It is unlikely that he really had the power to do so.

[45] In the late 1950's the Democratic Study Group (DSG) imitated the political parties by creating its own whip organization. DSG whips are also organized on geographical lines, although each regional subwhip is responsible for only four to six members.

assistants. By fiscal 1967 each Whip had a budget of $67,000 with which to staff and operate his office.[46]

The Whips have not developed independent power. Leaders and members of both parties understand that the Majority Whip serves the Speaker and Majority Leader, while the Minority Whip serves the Minority Leader. Neither party has developed a pattern of succession that automatically promotes a Whip to more important leadership positions. No Republican Whip and only three Democratic Whips have held higher leadership positions.[47]

## ASSISTANT WHIPS

The assistant whips of both parties, the primary direct contacts with rank-and-file members, vary considerably in their voting loyalty. Table VI shows the support the Democratic assistant whips gave the leaders and the administration on seventeen key votes in 1962 and 1963, and the support given by all Democrats in each whip zone on the same votes. In general, the assistant whips tended to be more loyal to the administration than all Democrats, and variations in their individual loyalty tended to reflect the normal variations by zone. Analysis of the performance of Republican assistant whips produces the same general conclusions.[48]

[46] The statement about office space in the Capitol is based on the floor plans contained in the *Congressional Directory*. The information on staff comes from the Legislative Appropriations Acts in the *U.S. Statutes at Large*. When the Republicans captured the House in the 1952 elections John McCormack was slated to move from Majority Leader to Minority Whip. He asked Speaker Martin, Majority Leader Halleck, and Minority Leader Rayburn if he might keep one of his longtime employees as administrative assistant. He and the Republican Whip, Leslie Arends, then agreed that they would both have administrative assistants.

[47] Only one of the three Democrats, Carl Albert, moved directly from Whip to Majority Leader. Ten years elapsed between the time Oscar Underwood was Whip and the time he was Majority Leader. John McCormack was Majority Leader for seven years *before* he first became Minority Whip because of election results putting the Democrats in the minority. He again became Majority Leader when the Democrats regained control of the House.

[48] Warren C. Ogden, Jr., "The Whip Systems of the United States House of Representatives" (B.A. thesis, University of North Carolina, 1964), pp. 40-41.

The problem of "disloyal" assistant whips is especially troublesome for the Democrats. The power to appoint and replace them rests exclusively with the state delegations, but even if the Whip had the power to remove assistants, their roll call voting record would not be an infallible test of performance. For example, in 1962 one Democratic assistant whip supported the administration only rarely and yet did an excellent job in reporting ac-

TABLE VI

### Voting of Democratic Assistant Whips and Members of Their Zones, 1962–63

*Part I: Percent Support of Administration on Seventeen Key Roll Calls*[a]

| States in Whip Zone | 1962 | | 1963 | |
|---|---|---|---|---|
| | Assist-ant Whips | All Zone Members | Assist-ant Whips | All Zone Members |
| Massachusetts, Connecticut, Rhode Island | 100% | 95% | 100% | 97% |
| New York | 100 | 95 | 100 | 97 |
| Pennsylvania | 100 | 98 | 90 | 95 |
| New Jersey, Delaware, Maryland | 100 | 92 | 100 | 99 |
| Virginia, North Carolina[b] | 43 | 53 | 60 | 56 |
| Georgia, South Carolina | 86 | 62 | 89 | 74 |
| Michigan, Wisconsin, Minnesota | 100 | 97 | 100 | 97 |
| Indiana | 100 | 96 | 100 | 97 |
| Ohio, West Virginia | 57 | 83 | 100 | 93 |
| Tennessee, Kentucky, Arkansas | 71 | 81 | 90 | 90 |
| Mississippi, Louisiana[b] | 86 | 41 | 100 | 53 |
| Alabama, Florida[b] | 67 | 62 | 78 | 70 |
| Missouri, Iowa | 100 | 80 | 100 | 81 |
| Illinois[b] | 100 | 98 | 100 | 98 |
| Texas[b] | 29 | 51 | 100 | 70 |
| Oklahoma (Kansas and Montana in 1962) | 100 | 78 | 90 | 90 |
| Washington, Oregon, Alaska, Hawaii, Arizona, New Mexico, Utah, Colorado, Idaho, Nevada (Montana in 1963) | 67 | 86 | 100 | 92 |
| California | 100 | 98 | 100 | 97 |
| Average (mean) | 84 | 79 | 94 | 85 |

[a] The seventeen votes are those on which the whip organization took a poll.
[b] Assistant whip changed during the two-year period.

## TABLE VI *(Continued)*

*Part II: Percent Support of Specific Legislation*

| Year and Legislation | Support by all Assistant Whips | Support by all Democrats |
|---|---|---|
| 1962: | | |
| Urban Affairs | 61% | 55% |
| Tax Bill | 94 | 86 |
| Debt Limit | 89 | 84 |
| Farm Bill | 78 | 81 |
| Trade Expansion Act | 89 | 83 |
| Public Works | 89 | 82 |
| U.N. Bonds | 87 | 81 |
| 1963: | | |
| Rules Committee | 83 | 81 |
| Public Works Appropriation | 94 | 86 |
| Medical Student Loans | 95 | 87 |
| Feed Grains Program | 93 | 88 |
| Debt Limit (May) | 100 | 87 |
| Area Redevelopment | 83 | 77 |
| Debt Limit (August) | 100 | 93 |
| Tax Bill | 100 | 90 |
| Debt Limit (November) | 100 | 85 |
| Cotton Bill | 93 | 79 |

curately and also in indicating ways in which each member might be induced to support the administration on a given bill. His successor in 1963 always voted with the leaders and administration but often failed to report on his zone. Voting loyalty is far less important than accuracy and thoroughness.

The Democratic assistant whips have a great deal of discretion in deciding whether they will attempt to persuade their zone members to support the administration position. The Republicans look on their assistant whips as definite agents of the leadership. The method of appointment—by the chief Whip—insures some accountability to the leadership.

## *Party Caucuses*

The party leaders have at times been able to use caucuses or conferences to develop their own resources for influencing legislative results. The caucuses of both parties have afforded some of the leaders a psychological climate conducive to party unity. They have also given the leaders an important opportunity for collecting information on the range of opinions in the party and for disseminating their own views.

## THE DEMOCRATIC CAUCUS

Party caucuses have been used for organizational purposes since the beginning of Congress and for legislative purposes at least as early as the Jefferson presidency.[49] The Democrats after the Civil War tended to meet only for purposes of organization. But in 1909, after a number of them had defected and voted with most of the Republicans to retain Speaker Cannon's rules intact, the Democrats met in caucus for the purpose of providing punishment for members bolting party positions in the future. They adopted rules that allowed Majority Leader Oscar Underwood to use the caucus as a device for binding the Democrats together in support of legislation from 1911 to 1915 (see pages 95-98).

Even during the period of caucus-aided success on domestic legislation in 1913 and 1914, President Wilson's attention was increasingly directed to foreign affairs. Border trouble with Mexico and the beginning of the Great War in Europe were his major problems. The increasing involvement of the United States in the War and the accession to the Majority Leadership of Claude Kitchin, who did not agree with Wilson on the War, destroyed the usefulness of the binding caucus as a tool for gaining majority party victories.[50] It was used sporadically in the 1920's and early 1930's as a legislative device. Since the Seventy-third Congress (1933-35), no Democratic leaders have used a binding caucus, although the party rules still permit it. They fear it would widen differences between the regional and ideological groups in the party.

[49] Berdahl, "Party Membership," p. 310.

[50] Alexander L. George and Juliette L. George, *Woodrow Wilson and Colonel House* (John Day, 1956), p. 142; Wilfred E. Binkley, *President and Congress,* 3rd. ed. (Vintage, 1962), p. 262.

A Democratic member of Congress from California from 1937 to 1947, Jerry Voorhis, described the general use of the caucus during his period of service: "Democratic caucuses have been almost non-existent, except for occasions when it was necessary to choose a majority leader or a candidate for Speaker or to elect a member of the Ways and Means Committee."[51] The one exception came in 1939, when the Democrats were beginning to realize the seriousness of their North-South split. They held five caucuses that year to discuss party unity.[52] The pattern described by Voorhis has continued: caucuses are used almost exclusively to elect the Speaker and Majority Leader (or Minority Leader) and Democratic members of the Ways and Means Committee, and to ratify perfunctorily the decisions of the Committee on Committees.

On rare occasions the Democratic caucus still discusses legislation. In 1953, when they were in the minority, the Democrats met on the Republican tax bill. In 1959, Democratic liberals used the threat of a caucus to stall floor action on a bill abolishing the ceiling on long-term interest rates. They got enough signatures to call a caucus, and confronted Majority Leader McCormack and Ways and Means Committee chairman Wilbur Mills of Arkansas, who acquiesced by postponing consideration of the bill until Speaker Rayburn returned from Texas. These instances seem to be the only legislative uses the Democrats made of their caucus in the 1953-67 period. McCormack made a more general use of it by pleading for party unity after his nomination for Speaker in 1962.[53]

In 1965 the caucus played the unusual role of punishing two Democrats who had supported the Republican candidate for President in the 1964 election. Both men were stripped of seniority, although allowed to remain in the party and on their committees.

[51] Jerry Voorhis, *Confessions of a Congressman* (Doubleday, 1947), p. 59.

[52] See Berdahl, "Party Membership," pp. 730-31; Floyd M. Riddick, "Political Procedure in the First Session of the Seventy-sixth Congress," *South Atlantic Quarterly*, Vol. 39 (January 1940), pp. 1-17. For accounts of some of these caucuses see the *New York Times*, February 15, July 26, and July 29, 1939.

[53] *Congressional Quarterly*, January 12, 1962, p. 31.

## THE REPUBLICAN CONFERENCE

The Republicans have never made as intensive use of their caucus as the Democrats under Underwood. Yet the Republican conference (as it is now officially known) has also had a changing role in the internal government of the House Republican party. Speaker Reed occasionally used it to debate issues and reach a party position. A nearly even division in the Republican caucus was no bar to near unanimity on the floor.[54]

There is conflicting evidence on the use of the caucus by Speaker Cannon at the beginning of the century. Most commentators indicate that it was not used a great deal, but it was used enough to be an additional aggravation to insurgent Republicans.[55] George Norris of Nebraska, one of the principal insurgents, testified about his experiences as a new member: "I soon lost my good standing with the leading politicians of my party. The direct cause was my resentment against the party caucus. When I first reached Washington it was the general practice of members to follow implicitly the decisions of the caucus."[56] Cannon deliberately made vague references to both conferences and caucuses when calling a meeting. Conferences were not binding; caucuses were. His opponents claimed he would call a conference and then later indicate that he considered it a binding caucus.[57]

One particular use of the caucus by Cannon infuriated the progressives in his party. In 1908 a Republican currency bill to which the Democrats were almost unanimously opposed, was one

[54] See, for example Chiu. *The Speaker*, p. 290; McCall, *Reed*, pp. 175-76.

[55] Wilder H. Haines, "The Congressional Caucus of Today," *American Political Science Review*, Vol. 9 (November 1915), p. 696. Joseph Cooper in "Congress and Its Committees" (Ph.D. dissertation, Harvard University, 1960), page 351, footnote 7, says: "In general, the Republican Party under Cannon did not rely on the caucus but accepted party policy as defined by the party leadership. However, caucuses were used at the start of a session to elect the leadership and at times when formidable opposition within the party existed as a means of binding recalcitrant members to the position of the leadership."

[56] George Norris, *Fighting Liberal* (Collier, 1961), p. 97. See also George R. Brown, *The Leadership of Congress* (Bobbs-Merrill, 1922), p. 178.

[57] Mayhill, "Cannon," *passim*.

of the main topics of controversy in the House.[58] To add to Cannon's difficulties, the Republican chairman of the Banking and Currency Committee, Charles Fowler of New Jersey, was not in sympathy with the policy position of the leaders, and his committee submitted another bill. The leaders convened a Republican caucus to consider the issue, and when Fowler still refused to abandon his position, the Speaker appointed a special committee to report satisfactory legislation.[59] Cannon shortly removed Fowler from his chairmanship.[60]

After being thrust into minority status in 1911, the Republicans dropped the caucus with its implication of binding power over the members and replaced it with a conference that had no binding power. The conference did little until 1921 except nominate the Republican candidate for Speaker.[61] In the Sixty-seventh Congress (1921-23), when the party had a majority in both houses and held the White House too, attempts were made to use the conference on legislative matters, with little success.[62]

In 1925, at the opening of the Sixty-ninth Congress (1925-27), the Republicans returned briefly to a caucus with its potential of binding actions. After electing leaders, its first act was to discipline those who had supported the 1924 presidential candidacy of Progressive Robert LaFollette. However, the caucus was not used for discussion of legislative matters, and the Republicans returned to the conference almost immediately.[63]

The conference performed only its normal electoral functions until 1939, when some Republican successes in the preceding Congress prompted the new Minority Leader, Joseph Martin, to call it together more often to discuss legislation, usually to encourage opposition. In that year the conference met ten times.[64]

[58] Hasbrouck, *Party Government*, p. 28.

[59] See J. Lawrence Laughlin, "The Aldrich-Vreeland Act," *The Journal of Political Economy*, Vol. 16 (October 1908), pp. 489-513.

[60] For Cannon's defense of his actions, see Brown, *Leadership*, p. 161.

[61] Luce, *Legislative Procedure*, p. 513; Chiu, *Speaker*, p. 329.

[62] For example, the conference voted 94 to 76 to increase the size of the House in a new apportionment bill, but the bill lost on the House floor when the dissenting Republicans maintained their opposition. Hasbrouck, *Party Government*, pp. 28-29, 31-32.

[63] *Ibid.*, p. 29; Berdahl, "Party Membership," pp. 497-503.

[64] Riddick, "Political Procedure," p. 7.

From 1939 to 1963, the conference developed no attributes of a truly deliberative body, although it met more often on legislation than the Democratic caucus. It served mainly as a forum for the leaders to urge a specific legislative course on the members. This lack of deliberation, coupled with the general lack of leadership consultation with members, helped cause a revolt in the organizational conference in January 1963. An older member who chaired the conference in accord with the wishes of the Minority Leader was replaced with a younger, more vigorous man who promised to make the conference a deliberative body.[65]

In the following two years, the new conference chairman, Gerald Ford of Michigan, called few general meetings to debate legislation, in part because of the lack of Republican consensus on matters that could have been discussed. The conference was considered more as a vehicle for publicizing party consensus than for revealing differences. Some conference subcommittees were appointed to make policy studies of specific issues and recommend Republican positions. In 1965, Ford became Minority Leader and was succeeded as conference chairman by Melvin Laird of Wisconsin, another young and aggressive member. Laird has sought to develop the conference as a deliberative body.

## Party Committees

At various periods since 1861 several party committees have also been important in allowing the party leaders more influence on the legislative behavior of their members. As explained previously, both the campaign committees and the committees on committees give the leaders some authority over the crucial tangible preferments of campaign money and standing committee assignments.[66]

---

[65] See *Congressional Quarterly*, February 8, 1963, pp. 149-56, for a discussion of the state of the House Republican party at this time.

[66] The committees on committees are much more important than the campaign committees. The latter, even when strong, are peripheral to most legislative business. Most of the time they have been weak. See Hugh A. Bone, *Party Committees and National Politics* (University of Washington Press, 1958), pp. 128-42, for

There have also been occasional efforts in both parties to construct a steering or policy committee. Those proposing such committees envision a small group being formally placed in a leadership capacity. The motivation behind such proposals is twofold and paradoxical: a desire to restrain the leaders, while at the same time making them more effective in producing a unified party.

## THE DEMOCRATIC STEERING COMMITTEE

In 1933 the Democrats established a Steering Committee, but it never played a significant role. Theoretically designed to reflect the policy preferences of all Democrats and allow them, through representatives, to help shape party policy, it continued its formal existence until 1956. Its last chairman explained simply why it was not needed: "Mr. Sam [Speaker Sam Rayburn] decides what will be done."[67]

When Rayburn died in late 1961, the liberal members of the party campaigned to reconstitute a steering committee to represent a broader range of party opinion. The new Speaker, John McCormack, acceded to their wishes. In 1962 a Steering Committee was formally established with eighteen members chosen by regions identical with the whip zones. Sitting as *ex officio* members are the Speaker, Majority Leader, Whip, chairman of the caucus, secretary of the caucus, and chairman of the Congressional Campaign Committee. From 1962 through 1966 the new committee seldom met and had no effect on legislation or party tactics. As its chairman said, "There just haven't been any issues

---

a description of these committees. At present the Democratic campaign committee has some discretion in distributing funds. The Republican campaign committee has more funds but now seems to distribute them largely on the basis of a formula that eliminates discrimination on the basis of loyalty. This is a reversal of the previous pattern. See the *Evening Star* (Washington), March 4, 1965; and the *Washington Post*, March 5, 1965.

[67] For more information on the Steering Committee created in 1933 see Herring, "First Session of the Seventy-third Congress"; and Walter E. Beach, "The Democratic Steering Committee in the United States House of Representatives" (M.A. thesis, George Washington University, 1961). For the text of the resolution establishing it see Floyd M. Riddick, *Congressional Procedure* (Chapman and Grimes, 1941), p. 364. The statement by the last chairman is quoted in Beach, p. 35.

that the members wanted to discuss."[68] Although formally labeled "advisory," the group was not even allowed to perform this limited—and perhaps meaningless—function. It did, however, have a large enough budget ($41,825 in fiscal year 1967) to hire a capable staff man to work for the leaders on legislative problems.

REPUBLICAN STEERING AND POLICY COMMITTEES

The Republicans have twice created a Steering Committee that has had substantial impact on the party's legislative decisions. The first committee had its origins in 1917, when an advisory committee of five members was appointed by the conference to aid Minority Leader James Mann. Many members did not trust the centralized power he had wielded since 1911. The advisory committee was a prelude to the general dispersion of power within the Republican party in 1919, when the Steering Committee was formally created, first with five members and later with eight. Intended as a device to decentralize power and promote party unity, it helped make scheduling and policy decisions until 1925, but rapidly lost importance thereafter because the new Speaker ignored it, although it continued in existence.[69]

In 1949 the name of the Steering Committee was changed to the Policy Committee and its membership was expanded to twenty-two.[70] Subsequent expansions to make it more representative increased the size to thirty-five. But the Policy Committee was largely ineffective until 1959, when John Byrnes of Wisconsin became its chairman. Over the next six years it became an integral part of the Republican leadership, stating policy positions and advising the Minority Leader. It overshadowed the conference for these six years, but was in turn overshadowed by it after 1965.

[68] Quoted in Daniel M. Berman, *In Congress Assembled* (Macmillan, 1964), p. 239.

[69] For general discussions of the Republican Steering Committee in the 1920's see Brown, *Leadership,* pp. 200-20; and Chiu, *Speaker,* pp. 329-35.

[70] On the post-1949 Policy Committee see Charles O. Jones, *Party and Policy-Making: The House Republican Policy Committee* (Rutgers University Press, 1964). For the text of the resolution creating it see George B. Galloway, *The Legislative Process in Congress* (Crowell, 1953), p. 334.

The Republican Steering Committee of 1919 to 1925 and the Policy Committee of 1959 to 1965 both used psychological preferment and control of communications in attempting to mold a united party behind specific policy positions. In part, the floor leader could use the Steering Committee or Policy Committee members as his assistants. But he was also bound by their collective decisions. Active steering or policy committees almost inevitably have strained relations with the single most important leader of a party because they diminish his authority. This explains why an active and powerful committee is an unusual phenomenon in both parties.

## *Party Development and the Institutionalization of the House*

The development of party offices, caucuses, and committees since 1861 occurred in three main stages. In the first, power was centralized in the hands of the Speaker and a few close lieutenants. In the second, the House acquired the main characteristics of an institution, including, crucially, a membership more dedicated to career service and a virtually automatic rule of seniority for apportioning rank (and its accompanying power) on standing committees. In the third stage, the parties became more bureaucratized.

### CENTRALIZATION OF POWER

The four Speakers who contributed most to the centralization of power in the House—Randall, Carlisle, Reed, and Crisp—all served between 1875 and 1895. They were reacting to the confusion and resulting lack of legislative accomplishment in the national government during much of this period. They sought to make their parties effective by acquiring power to produce unity. For only six of the years between 1875 and 1895 did a single party control the White House, Senate, and House. In 1881-83, the Republicans held all three, and were able to pass a major tariff increase. They had similar control in 1889-91, and again passed a tariff increase. The Democrats controlled the national government in 1893-95 and passed a tariff reduction. Little else was achieved legislatively during these two decades. Often the House could not conduct even routine business because of the minority party's power to disrupt the proceedings.

The House doubled in size between 1861 (178 members, although there had been 237 members before the southerners left) and 1893 (357 members). This put additional strains on the leaders as they attempted to keep a tightly knit legislative party. New methods of keeping track of the preferences, movements, loyalties, and behavior of the members were needed. Furthermore, between 1876 and 1896, eight new western states entered the Union, sending representatives to the House who were less tied to traditional party positions than the representatives of the older states.[71] This development also pushed the leaders toward exercising more centralized power.

An internal House development that drove the leaders to seek greater centralized power for themselves was the division of the appropriations function. From 1865 to 1877 the Appropriations Committee handled all appropriations bills. Between 1877 and 1885 the House transferred eight of its fourteen bills to the jurisdictions of other standing committees.[72] A unified jurisdiction was not restored until 1920. The Speakers in the late nineteenth century were concerned that appropriations not exceed revenue. When they had to deal with a single committee they could influence developments in the field much more easily than when they had to deal with a number of committees.[73] Thus they developed some of their powers, such as recognition, specifically to protect the Treasury from raids by the numerous substantive committees with appropriating power.

[71] See George H. Mayer, *The Republican Party, 1854-1964* (Oxford, 1964), pp. 223-24.

[72] For a brief discussion of the events of 1877 to 1885 see Richard F. Fenno, Jr., *The Power of the Purse* (Little, Brown, and Co., 1966), pp. 43-44. It should be stressed that personal hostility to Appropriations Committee Chairman Samuel Randall played a large part in the 1885 decision to take six bills away from the committee.

[73] See L. Dwaine Marvick, "Congressional Appropriation Politics" (Ph.D. thesis, Columbia University, 1952), pp. 27-31.

INSTITUTIONALIZATION OF THE HOUSE[74]

In the late nineteenth century members of the House began to serve longer than their predecessors. Data already presented on the age and prior service of Speakers and Minority Leaders show 1899 to be a clear dividing line between younger, relatively junior Speakers and Minority Leaders and older, relatively senior Speakers and Minority Leaders. Freshmen in the Congress convening in 1899 represented the smallest percentage (30.1) of the total number of members in the history of the House to that date. In 1901, for the first time in history, the mean period of service of all members exceeded three terms. Five-Congress averages show 1899 to be an important watershed:

| Congresses | Years | Percentage of Freshman Members | Mean Period of Service (terms) |
|---|---|---|---|
| 41st–45th | 1869–78 | 50.5 | 2.05 |
| 46th–50th | 1879–88 | 39.8 | 2.39 |
| 51st–55th | 1889–98 | 41.3 | 2.51 |
| 56th–60th | 1899–1908 | 25.9 | 3.22 |

These figures represent a determination on the part of a much greater number of members to make a career of membership in the House. Before 1899 it was usual for even Speakers and committee chairmen to leave to accept a Senate seat or Cabinet position. After 1899 this was rare.[75]

[74] This discussion is based on data collected by the author and on data and arguments presented by Nelson W. Polsby, "The Institutionalization of the U.S. House of Representatives" (paper prepared for delivery at the 1966 meeting of the American Political Science Association); H. Douglas Price, "The Congressional Career—Risks and Rewards" (unpublished paper); and T. Richard Witmer, "The Aging of the House," *Political Science Quarterly*, Vol. 79 (December 1964), pp. 526-41.

[75] The reasons for the relatively sudden increases in years of service and the emergence of a true "House career" are unclear. Possibilities that should be explored include the greater attractiveness of service in the House because of the order established by the Speakers by 1895, the greater ease with which incumbents began winning elections, the greater ease with which incumbents could obtain campaign money, and the great reduction in the number of contested

Until 1911 the Speaker appointed all members of committees and designated the chairmen. He often followed seniority, but was not obliged to do so and the members did not expect him to do so consistently. As long as most members did not expect to serve in the House for the rest of their political careers this power was acceptable to them. When they began to look to a career in the House their definition of acceptability changed. To make their careers profitable in terms of power and influence, they had to be sure that there was a secure, orderly path of advancement open to them. With an arbitrary Speaker who might, for some reason, dislike them, the path could be closed permanently by unfavorable committee assignments or denial of chairmanships. New awareness of these possibilities was partially responsible for the revolt against Speaker Cannon and the rules changes in 1910 and 1911.

Between 1911 and 1921 seniority rapidly became the "rule" (unwritten, but well understood) for advancement to chairmanships. The leaders during this decade occasionally violated seniority and thus tried to keep the members in line for chairmanships from being violently anti-party in their behavior.[76] But since 1921 neither party has violated seniority, except for three

---

seats. On the latter point, it is interesting to note that 1899 again marks a turning point.

| Congresses | Years | Percentage of Contested Seats per Congress |
|---|---|---|
| 41st–45th | 1869–78 | 5.28 |
| 46th–50th | 1879–88 | 3.72 |
| 51st–55th | 1889–98 | 5.02 |
| 56th–60th | 1899–1908 | 2.20 |
| 61st–65th | 1909–18 | 1.72 |
| 66th–70th | 1919–28 | 1.06 |

[76] Changes in the chairmen and ranking minority members of nineteen House committees between 1911 and 1925 were studied to ascertain how many times seniority was violated. During this period the Democrats violated seniority five times, all before 1915 (three times in 1911, once in 1913, and once between 1913 and 1915). The Republicans violated seniority three times (once in 1913 and twice in 1921). In 1915, 1917, 1919, 1923, and 1925 (with the exception of the LaFollette mavericks in the last year) neither party violated seniority at the highest levels of committee succession. See Michael E. Abram, "The Rise of the Modern Seniority System in the House of Representatives" (unpublished senior honors thesis, Harvard College, 1966).

isolated instances in which members were removed from committees or reduced in rank primarily because they supported the presidential nominee of another party.

## BUREAUCRATIZATION OF THE PARTIES

The hardening of the seniority rule decreased the power of the leaders and made them seek other ways and methods for influencing their members. One of the methods they chose was to encourage the development of party organizations and committees that could help them work for unity. Since the 1930's, the leaders of both parties have encouraged the development of a large whip organization and have made increasing use of it.

The leaders of both parties have also experimented with steering and policy committees and the caucus or conference. Sometimes such committees or caucuses have proved to be ineffective, on other occasions they have provided a useful increment to the power of the leaders. Some of these experiments have failed; but the important point is that many of the leaders have been willing to experiment with various forms of organization in an attempt to overcome the anti-party effects of seniority and autonomous standing committees.

# ☆ 3 ☆

# Functions of the Leaders

Since 1861 the party leaders in the House have consistently performed six major legislative functions:[1] (1) organizing the party, (2) scheduling the business of the House, (3) promoting attendance of members for important votes on the floor, (4) distributing and collecting information, (5) persuading members to act in accord with their wishes, and (6) maintaining liaison with the President and his top advisers. The performance of these functions is dynamically interrelated; typically, several leaders share in the execution of a number of them simultaneously in an effort to influence legislative results. For purposes of clarity, however, the relation of individual leaders, caucuses, and committees to each function will be analyzed separately.

## *Organization of Party*

### THE SPEAKER

The Speaker has a large role in all organizational decisions made by the majority party. He has usually operated behind the scenes to assure the election of Majority Leaders he favors, although both parties formally select their Leader in the caucus or

[1] This chapter is concerned specifically with the *legislative* functions of the leadership. The leaders may perform other functions, such as helping members gain re-election, that are not primarily legislative in immediate impact.

conference. Since 1925, Speakers have been successful in this endeavor through a variety of approaches. In 1933, Henry Rainey of Illinois picked Joseph Byrns of Tennessee as Democratic Majority Leader by making a trade—in return for support for his bid for Speaker, Rainey and his followers supported Byrns for Majority Leader.[2] Two years later, after Rainey's death, Byrns remained technically neutral while eight candidates battled for the job of Majority Leader. William Bankhead of Alabama, Byrns' preference, won. In 1940, Sam Rayburn encouraged John McCormack in his attempt to win the post.[3]

When a new Majority Leader was chosen in 1962, McCormack made no formal statement of his preferences. However, the belief that he backed Carl Albert of Oklahoma was so prevalent among Democrats and newsmen that Richard Bolling of Missouri, the only other announced candidate for the office, withdrew before the caucus.[4]

The Democratic Whip is formally named by the Majority Leader, but the Speaker often has the commanding voice in making the appointment. In 1935, because Senator Joseph Guffey of Pennsylvania had helped persuade House members from his state to vote for Byrns for Speaker, Byrns named a Pennsylvanian, Patrick Boland, as Whip.[5] Speaker Rayburn was instrumental in selecting all of the Whips who served under him. When it was suggested that Carl Albert run against McCormack for Speaker in 1962, Albert replied, "I would never do that against John McCormack. Mr. Rayburn and Mr. McCormack picked me and made me Whip, and to run against Mr. McCormack would have been the act of an ingrate."[6]

Rayburn also created a new formal leadership post of deputy whip in 1955 and picked one of his younger favorites, Hale Boggs of Louisiana, to fill it. McCormack wanted to promote Boggs to Whip in 1962, and Albert, who had the formal power of

[2] E. Pendleton Herring, "First Session of the Seventy-third Congress," *American Political Science Review*, Vol. 28 (February 1934), pp. 65-83.

[3] C. Dwight Dorough, *Mr. Sam* (Random House, 1962), pp. 300-01.

[4] Nelson W. Polsby, "Two Strategies of Influence: Choosing a Majority Leader, 1962," in Robert L. Peabody and Nelson W. Polsby, *New Perspectives on the House of Representatives* (Rand McNally, 1963), pp. 245-47.

[5] Dorough, *Mr. Sam*, pp. 253-54.

[6] Quoted in Polsby, "Two Strategies," p. 246.

appointment, agreed. At the same time, McCormack promised the senior California Democrat that the post of deputy whip would go to a member from his state. Boggs, with formal power to make the appointment, saw no reason to dissent from the Speaker's position and they agreed on John Moss.

Since the mid-1920's, then, the Democratic Speaker has been predominant in choosing men to fill the other leadership positions. During this same period a limited pattern of leadership advancement has been solidifying inside the party: the Majority Leader has, without exception, become Speaker when the old Speaker died or left the House. In the latest Democratic leadership change (1962), the Whip and deputy whip also both moved up one notch.

The two Republican Speakers since the mid-1920's have both picked their own Majority Leader, but have had no chance or necessity to pick their own Whips. Both Nicholas Longworth and Joseph Martin were faced with incumbent Whips when they became Speaker, and neither saw any reason to ask the party for a change.

The Republicans have been in the minority during most of the period since 1925, and the expectations of rank-and-file members about who would become Speaker if they should achieve a House majority are unclear. In 1919 they denied the Speakership to their Minority Leader of eight years. In 1925 they promoted their Majority Leader, and in 1947 and 1953 they promoted their Minority Leader. Since the last Republican Speaker, however, there have been two close, hard-fought, and rancorous struggles for the post of Minority Leader (1959 and 1965).

The Speaker's influence on other important aspects of party organization is less direct. Democratic Speakers have substantial influence over assignments to the Ways and Means Committee, which also acts as the Committee on Committees. The Ways and Means members are elected by the caucus, but only three times in recent decades have candidates other than those supported by the Speaker won.[7] The Speaker's influence on assignments to the

---

[7] The two most recent cases of non-leadership candidates being successful in their bid for a seat on Ways and Means were Burr Harrison in 1951 and Pat Jennings in 1963. Both are Virginia Democrats. On Jennings' defeat of the leader-

other standing committees is not as clear. Democratic and Republican Speakers both control new appointments to the Rules Committee; however, Republican Speakers have more control over Appropriations Committee appointments than do Democratic Speakers.

Aside from Rules, Ways and Means, and Appropriations, the Speaker picks his spots for influencing committee assignments. Speaker Martin limited his efforts to "important" committees: "In the four years that I served as Speaker no Republican went on an important committee without my approval."[8] Even if this claim is taken at face value, it suggests that there were less important assignments that he let the Committee on Committees handle in normal fashion by bargaining between the various large states and geographical areas. Democratic Speakers work much the same way. Members of the Committee on Committees have indicated that the Speaker intervenes only occasionally in the normal bargaining for choice assignments.

## FLOOR LEADERS

The floor leaders have substantial influence in the organization of their parties. Democratic floor leaders formally appoint the Whip (although, as indicated above, the Speaker may actually control the appointment). Republican floor leaders chair their party's Committee on Committees and are important in its decisions. Democratic floor leaders have not served on their Committee on Committees since 1919.

In recent years the Minority Leader has tried to influence the other top choices for leadership positions in the Republican party. In 1959 Charles Halleck helped John Byrnes become chairman of the Policy Committee as part of the price for getting the necessary support to oust Joe Martin as Minority Leader. In 1965 the new Minority Leader, Gerald Ford, felt it his duty to try to influence the choice of a Republican Whip. He announced

ship candidate see Richard Bolling, *Defeating the Leadership's Nominee in the House Democratic Caucus* (Bobbs-Merrill, 1966), Inter-University Case Program Case No. 91.

[8] Joe Martin, *My First Fifty Years in Politics* (McGraw-Hill, 1960), p. 181.

support for another candidate against a man who had been Whip for twenty-one years and was the second senior Republican in the House. In the ensuing fight, the Republicans rebuffed their new Leader by retaining the incumbent Whip, thus demonstrating convincingly that Ford would not have a completely free hand in reshaping the party organization.

Both the Majority and Minority Leaders tend to be more effective in influencing less visible appointments. Their good will is eagerly sought by incoming freshmen seeking good committee assignments and by veteran members who wish to change committees.

### PARTY CAUCUSES AND COMMITTEES

The Democratic caucus chooses the party's candidate for Speaker. It has also elected the floor leader ever since the post emerged. Since 1911 it has elected the party's members of the Ways and Means Committee.

Only once has the Democratic caucus taken disciplinary action involving party organization. In 1965, it voted to punish two members by stripping them of their seniority after they supported the Republican candidate for President in 1964.

The Republican conference has also chosen candidates for Speaker and, since 1923, has elected Majority Leaders. It has always possessed the residual power to choose the Whip, although it gave automatic approval to the choice of the Committee on Committees until 1965.

The conference ventured into the realm of discipline only once, in 1925, when thirteen Republicans who had supported the candidate of a third party for President were stripped of some committee assignments and seniority on those they retained.

The Committees on Committees of both parties have performed a major organizing task since their creation in 1911 (Democratic) and 1917 (Republican).[9] The power in the Republican committee is wielded by a few representatives from the states with the most Republicans who serve on a subcommittee

---

[9] See Nicholas Masters, "Committee Assignments in the House of Representatives," *American Political Science Review*, Vol. 55 (June 1961), pp. 345-57.

of the Committee on Committees. There, as in the full committee, they cast one vote for each Republican from their state. The
senior conservatives who serve on the subcommittee discipline
members for lack of party loyalty, even though the party leaders
may prefer not to have committee assignments used consistently
in this way. To have an impact on the assignment process, the
leaders must be able to influence the subcommittee members.

In the Democratic Committee on Committees each member
has one vote, regardless of the number of Democratic Representatives from his state. Every Democrat has a geographically
based spokesman who must nominate him for committee assignments. The leaders and the committee chairmen may make their
wishes known in a few cases, but the process is usually left to the
judgment of the Committee on Committees (although, as one
committee member put it, the leaders know that "we won't deliberately do violence to their wishes and preferences").

The power of chairmen to govern assignments to their own
committees varies with the man. At times, the Committee on
Committees may pack a committee to limit the powers of its
chairman. Some chairmen are successful in designating new
members of their committee and vetoing some possible choices.
Other chairmen may stay aloof from the process, partly by choice
and partly because they are not consulted. One chairman explained, "The Committee on Committees does not check with
me ahead of time to see if any of the men they want to assign to
my committee are possibly unsatisfactory to me. I raised hell
about one member they gave me last year. But I was stuck with
him. There was nothing I could do."

The degree to which individual members, both freshmen and
incumbents, campaign for committee seats varies widely. Some
write a request to the Committee on Committees. Others mount
extensive campaigns, complete with letters from important party
leaders.

An analysis of the Democratic assignment process in 1963 suggests the role of the leaders and the patterns of communications
that develop. This analysis is based on the files of a member of
the Committee on Committees, which contained summary sheets
of vacancies and applications prepared for the committee prior
to its mid-January meeting. The summary sheets reflect verbal

applications, although many verbal communications on pending applications are not recorded.

The committee had to find assignments for each of the thirty-six Democrats who entered the Eighty-eighth Congress as freshmen. Of these, only sixteen applied for specific seats before the committee met. Apparently the other twenty were willing to trust either fate or the judgment of their zone representatives. Some of the sixteen requested only one committee; others listed four or five choices, indicating preferences.

Of the 222 Democrats returning to the Eighty-eighth Congress, twenty-one applied for specific changes of committee assignment. Twelve of them got new or additional assignments (ten received the assignment they requested); nine of them got no new assignment. The remaining 201 Democrats did not apply in writing for a change in assignment, but twenty-four of them were moved. The extent to which the committee acted contrary to the wishes of the members suggests its independence and strength.

These data also provide a clue to the committee's consideration of party loyalty in making assignments. As indicated, ten of the twenty-one incumbent members who applied for new assignments got their first choice. Another member received his second choice, which, surprisingly, was the Appropriations Committee, generally the most prized assignment next to Ways and Means itself. These eleven men "succeeded." The other ten "failed": nine of them got no change and one received an assignment he did not desire. Averaging party loyalty scores for the two groups in the previous Congress produced the following results: the eleven "successes" had a score of 67 and the ten "failures" had a score of 34.[10]

As might be suspected from the average loyalty scores, the committee was kinder to northerners and westerners than to southerners. Of eight southerners applying for a change, only two were successful. Five out of seven northerners and four out of six westerners were successful.

[10] The party loyalty score is the result of subtracting *Congressional Quarterly's* party opposition score from its party unity score. These represent the percentage of the time a member voted for and against the majority of his party when the majorities of the two parties were opposing each other.

For freshman members, the clearest lesson is to apply early. Of the sixteen incoming Democrats who applied before the Committee on Committees met, ten got their first choice and four got their second choice. The two who were unsuccessful were southerners who had campaigned for office on anti-administration platforms.

Some members who applied early merely stated their preferences; others solicited letters of support from their deans, their delegations, the committee chairman concerned, their Ways and Means representative, and (in one case each) the Speaker and a Senator. Those who received support from committee chairmen were successful in all but one case, which involved a sitting member who often opposed the administration and the leaders. Delegation support tended to help only if the delegation was generally loyal. Seniority did not seem to be important: the unsuccessful incumbents had served an average of 3.4 terms; the successful incumbents averaged 3.2 terms.

Appeals used by those seeking assignments and by their supporters usually stressed the importance of regional or state representation on a given committee. They pointed out that a departing member of the committee was from the same state or region, or that the state or region had been represented on the committee for some time. They cited qualifications they felt were particularly relevant to the desired assignment and indicated the support they had obtained for the assignment.

## Scheduling Business

### THE SPEAKER AND THE MAJORITY LEADER

The scheduling of business for the House is formally the job of the Majority Leader. His responsibility is carried out in constant consultation with the Speaker, who makes scheduling commitments of his own to the White House or to committees or subcommittee chairmen.

Scheduling is often a delicate political decision. Bills favored by the majority party leadership (and President, if of the same party) must be scheduled at the most advantageous times. In the fight over increasing the size of the Rules Committee in 1961, for example, Speaker Rayburn gave his supporters a vital four extra days to line up needed votes.[11] Similarly, if the leaders do not favor certain bills, but cannot avoid letting them come to the floor, they will try to schedule them at the most inopportune time for the supporters.

Most bills are scheduled when the substantive committee reports them. In the case of bills requiring a rule for floor consideration, the chairman of the standing committee may inform the Speaker even before a rule is requested that a bill is ready for floor action, and suggest the timing that he would prefer. When it is clear that there will be no opposition in the Rules Committee, the Speaker usually tries to accommodate him.

The Speaker also exercises discretion about bringing bills to the floor under suspension of the rules. This procedure limits debate to forty minutes but requires a two-thirds vote for passage. Suspensions are usually in order only two Mondays a month, but during the last six days of the session the Speaker may bring any bill to the floor under suspension of the rules. Thus, in effect, he largely determines which bills may be passed and which must await a new session or even a new Congress, when they must again go through the entire legislative process.

Usually the Speaker carefully calculates his objectives before he schedules a bill. Casual scheduling may risk serious legislative setbacks. Speakers or committee chairmen who acquire the reputation for losing too many bills make subsequent defeats more likely.

In scheduling the business of the House, the Speaker also attempts to cooperate with the Minority Leader. Generally he will not approve scheduling that the Minority Leader considers unfair. On occasion, rank-and-file members of both parties can devise ways, either planned or spontaneous, to force scheduling decisions by the Speaker. A month before the 1964 election, for example, House members greeted a demand for adjournment with an ovation and voted against the leaders on an important roll call, in effect forcing a decision to adjourn rapidly.[12]

In scheduling the routine business of the House, the Majority

---

[11] See Neil MacNeil, *Forge of Democracy* (McKay, 1963), p. 43 and Chapter 15.
[12] *Washington Post*, October 2, 1964.

Leader operates in a set pattern. His legislative assistant makes up a draft of the program for the following week late on Wednesday or early Thursday. The draft is based on commitments made to various committee chairmen by the Speaker and Majority Leader. It also includes information from the Speaker's office on what bills are to be put on the suspension, consent, and private calendars, and what legislation is coming from the privileged committees that do not need a rule from the Rules Committee. The draft is then submitted to the Speaker for any changes he cares to make. Late Thursday afternoon, in a colloquy on the floor with the Minority Leader, the Majority Leader outlines the program, reserving the right to change it and bring up conference reports.

Committee chairmen can play a major role in scheduling. The schedule for appropriations bills in 1964, for example, was framed by the chairman of the Appropriations Committee, Clarence Cannon of Missouri. The Majority Leader was delighted to follow the schedule without deviation, and these bills, which had frequently been delayed in previous years, were all completed in the House before the fiscal year ended on June 30.

Also in 1964, the White House asked the Majority Leader to follow with particular care six annual authorization bills that had been delayed too long in 1963 and other preceding years. The Majority Leader assigned a staff member to call each of the relevant committees weekly to check the progress of the bills until they reached the floor. The effectiveness of these calls may be judged from the following comparison of the dates of floor action in 1963 and 1964:

| | Date of Floor Action | |
| Authorization Bill | 1963 | 1964 |
| --- | --- | --- |
| Defense procurement—ships, missiles, aircraft, R&D | March 13 | February 20 |
| Defense—military construction | June 5 | March 18 |
| AEC—operations and construction | July 8 | May 7 |
| NASA—operations and construction | August 1 | March 25 |
| Foreign aid | August 23 | June 10 |
| Peace Corps | November 13 | March 4 |

PARTY CAUCUSES AND COMMITTEES

From 1911 to 1915, the Democratic caucus decided when the House could act on important bills. A resolution of the issues involved was necessary in the caucus before the legislation was permitted to go to the floor.

The Republican conference never played a similar role, although from 1919 to 1925 the Steering Committee met daily and agreed (usually on the advice of the Majority Leader) on what the House should act. In 1949, the Republican majority adopted a resolution that seemed to give the conference a major role in scheduling. It stated: "No issue of major importance affecting national Republican policy shall be brought to the Floor of the House with the consent of the Republican leadership until after a Republican conference has been held, with adequate time for a full discussion of the subject . . ."[13] However, the party has held a majority for only two years since the adoption of the resolution, and Speaker Joseph Martin and Majority Leader Charles Halleck were not disposed to give the conference such a role.

## Promoting Attendance

The primary function of the party whip organizations is to ensure maximum attendance on the floor when critical votes are taken.[14] This involves keeping the members in Washington and getting them to the House chamber for the votes. The assistant whips check probable attendance by asking members if they will be in town on specific days. The results show which members should be asked to change their travel plans, or which days seem most favorable for floor action.

[13] George B. Galloway, *The Legislative Process in Congress* (Crowell, 1953), p. 334.
[14] Other party officials also promote attendance, but they have no machinery to do so systematically. The Republican Policy Committee from 1959 to 1965 helped promote maximum Republican attendance.

On the day of a floor vote, the Whip's office compares its attendance check against absentees on the day's first quorum call to indicate which members need to be called. Only those thought to be friendly to the leadership position will be alerted. As the time of the vote approaches, calls go out from the Whip's office specifying what is being voted on and indicating that the leaders desire the members' presence. To get members to the floor for crucial votes, the Whip's office uses every available means, from airplanes to wheel chairs.

While the importance of the issue obviously affects attendance on a specific vote, the whip organization helps to produce a high voting turnout. On the seventeen bills in 1962 and 1963 on which the whip organization was fully active, total Democratic voting participation was 94 percent. On all roll calls, Democratic voting participation was 83 percent in 1962 and 84 percent in 1963.[15]

## *Distribution and Collection of Information*

### THE SPEAKER

The Speaker helps other party leaders collect information from the rank-and-file members and distributes information to them. While the whip organization is responsible for systematic collection of information from the membership, he decides when a poll should be taken. Formal responsibility for distributing information is generally given to the Majority Leader and Whip, and sometimes to a substantive committee chairman, but occasionally the Speaker also sends letters to all party members with information on upcoming legislation.

Thus the Speaker's informational activities are largely informal, but extremely important. In constant contact with commit-

[15] *Congressional Quarterly,* June 16, 1961, pp. 993-94, suggests that the whip organizations help promote high voting turnout. The assistant whips had attendance records much like those of all Democrats on all roll calls, but on seventeen key votes on which the whip organization was active they did somewhat better than the rank-and-file. The assistant whips voted 83.4 percent of the time on all roll calls in 1962, and 84.7 percent in 1963. But on the seventeen key votes their voting attendance rose to 96 percent.

tee chairmen, he learns of their legislative progress and plans and makes his own views known to them. He is also in regular contact with other senior members of his party and some more junior members. He usually maintains ties with some members of the minority to keep informed of their plans and prospects.[16]

The Speaker can change his communications network on any given legislative fight. He always is in touch with his Majority Leader and Whip. Depending on the issue and committee personnel, he may choose to work with the committee chairman involved, or bypass him and work with another majority member. For example, during Howard Smith's chairmanship of the Rules Committee, both Rayburn and McCormack worked with more junior, liberal Democrats. Thus Homer Thornberry of Texas and Richard Bolling of Missouri were the "Speaker's men" on the Rules Committee for Rayburn. McCormack continued to rely on Bolling on some matters, and also looked to Thomas O'Neill of Massachusetts and B. F. Sisk of California for special aid.

## THE FLOOR LEADERS

The Majority and Minority Leaders are responsible for transmitting certain information to their members and for eliciting information from them. For example, they have much to say about when whip polls will be taken and they also interpret and use the results.[17] Both floor leaders send information to their members about bills before the House.

The Majority Leader also maintains a steady flow of information between the White House, the Speaker, and committee chairmen. His office is the central point for collecting and transmitting accurate details on what is coming up for House consideration.

The Minority Leader has a special informational role to play because he is the chief spokesman for minority policy positions

[16] See Booth Mooney, *Mr. Speaker* (Follett, 1964), pp. 132-33, for a good description of Rayburn's attempts to know what was happening in the House.

[17] Minority Leader Champ Clark was apparently the first to use a polling technique. See Champ Clark, *My Quarter Century of American Politics* (Harper, 1920), Vol. 2, p. 382.

in the House. (The Majority Leader takes some part in stating majority positions, although he is clearly inferior to the Speaker in this regard.) His freedom to state party positions varies. In the Republican Eighty-third Congress (1953-55), Sam Rayburn took the lead in stating Democratic positions. He checked these positions with a few close advisers, but felt no need to use a Democratic caucus or any kind of steering or policy committee to advise him. In the Eighty-seventh and Eighty-eighth Congresses (1961-65), on the other hand, Minority Leader Halleck was generally obliged to check with the Republican Policy Committee before taking positions for the party on major bills.[18]

## THE WHIPS

The Whip in both parties is routinely responsible for giving party members written notice of each week's floor schedule. His office also provides information on the substance of important bills.

To ascertain how members will vote on important legislation, the principal device is the poll. This is conducted by the whip organization after the leaders decide that one is needed. Assistant whips or designated staff members in their offices contact each member's office and ask for a response to a specific question: "Will you vote for final passage of H.R. 777, the social security amendments?" These responses are then reported to the Whip's office for tabulation and appropriate action. Some Democratic assistant whips are reluctant to report the names of those opposing the leadership. A few report by number, not name. In the Eighty-eighth Congress only one zone (containing 16 of the 257 Democrats) reported in this unsatisfactory manner and the assistant whip was usually willing to divulge the names privately to the Whip's administrative assistant, whom he trusted. By 1966 this problem had become acute, however, and four assistant whips (responsible for 72 of the 294 Democrats) generally refused to report members' positions by name. The Republican party

[18] Unfortunately for Halleck, he apparently did not check enough before announcing policy positions to satisfy many of his critics. See Meg Greenfield, "Charles A. Halleck and the Restless Republicans," *Reporter*, March 29, 1962, pp. 27-30.

does not have this problem because its Whip appoints his own assistants and would not tolerate such behavior.

A poll is usually taken after a bill has been reported from the committee and before it is scheduled for floor action. Ordinarily a poll is completed within two days to two weeks. Naturally, the longer the time available, the more accurate its results. Accuracy also depends on the clarity and specificity of the questions asked. A poll on a relatively uncomplicated bill may be simply on final passage. If legislation is extremely complex, a simple response for or against the bill may hide important feelings about amendments. Therefore, polls are often taken on specific provisions, proposed amendments, and the recommittal motion to be offered by the minority. The most effective assistant whips probe the sentiments of their members about specific provisions. If a current of opinion develops against a certain feature, the legislation may be changed in time to save it from defeat.

The results of a poll taken by the presidential party are usually supplemented by and shared with officials from the White House and executive branch. Lobbyists are additional sources of information for both parties.[19]

Poll results require sensitive and knowledgeable interpreters who have the experience to tell when a report from a member is of dubious validity and when it can be accepted at face value.[20] Such knowledge is vital, since decisions about provisions in the

---

[19] During 1962-63 the White House or department concerned rarely had information as accurate as that which the whip organization had collected. Lobbyists often had an even more distorted picture of voting probabilities. See Raymond Bauer, Ithiel de Sola Pool, and Lewis A. Dexter, *American Business and Public Policy* (Atherton, 1963), p. 352, for an instance of the same lack of accuracy a decade earlier. Outsiders from the executive branch or interest groups know less about the peculiarities of individual members and are likely to arouse resentment among members. The Whip, White House, and friendly lobbyists usually exchange their poll results, producing a composite poll.

[20] There are several reasons for a member to make an inaccurate report of his position. He might want to avoid leadership pressure by not alerting anyone to his opposition. He might be annoyed at the inconvenience of repeatedly reporting his position. Finally, he might use the report of opposition as a bargaining device. For example, on the poll on the debt limit increase in May 1963, a usually loyal Democrat from the midwest reported "doubtful" and, at the same time, indicated his eagerness for final Treasury confirmation that a new Internal Revenue Service installation would be located in his district.

TABLE VII

## Accuracy of Democratic Whip Polls, 1962–64

| Year and Subject | Percent of Members Correctly Reported | Number of Members Correctly Reported | Number of Members Incorrectly or Not Reported |
|---|---|---|---|
| **1962:** | | | |
| Urban Affairs | *87%* | 226 | 34 |
| Tax Bill | *81* | 212 | 49 |
| Debt Limit | *90* | 237 | 25 |
| Farm Bill | *82* | 216 | 46 |
| Trade Expansion | *92* | 241 | 21 |
| Public Works | *87* | 228 | 33 |
| U.N. Bonds | *87* | 227 | 34 |
| **1963:** | | | |
| Rules Committee | *96* | 247 | 10 |
| Public Works Appropriation | *91* | 233 | 23 |
| Medical Student Loans | *94* | 240 | 16 |
| Feed Grains | *84* | 214 | 42 |
| Debt Limit (May) | *93* | 239 | 17 |
| Area Redevelopment | *91* | 232 | 23 |
| Debt Limit (August) | *85* | 218 | 38 |
| Tax Bill | *96* | 246 | 10 |
| Debt Limit (November) | *92* | 235 | 21 |
| Cotton Bill | *84* | 214 | 42 |
| **1964:** | | | |
| Food Stamp | *84* | 215 | 40 |
| Wheat-Cotton | *84* | 214 | 41 |
| International Development Assn. | *87* | 219 | 34 |
| Pay Raise | *87* | 220 | 33 |
| Excise Tax | *85* | 214 | 39 |
| Mass Transit | *91* | 230 | 23 |
| Poverty | *92* | 234 | 19 |

bill, its scheduling for floor action, and attempts to change votes are based partially on poll results. The accuracy of Democratic whip polls presented to the leaders in 1962, 1963, and 1964 is shown in Table VII. A similar analysis of Republican polls was not possible, because they did not file their results.

The percentages in Table VII do not indicate adequately the utility and reliability of the polls. More detailed analysis of the 1963 polls and final roll calls offers additional evidence.

There were ten polls in 1963, and the leaders won nine of the roll calls that followed.[21] On all ten votes the whip organization tried to ascertain how 256 Democratic members would vote. It was successful 90.5 percent of the time in predicting whether a member would be absent and how he would vote if present. The whip organization failed to provide correct prior information on the individual's voting behavior 9.5 percent of the time.

The leaders in 1963 always knew how 123 of the 256 Democrats would vote, but 133 (52 percent) party members surprised the leaders one or more times. Two members voted contrary to advance reports six times, one member did so five times, seven members four times, nineteen members three times, thirty-six members twice, and sixty-eight members once.

To show what type of member was reported reliably, average presidential support and presidential opposition scores were computed for members grouped according to the number of times they were reported inaccurately on the whip poll.[22] The results show little difference in average scores for members who were reported inaccurately two or more times. Those inaccurately reported only once were considerably more consistent in their party support, and those who were never reported inaccurately were the most loyal of all.

| Number of Times Reported Inaccurately on Whip Poll | Number of Members | Presidential Support Score | Presidential Opposition Score |
|:---:|:---:|:---:|:---:|
| 6 | 2 | 59 | 36 |
| 5 | 1 | 63 | 31 |
| 4 | 7 | 59 | 26 |
| 3 | 19 | 54 | 29 |
| 2 | 36 | 58 | 26 |
| 1 | 68 | 71 | 15 |
| 0 | 123 | 82 | 5 |
| Average | | 72 | 14 |

[21] The subject matter of these ten polls is indicated in Table VII. The loss was on area redevelopment.

[22] *Congressional Quarterly* computed presidential support and opposition scores on the basis of roll call votes on items on which the President took a position.

The categories of reliability were also analyzed regionally. Southern Democrats were over-represented increasingly in categories containing larger numbers of inaccurate reports. Except for the few members in the most unreliable categories, western Democrats were represented roughly in proportion to their numbers in all of the other categories. Northern Democrats were under-represented in all categories except the one reflecting complete accuracy and reliability.

| *Number of Times Reported Inaccurately on Whip Poll* | *Total Number of Members* | *House Democrats* | | | | | |
|---|---|---|---|---|---|---|---|
| | | *Southern* | | *Western* | | *Northern* | |
| | | *No.* | *%* | *No.* | *%* | *No.* | *%* |
| 6 | 2 | 2 | *100* | 0 | *0* | 0 | *0* |
| 5 | 1 | 1 | *100* | 0 | *0* | 0 | *0* |
| 4 | 7 | 5 | *71* | 1 | *14* | 1 | *14* |
| 3 | 19 | 15 | *79* | 4 | *21* | 0 | *0* |
| 2 | 36 | 21 | *58* | 7 | *19* | 8 | *22* |
| 1 | 68 | 30 | *44* | 18 | *26* | 20 | *29* |
| 0 | 123 | 21 | *17* | 28 | *23* | 74 | *60* |
| Total | 256 | 95 | *37* | 59 | *23* | 102 | *40* |

The members most consistently opposing the leadership were more predictable and were reported more reliably and more accurately than those with a moderate record of support and opposition. Those most difficult to report prior to a vote tended to be ideologically uncommitted members who wavered from vote to vote with their perceptions of how much loyalty to the Democratic program their constituencies would tolerate. The average presidential opposition score of the fifty-one Democrats who were the strongest opponents to the President's program in 1963 was related to the seven categories of accuracy.[23] The concentration of the most consistent Democratic opponents of the President came in categories of fairly great accuracy, especially in those categories where only one or two mistakes were made.

[23] These fifty-one Democrats were labeled as the strongest opponents of the President's program because they had a presidential opposition score of 25 or higher. This means that they opposed the President on more than a quarter of the issues on which he took a position.

| Number of Times Reported Inaccurately on Whip Poll | Number of all Democrats | Number of Strong Opponents | Average Presidential Opposition Score of Strong Opponents |
|:---:|:---:|:---:|:---:|
| 6 | 2 | 2 | 36 |
| 5 | 1 | 1 | 31 |
| 4 | 7 | 5 | 30 |
| 3 | 19 | 13 | 38 |
| 2 | 36 | 14 | 47 |
| 1 | 68 | 14 | 49 |
| 0 | 123 | 2 | 26 |
| | — | — | — |
| Total | 256 | 51 | 42 |

This table indicates that the leaders can identify the most con-sistent opponents and take their reports at face value, if time is limited and can be devoted to only a few members. Identifying the unreliable members quickly through the whip polls thus in-creases the leaders' chances of success.

## PARTY CAUCUSES AND COMMITTEES

Both the Democratic caucus and the Republican conference supply their members with limited information about what is happening legislatively. Only in the 1911-15 period did the Democratic caucus consistently debate the substance of legisla-tion, determine the party position, and inform the members of that position. The Republican conference has never operated in similar fashion, although in the Eighty-ninth Congress (1965-67) it began to meet more often to discuss pending bills.

During the 1959-65 period, the Republican Policy Committee met weekly and discussed forthcoming bills with Republicans who chose to attend, but in the Eighty-ninth Congress it cur-tailed its operations and acted primarily as a satellite of the con-ference. The Research and Planning Committee assumed the policy research and development task, formerly the province of the Policy Committee's Subcommittee on Special Projects.

## *Persuasion*

Persuasion can involve both bargaining (an exchange of considerations) and pressure (the threat of sanctions, tangible or psychological). Much persuasion by the leaders consists of personal appeals to members for help. In such situations, the only considerations that are exchanged involve long-term credits (mutual good will), not specific tangible items (a dam for a vote); the only sanction that the leaders use is an implied threat to withdraw personal esteem.

Party leaders use all of their resources in trying to persuade their members to act in specific ways. Specific examples may be found in every chapter; only a few additional notes are needed here.

### THE SPEAKER

The Speaker is the chief persuader for his party. Joe Martin has described his role during his four years as Speaker:

> The details of leadership are handled by the chosen floor leader . . . but the Speaker himself is the grand strategist and guiding spirit. Each Speaker, of course, exercises his leadership according to his own character and the prevailing political situation. For my own part I was never dictatorial. I worked by persuasion and drew heavily on long-established personal friendships. I found that I could best keep my members with me by tact and discretion. Unless it was absolutely necessary I never asked a man to side with me if his vote would hurt him in his district. Whenever I could spare a man this kind of embarrassment I did so and saved him for another time when I might need him more urgently. In fact I often counseled members against taking positions on legislation that would cost them the next election.[24]

Data on the activities of Speaker McCormack on four 1963 bills show how he operated. The votes involved a resolution to enlarge the Rules Committee in January and bills to extend and

[24] Martin, *Fifty Years*, pp. 182-83.

increase the national debt limit in May, August, and November. The Speaker seriously endeavored to change the minds of about twenty Democrats before each of the roll calls. He received varying responses, ranging from flat refusals to all-out promises of support. On each of the debt limit bills he was able to obtain eight to ten "pocket" or reserve votes, which he could call upon if absolutely needed to pass the bill.

Persons contacted were generally from the southern or border states, but none was a bitter opponent of the administration. Over a third of those contacted on any one impending vote were contacted on at least one of the other three. But the majority of those contacted directly on each vote, did not receive a special appeal on any of the other votes. Nor did the Speaker press the same people too often for pocket vote commitments. Only three members gave more than one pocket vote to the Speaker on the four roll calls.

THE FLOOR LEADERS

The Majority and Minority Leaders have two principal tasks in relation to persuading their members to behave loyally. First, they negotiate behind the scenes with individual members, state delegations, and, occasionally, ideological groups. Both floor leaders are constantly calling members, seeing them in their offices or in the leaders' offices, or seeing them on the floor. What is said in these encounters varies with the style of the individual leader. Carl Albert, for example, generally uses a straightforward appeal: "Can't you help us; we need your vote." He also takes care to be informed on the details of bills, so that he can argue with individual Democrats who want to dissent. He rarely asks members to vote against what they seriously believe to be the desires of their constituency. Charles Halleck, according to testimony offered by Republicans in interviews, was much less understanding in his appeals.

Second, floor leaders protect the interests of their party on the floor. They conduct most of the procedural debates, the Minority Leader ever ready to cry "foul" and the Majority Leader, in the graphic words of a 1916 observer, "exhibiting an irresistible desire to club any captious interference with the plans and purposes of the majority."[25] The floor leaders also conduct a good deal of the substantive debate and are expected to be persuasive orators.

## THE WHIPS

The whip poll results are important in helping the leaders determine where to apply pressure and with whom to bargain. Among contemporary democrats, for example, the polls form the basis for a division of labor at meetings of the Speaker, Majority Leader, Whip, deputy whip, White House and departmental liaison officials, and the relevant committee chairman three weeks to three days before a bill comes to the floor.

There is no systematic way of charting the effectiveness of poll-guided persuasion, since the ultimate test would compare what happened with what otherwise might have happened.[26] Some incidents involving the Democratic whip organization and important legislation in 1962 give a sample of the work done and its effectiveness.

The whip organization successfully identified the trouble spots on the omnibus tax revision bill that was aimed primarily at aiding business. One particularly difficult area was the New York delegation, which was finally brought into line with the loss of only three votes. Several southern delegations were initially opposed, but a caucus of the North Carolina delegation

[25] DeAlva S. Alexander, *History and Procedure of the House of Representatives* (Houghton Mifflin, 1916), p. 109.

[26] Some inferences might be drawn from a comparison of the winning percentage on roll calls used by *Congressional Quarterly* in computing its presidential support index with the administration's record of success on the key votes analyzed here. The question could be put whether the President won a greater percentage of the time when the Democratic whip organization was fully engaged in the battle. On the seventeen key votes in 1962 and 1963, the President won fourteen times—82 percent support—as against an over-all 85 percent winning record (on 60 roll calls) in 1962. From this it might be argued that the whip organization made no material difference, since the winning percentages are about the same. But it might also be argued that since the roll calls used here represent the "toughest" of the more numerous roll calls chosen by *Congressional Quarterly*, the winning percentage is higher than could be expected without concentrated whip activity.

and the effective work of the assistant whip for Texas helped hold southern losses to fifteen votes. At the last minute, during the floor debate, the secretary in the Whip's office discovered that some of the members from a midwestern state were wavering in their support. When this message was transmitted to Boggs on the floor, he escorted a member of the delegation to the Speaker's office where both the Speaker and the President (on the telephone) convinced him of the need for his support.

Before the vote on increasing the national debt limit, the Whip enlisted Francis Walter of Pennsylvania to use some of his credit with the southerners to persuade a major southern delegation. As a result, only three Democrats from that state voted against the bill.

In late June, the whip poll showed that the Republican motion to recommit the trade bill with instructions to continue the reciprocal trade agreements program for another year might attract as many as eighty Democratic votes. Hard work on the part of the President, chairman Wilbur Mills of Ways and Means, Secretaries Arthur Goldberg (Labor) and Luther Hodges (Commerce), Under Secretary Willard Wirtz (Labor), and Assistant Secretary Hickman Price (Commerce), the Speaker, Majority Leader, and Whip reduced eventual Democratic losses on the motion to forty-four.

In 1966, the relation of the whip polls to persuasion was highlighted when twenty-six western Democrats reacted against the pressures brought by executive officials and group lobbyists who had seen whip polls identifying potential dissenters from the party position. They voted unanimously to have their assistant whip report only numbers, not names, in future polls, and their dean wrote a strong letter to the Speaker protesting the use of poll information by outsiders.[27]

PARTY CAUCUSES AND COMMITTEES

The only kind of pressure that the full membership assembled in caucus can exert is the psychological force of a large meeting. When the 1911-15 Democratic caucus made a binding decision,

[27] See the *Washington Post,* April 5 and 6, 1966.

dissenters were required to stand up and announce that they would not be bound. Few took this option. The Republican caucus since 1910 has not taken binding positions, but its "advice" is a form of pressure on the Republican members to conform.

The Republican Steering Committee from 1919 to 1925 was clearly involved in persuasion. Its members were recognized as agents of the leadership and hence could bargain with or apply pressure on other Republicans. The Republican Policy Committee in 1959-65 was also an agent of persuasion. It took positions that it then attempted to explain in short papers circulated to all Republicans. This was a clear indication that party leaders wished them to act accordingly.

## Liaison with the White House

Liaison with the White House is performed principally by the Speaker or Minority Leader, depending on the President's party.[28] Cannon was the first post-1861 Speaker to meet regularly with the President. These meetings were more than routine or ceremonial: he and Theodore Roosevelt discussed major bills and agreed on position, strategy, and tactics.[29]

Not until Longworth's regime did regular meetings between Speaker and President again focus on knotty legislative questions. Franklin Roosevelt met with the Speakers during his first term, but tended to dictate to them. By late 1937 the necessity for regular meetings and for discussion, not dictation, became evident when the Speaker and President made contradictory statements in public:

It had been common during the early part of the speakership of Mr. Bankhead for the Speaker to announce to reporters at his morning press conference that he did not expect any message from the

[28] In 1959 and 1960 the Republican Policy Committee became indirectly involved in liaison with the White House. The House Republican leaders would meet with the Policy Committee shortly after their weekly meeting with President Eisenhower to tell the committee members what had transpired.

[29] L. White Busbey, *Uncle Joe Cannon* (Holt, 1927), pp. 218-19.

White House during the day. Then after the lapse of an hour a message from the White House to Congress would arrive, an embarrassing predicament for the Speaker. Further, the President was regularly making legislative proposals to Congress which were so far-reaching and unprecedented without first consulting the leaders that they were unable to sell such bills of fare to the membership; in fact, it was embarrassing to present them. . . . No records are available as to the origin of these conferences, but since they were started with the rise of Sam Rayburn to the floor leadership, it is only natural to believe that Mr. Rayburn's contribution to their conception and development is not secondary.[30]

After Rayburn became Speaker in 1940, the Speaker and President worked closely to inform each other on legislative matters. Speaker Martin worked in much the same manner during his one term when the Republicans also controlled the White House. McCormack has continued the same practices. Both at White House meetings and in phone conversations, the Speaker (usually with the Majority Leader and Whip) and the President shape the strategy of the Democratic party in the House.

## *Present Allocation of Functions: Summary*

The present (1966) allocation of primary responsibility for performing the six leadership functions in both parties is summarized in Table VIII and underlines the central importance of the information and persuasion functions. Most of the leaders and committees in both parties perform part of these two functions. Because they are the most complex of all the functions, they receive more widespread and concentrated attention.

Information and persuasion are intertwined. Accurate information about bargains and the use of pressure (the two principal forms of persuasion) is essential to leadership success. The whip organizations in both parties (and the Republican Policy Committee since 1959) give the leaders news of various bargains

[30] Floyd Riddick, "Sam Rayburn," in J. T. Salter, *Public Men in and out of Office* (University of North Carolina Press, 1946), pp. 161-62. See Chapter 1, footnote 3, above.

TABLE VIII

*Responsibility for Leadership Functions, 1966*

| Functions | DEMOCRATS | | | | |
| --- | --- | --- | --- | --- | --- |
| | Speaker | Majority Leader | Whip | Caucus | Committee on Committees |
| Organization of party | X | — | — | X | X |
| Scheduling of business | X | X | — | — | — |
| Promoting attendance | — | — | X | — | — |
| Distribution and collection of information | X | X | X | — | — |
| Persuasion | X | X | X | — | — |
| Liaison with the White House | X | — | — | — | — |

| Functions | REPUBLICANS | | | | |
| --- | --- | --- | --- | --- | --- |
| | Minority Leader | Whip | Conference | Policy Committee | Committee on Committees |
| Organization of party | X | — | X | — | X |
| Scheduling of business | (primarily a majority function) | | | | |
| Promoting attendance | — | X | — | — | — |
| Distribution and collection of information | X | X | X | X | — |
| Persuasion | X | X | X | X | — |
| Liaison with the White House | (primarily a majority function) | | | | |

struck between party members on legislative matters, spot wavering members, and provide indications of the type of persuasion that may be necessary to bring some of the waverers into line. Such information is incomplete, but without it the leaders would be unable to make informed judgments on the state of their membership and their prospects for legislative success.

# ☆ 4 ☆

# Patterns of Leadership

Sometimes it is assumed that the leadership of the majority party in the House has been cast in two basic patterns: the pre-1910 pattern of an autocratic Speaker with a united party, and the post-1910 pattern of a Speaker bound by certain rules and surrounded by a more or less constantly bickering party that he can lead only part of the time. The minority party is also assumed to have been united by an autocratic leader before 1910, and much less united after 1910.

The thesis of this chapter is that both parties have experimented with four different patterns of leadership in the majority, and three patterns in the minority. A close examination of House leadership from 1861 through 1967 provides no support for simpler assumptions, nor does it reveal that the leadership of either party has become stabilized in any unchangeable pattern. History suggests that both parties will continue experimenting and changing in the future.

If the congressional parties are *deliberately* experimental in mood and outlook, this has important consequences for the place of Congress in the federal establishment. Only by conscious changes can Congress maximize its power in relation to the growing power of the President and the bureaucracy. In at least this one area of party leadership Congress has been willing to make such changes, although not all of the specific changes have led to the desired results.

## *Majority Party Patterns*

The four basic patterns of majority party leadership are (1) leadership by the Speaker, (2) leadership by the Majority Leader, (3) leadership by a collegial group, and (4) leadership by the President. Table IX shows these patterns from 1861 to the present.

The patterns are differentiated by the way party leaders most consistently made important decisions about legislative strategy and tactics. Such decisions shape the general flow and timing of business coming to the House floor and set the limits and nature of bargaining on any one bill. None of the patterns is "pure": even relatively unimportant Speakers have been involved in a number of these decisions, there are elements of collegial decision-making in all patterns, and, in recent decades, the President has been increasingly involved. To understand the shifting nature of party leadership, however, the four patterns are both accurate and useful.

### LEADERSHIP BY THE SPEAKER

In periods of "leadership by Speaker," he was the principal majority party leader making decisions about legislative strategy and tactics. No Speaker has ruled entirely by himself; all have had at least one or two top aides. Three have come close to exercising complete control over the House's conduct of its legislative business. These were Republicans Blaine, Reed, and Cannon. Blaine tried, but in legislative terms did not succeed. Reed tried and succeeded. Cannon tried, succeeded for a short time, and then, as result of his excesses, was brought down by the opposition and some members of his own party. Seven other Speakers have been dominant figures in their party without harboring the illusion that they could rule alone: Randall, Carlisle, Crisp, Longworth, Garner, Rayburn, and Martin.

## LEADERSHIP BY THE MAJORITY LEADER

Periods of "leadership by Majority Leader" occurred when he (or an important committee chairman who, in effect, served as Majority Leader) made the bulk of the strategic and tactical decisions affecting legislation in the House. Two Majority Leaders, Underwood and Rayburn, and two committee chairmen, Thaddeus Stevens and William Kelley, have led their party. Stevens was successful in leading the Civil War and postwar Republican House because of his intelligence and forcefulness, despite his vindictive nature. He was also aided by having Speakers whom he could easily dominate. Kelley led because of the incompetence of the Speaker. Rayburn did not exercise the power that Stevens did, but served as the rallying point for his party during a period when the Speaker was ill much of the time.

Underwood was the most effective of these Majority Leaders. He overshadowed the Speaker and was highly successful in revitalizing the caucus as an instrument to attain party ends. His period of greatest achievement came through working with a vigorous Democratic President and a cooperative Senate leadership.

## LEADERSHIP BY A COLLEGIAL GROUP

If an identifiable and relatively stable group of leaders made most of the strategic and tactical decisions about legislative matters in any one period, this period was designated as "leadership by collegial group." This pattern has been tried by the majority party on three different occasions, in three varying forms. From 1899 to 1903, the Republicans, in the midst of the Reed-Cannon era, elected an ineffective Speaker and, in effect, turned control of party fortunes over to important committee chairmen and the majority members of the Rules Committee. From 1919 to 1925 they again elected an unimpressive Speaker and then devised an elaborate distribution of power, principally to a Steering Committee, to guide the party in legislative matters. From 1962 until the present, the Democrats have relied on three principal leaders

## TABLE IX

## Patterns of Majority Party Leadership in the House, 1861–1967

| Years | Pattern | Party | Chief Party Leaders in House and Positions[a] | Reason for End of Period |
|---|---|---|---|---|
| 1861–69 | Majority Leader | R | Stevens, W&M, Approp. | Death of Stevens |
| 1869–75 | Speaker | R | Blaine, Spk.; Garfield, Approp.; Dawes, Approp., W&M | Party became minority |
| 1875–81 | Speaker | D | Randall, Spk.; Morrison, W&M; Wood, W&M | Party became minority |
| 1881–83 | Majority Leader | R | Kelley, W&M; Reed | Party became minority |
| 1883–89 | Speaker | D | Carlisle, Spk.; Morrison, W&M; Mills, W&M | Party became minority |
| 1889–91, 1895–99 | Speaker | R | Reed, Spk.; McKinley, W&M; Dingley, W&M; Cannon, Approp.; Tawney, Whip | Party became minority ('91); resignation of Reed; Senate domination of Speakership election |
| 1891–95 | Speaker | D | Crisp, Spk.; Wilson, W&M | Party became minority |
| 1899–1903 | Collegial | R | Cannon, Approp.; Dalzell & Grosvenor; Rules; Payne, W&M, M.L.; Henderson, Spk.; Tawney, Whip | Retirement of Henderson; Lack of Senate influence on choice of new Speaker |
| 1903–11 | Speaker | R | Cannon, Spk.; Payne, W&M and M.L.; Hemenway & Tawney, Approp.; Watson & Dwight, Whip; Dalzell, Rules; Sherman | Progressive defeat of "Cannonism"; party became minority |
| 1911–15 | Majority Leader | D | Underwood, M.L., W&M; Clark, Spk. | Retirement of Underwood; World War I; personality of President Wilson |
| 1915–19 | President | D | Kitchin, M.L., W&M; Clark, Spk. | Party became minority |

TABLE IX *(Continued)*

| Years | Pattern | Party | Chief Party Leaders in House and Positions[a] | Reason for End of Period |
|-------|---------|-------|------------------------------------------------|---------------------------|
| 1919–25 | Collegial | R | Mondell & Longworth, M.L.; Steering Committee members (7) | Retirement of Speaker Gillett; personality of Longworth |
| 1925–31 | Speaker | R | Longworth, Spk.; Tilson, M.L.; Snell, Rules | Party became minority |
| 1931–33 | Speaker | D | Garner, Spk. | Retirement of Garner; personality of President Roosevelt |
| 1933–37 | President | D | Rainey & Byrns, Spk.; Byrns & Bankhead, M.L.; Greenwood & Boland, Whip | Death of Byrns; personality of Rayburn; increased opposition to New Deal |
| 1937–40 | Majority Leader | D | Rayburn, M.L.; Bankhead, Spk. | Death of Speaker Bankhead; election of Rayburn as Speaker |
| 1940–47, 1949–53, 1955–61 | Speaker | D | Rayburn, Spk.; McCormack, M.L.; Albert, Whip | Party became minority ('47, '53); death of Rayburn |
| 1947–49, 1953–55 | Speaker | R | Martin, Spk.; Halleck, M.L. | Party became minority |
| 1962– | Collegial | D | McCormack, Spk.; Albert, M.L.; Boggs, Whip | — |

SUMMARY (through 1966)
Pattern

| | Speaker | | Majority Leader | | Collegial | | President | |
|-------------|-----|-------|-----|-------|-----|-------|-----|-------|
| | No. | Years | No. | Years | No. | Years | No. | Years |
| Democrats | 5 | 36 | 2 | 7 | 1 | 5 | 2 | 8 |
| Republicans | 5 | 30 | 2 | 10 | 2 | 10 | 0 | 0 |
| Total | 10 | 66 | 4 | 17 | 3 | 15 | 2 | 8 |

[a] Abbreviations: Spk. (Speaker); M.L. (Majority Leader); W&M (Ways and Means Committee chairman); Approp. (Appropriations Committee chairman); Rules (Rules Committee member).

with an additional nineteen members important in the whip organization.

The "leadership by President" category indicates periods when the President and his top aides made the most important strategic and tactical decisions about legislation before the House. The President has often demonstrated leadership on the substance of legislation in other periods, but there have been only two periods—under President Wilson from 1915 to 1919 and under President Roosevelt from 1933 to 1937—when House leaders did not make a consistently major strategic or tactical input in planning the course of legislation.

USE OF THE PATTERNS

The summary figures on Table IX show the wide range of experience in both parties. Out of eight possible combinations, seven have been tried. The Republicans have not yet experimented with leadership by the President, which would be contrary to the legislative philosophy of most Republican Presidents. Six of the seven combinations of party and pattern have been tried on more than one occasion.

Leadership by the Speaker has been the pattern for sixty-six years out of 106, but during three-eighths of the period the majority party has assigned its Speaker a less than commanding role. From 1861 to 1911, leadership by the Speaker was the pattern for thirty-six out of fifty years, but even in this period the Republicans experimented three times with other forms of leadership. From 1911 through 1966, leadership by the Speaker was used for thirty years out of fifty-six. At six different times the majority party chose another way of arranging its leadership.

To explore the origins, nature, and legislative consequences of the majority party patterns, specific examples of those involving a central and active role for House leaders are discussed below.

## Examples of Various Kinds of Majority Leadership

### SPEAKER JOHN G. CARLISLE[1]

The Democrats controlled the House from 1875 to 1881 but were almost completely frustrated in their attempts to pass legislation. They were restored to the majority by the elections of 1882, but still faced the prospect of a bitter intra-party fight over the tariff that would render them legislatively impotent. The Democratic Speaker from 1876 to 1881, protectionist Samuel Randall of Pennsylvania, was still in the House and expected to be nominated for Speaker. The party decided otherwise, however, and nominated John G. Carlisle of Kentucky, a staunch low-tariff supporter. Carlisle served as Speaker from 1883 to 1889.

As Speaker, Carlisle was willing to experiment with his powers in an effort to gain party legislative ends. He relied on a loyal chairman of the Ways and Means Committee (William Morrison of Illinois, from 1883 to 1887; and Roger Q. Mills of Texas, from 1887 to 1889) and a committee membership chosen to help obtain the goal of tariff reduction. He recognized Randall's ability and support in the party by making him chairman of the Appropriations Committee, but did not rely on him for general legislative assistance. He created no new organs to promote party unity on legislation, but made greater use of his power of recognition to further party ends.

Despite Carlisle's efforts, the Democrats remained split and ineffective throughout most of his Speakership. The Senate remained narrowly Republican and the Democratic majority in the House dwindled in successive elections. When they had their largest majority (62 percent of the members of the House in 1883-85), a Republican (Chester A. Arthur) was President. Dur-

---

[1] This section is based in large part on material contained in James A. Barnes, *John G. Carlisle* (Dodd, Mead, 1931); and Festus P. Summers, *William L. Wilson and the Tariff* (Rutgers University Press, 1953).

ing Grover Cleveland's presidency, Democratic majorities shrank to 56 percent in 1885-87 and 52 percent in 1887-89.

In 1884 the Ways and Means Committee reported a tariff reduction bill to the floor, only to have it defeated by the defection of about forty Democrats. Randall led the defectors, and the group was promptly labeled "Randall and the forty thieves."[2] Two years later he and his followers were still able to block two efforts to consider a tariff bill.

The Democrats rallied during the Fiftieth Congress (1887-89). Carlisle himself acted as floor leader during debate on the tariff in Committee of the Whole, which is a "committee," designed to facilitate the disposition of legislative business. It contains all members of the House and has more lenient rules than the House. Chairman Mills and the majority members of the Ways and Means Committee made the issue completely partisan, excluding the Republicans from Ways and Means deliberations and not holding the customary public hearings. Finally, with the aid of President Cleveland's special message on tariff reform, the House passed the Mills bill with only four Democrats dissenting and Randall too ill to be present. The victory was shortlived as the bill died in the Republican Senate.

### SPEAKER THOMAS B. REED

In 1889 the Republicans achieved a majority in the House for two years after being in the minority for twelve of the preceding fourteen years. In 1895 they again became the majority, this time for sixteen years. Both times they chose Thomas B. Reed to be Speaker, a position he kept until he left the House in 1899. The desire of party members to accomplish something after being out of power, and an electoral base that made most Republicans unwaveringly loyal to policies favoring northeastern business and midwestern agriculture, gave Reed an opportunity to use his personal skills to forge a unified and productive party.

[2] The Democrats decided to strip Randall's committee of much of its power in 1885. Morrison, who had fought Randall for a decade, led the forces against him, which were successful in distributing the power to report specific appropriations bills among half a dozen substantive committees.

Many aspects of Reed's leadership have become legend. He was a strong believer in party unity on legislative matters. The rules changes he sponsored during his first term as Speaker (1889-91) were designed to allow him to pass legislation even though he had only a seven-seat majority. He did not rule alone, but worked with William McKinley (both as Ways and Means chairman and as President), President Benjamin Harrison, Joseph Cannon (chairman of Appropriations), and Nelson Dingley (chairman of Ways and Means). He also appointed the first Republican Whip, James Tawney of Minnesota, to aid him in keeping party members on the floor and voting correctly.

Reed led a basically united party, and thus produced major legislation that he and the Republican Presidents desired. Aided by chairman McKinley, and to some extent by Harrison, Reed induced the House to pass what became the Tariff Act of 1890. When Reed began his second term as Speaker in 1895, after witnessing the Democratic failures for the preceding two Congresses, he was even more sure of the necessity for majority party discipline.[3] He used personal persuasion, his control of committee assignments, and the aid of Dingley, Cannon, and President McKinley to pass a major tariff bill in 1897. Even on matters that split the Republicans in caucus, Reed was able to obtain virtual unanimity during final floor action. But he could not overrule the President. When his own preferences for a non-imperialistic foreign policy were ignored by McKinley and his advisers, Reed left Congress. Thus his career was marked by success with domestic legislation and personal frustration.

### SPEAKER JOSEPH G. CANNON

Joseph Cannon ran unsuccessfully for Speaker in 1881, 1889, and 1899.[4] Bitterly disappointed, he tried to obtain a Senate seat in 1900, but failed. When he finally became Speaker in 1903 he

[3] See Thomas B. Reed, "Two Congresses Contrasted," *North American Review*, Vol. 155 (August 1892), pp. 227-36.

[4] He lost in 1899 because of a split in the Illinois delegation. See Arthur Wallace Dunn, *From Harrison to Harding* (G. P. Putnam's Sons, 1922), Vol. 1, pp. 310-12.

was fully prepared, by long observation and by temperament, to use the powers of the office to gain his legislative ends.

Cannon revived the power of the Speakership after his immediate predecessor, David Henderson, had proved incapable of running the House.[5] He codified, solidified, and used with vigor the powers that Carlisle, Reed, and others had developed. He ruled the House Republicans with the help of a few close associates: the chairmen of Appropriations and Ways and Means, members of the Rules Committee, and the Whip. While he made no basic changes in the party organization, he made full use of the existing structures: the caucus or conference (he deliberately confused the distinction between the two) and the relatively new office of Whip. Cannon maintained strict control over the committee chairmen and would not hesitate to bypass them, or demote them, if they disagreed on important legislation. He used committee assignments to promote men whom he trusted. Though he allowed the Minority Leader to make the Democratic assignments from 1903 to 1908, he retained a veto.[6]

[5] Between Reed and Cannon the Republicans elected David B. Henderson as Speaker. In part his choice was dictated by important Republican Senators who wanted a House subservient to their legislative wishes. Without the personality or intelligence of Reed or Cannon, he lacked the capacity to run the House, and other Republicans on the Rules Committee often made decisions for him. Henderson was also subjected to pressures from other party members that sometimes led to reversals of position on upcoming legislation. Even when he took a definite position, he could sometimes be defeated by members of his own party. See Hubert B. Fuller, *The Speakers of the House* (Little, Brown and Co., 1909), p. 248; and Charles W. Thompson, *Party Leaders of the Time* (Dillingham, 1906), p. 153.

Henderson is usually overlooked by those assuming the Reed-Cannon era to be typical of the pre-1910 House.

[6] Cannon liked the Democratic leader, John Sharp Williams of Mississippi. In 1903, he decided that Williams could appoint minority members of committees, although he retained a veto for himself. Cannon felt this would be another method for solidifying Republican control and fracturing the Democratic ranks. He could reason that if Democrats were unhappy with assignments handed them by a Republican Speaker, Republicans would be the natural target of their anger, but if a Democrat had given them the assignments their anger would be aimed at him. From 1903 to 1908 Cannon had no need to stack the minority side of a committee, since the majority members were responsive to his wishes. But when some Republicans became less responsive and when the Democrats appointed a new leader, Champ Clark, who was not close to Cannon, the Speaker

Even with this strict control, however, a minority of Republicans was still capable of overruling the Speaker's wishes on important legislation by joining the Democrats. In 1905 a group of about sixty-five Republicans was successful in forcing a change in leadership plans for a statehood bill.[7] But the party was united enough to pass a major legislative program in the Fifty-ninth Congress (1905-07). Cannon met often with President Theodore Roosevelt during this Congress and agreed to work for part of his program (meat inspection, pure food legislation, and railroad rate legislation) in exchange for the President's promise not to pursue other parts of it (tariff reform and labor legislation).[8]

Republican unity gradually dissolved, in part because of Cannon's methods. He was eventually shorn of much of his power in 1910 because a sizable number of his own party voted with the Democrats.[9]

---

took back the power to appoint minority members. This reassumption of power increased Democratic and progressive Republican feeling against "Cannonism."

[7] Thompson, *Party Leaders*, p. 196.

[8] See George Roger Mayhill, "Speaker Cannon under the Roosevelt Administration" (Ph.D. thesis, University of Illinois, 1942), pp. 94-109, on how Cannon and other Republican leaders in both houses talked Roosevelt out of proposing tariff reform. See pp. 113-219 for what Cannon did and did not do for the Roosevelt program in the Fifty-ninth Congress.

[9] Roll call analysis has demonstrated that the 1890-1910 period was the high water mark of party loyalty, but not of uniformly high party regularity. The Democrats were disunited at the beginning, and the Republicans toward the end. The changing electoral base of the parties helped produce these changes. The Republicans, for about a decade before 1896, mainly attracted the votes of businessmen and midwestern farmers. With the 1896 election they began to attract far westerners, laboring men, and other groups that would, in another decade, produce insurgent members of the party.

The Democrats under Cleveland were split between northeastern sound money men and southern and western agrarians more interested in soft money. Gradually the northeasterners became Republicans until, by the turn of the century, the Democratic party was solidly based on the southerners and westerners. There were splits within the party on some issues, but fewer than before. In fact, Democratic unity in the House continued to grow until the 1913-15 period.

Julius Turner, *Party and Constituency: Pressures on Congress* (Johns Hopkins Press, 1951); A. Lawrence Lowell, "The Influence of Party Upon Legislation in England and America," *Annual Report of the American Historical Association*, H. Doc. 702, 57 Cong. 1 sess. (1902); Sondra B. Gamow, "Party Discipline: Its Nature and Extent in the United States House of Representatives, 1890-1910" (B.A. thesis, Radcliffe College, 1964).

### SPEAKER SAM RAYBURN

Sam Rayburn became Speaker in 1940 and held that post for all but four of the next twenty-one years. He had been the principal leader of the Democratic party since 1937 as Majority Leader, in part because Speaker William Bankhead was not in good health and had to delegate power. He faced a serious liberal-southern conservative split within the party during his entire tenure.

After Rayburn became Speaker, his method of operation was consistently highly centralized and highly personal. His preference was for close-lipped, tightly run individual control of his party, a preference clearly expressed in his opposition to the creation of party policy committees in 1946. He consulted with other leading Democrats, but on his own terms. Much party policy and many party decisions were made by him alone and communicated to his fellow Democrats at what he considered the proper moment. He liked to keep a few younger Democrats around him as lieutenants.

Rayburn used the whip organization less than his two immediate predecessors, who had helped to expand and formalize it. His party was disunited on many important issues and he felt that the best way to minimize disunity was to operate on a personal basis: bargaining with individuals rather than with the party as a whole, in caucus or through the whip organization. He also faced some committee chairmen hostile to his and the Democratic Presidents' legislative ends. Again he felt that a personal approach was the best. He worked closely with Presidents Roosevelt, Truman, and Kennedy to pass administration bills, but it was he who determined the strategy to pursue and the tactics to use in the House.

Rayburn battled the Rules Committee throughout his Speakership. He led the 1961 fight to enlarge the committee (for one Congress only) to permit its control by Democrats loyal to him and to the new Kennedy administration. This enlargement succeeded by five votes on the House floor.[10]

[10] Rayburn's successor as Speaker, John McCormack, solidified this gain and

Rayburn did not preside during a time of his party's legislative triumph in the domestic sphere. World War II, two Republican Congresses, a two-term Republican President, and continuing southern disaffection all intervened to prevent many of the Democratic programs from becoming law. But there was substantial achievement in foreign legislation and some in domestic legislation, enough to earn for Rayburn a reputation as an incomparable legislative wizard when faced with unfavorable odds.

THADDEUS STEVENS

Thaddeus Stevens served in the House for only fourteen years —four years from 1849 to 1853 and ten years from 1859 until his death in 1868. Yet he was one of the most powerful men ever to sit there. He became the Republican leader when he returned to the House in 1859. When he became chairman of Ways and Means in 1861, he was in full control of his party.[11] In 1865 he became chairman of the newly created Appropriations Committee, where he continued to dominate the House and threaten President Andrew Johnson.

Members who served with Stevens, as well as historians, are clear in their judgment that he ran the House much as he pleased. A Democratic leader said that

He had a will of audacious and intolerant quality. His humor . . . smacked of Voltaire. It had lurid lights. The intensity of his hatred was only next to infernal; but he seldom indulged it. He never hated a fair opponent. He did hate, bitterly, some of his own party who would not follow his doctrine, and obliterate states in order to territorialize and terrorize them. . . . In the House of Representatives, early in the first session of the Thirty-eighth Congress, on the 5th of

made it permanent in 1963, at the opening of the Eighty-eighth Congress. See Milton C. Cummings, Jr., and Robert L. Peabody, "The Decision to Enlarge the Committee on Rules: An Analysis of the 1961 Vote," and Robert L. Peabody, "The Enlarged Rules Committee," in Robert L. Peabody and Nelson W. Polsby, eds., *New Perspectives on the House of Representatives* (Rand McNally, 1963). See also Neil MacNeil, *Forge of Democracy* (McKay, 1963), Chapter 15.

[11] Ralph Korngold, *Thaddeus Stevens* (Harcourt Brace, 1955), pp. 101, 126. Even the biographer of the Speaker from 1863 to 1869 pictures Stevens as "the dominating personality in the House." Willard H. Smith, *Schuyler Colfax* (Indiana Historical Bureau, 1952), p. 189.

December, 1865, he arose to dictatorship. He commanded universal party obedience.[12]

George Boutwell, a Republican in Congress from 1863 to 1869 and later a Cabinet official under Grant, offers a convincing portrait:

> Mr. Stevens was a tyrant in his rule as leader of the House. He was at once able, bold, and unscrupulous. He was an anti-slavery man, a friend to temperance and an earnest supporter of the public school system, and he would not have hesitated to promote those objects by arrangements with friends or enemies. He was unselfish in personal matters, but his public policy regarded the state of Pennsylvania, and the Republican party. The more experienced members of the House avoided controversy with Stevens. First and last many a new member was extinguished by his sarcastic thrusts. As for himself no one could terrorize him. I recall an occasion near the close of a session, when as it was important to get a bill out of the Committee of the Whole, he remained upon his feet or upon his one foot and assailed every member who proposed an amendment. Sometimes his remarks were personal and sometimes they were aimed at the member's State. In a few minutes he cowed the House, and secured the adoption of his motion for the committee to rise and report the bill to the House.[13]

Stevens came much nearer to leading the House absolutely than any of his successors. Organization did not concern him. In the wartime setting and particularly in the postwar setting, charisma sufficed. Republicans opposed his policies only at their peril. Their careers, as well as their mental comfort, were at stake. He himself led the most important committees, and tolerated no dissent on major policies from chairmen of other committees. The Speakers with whom he served were pale figures compared to him. He could not dominate President Lincoln, although the policies of the two clashed during the war. After the war, Stevens' policies were irreconcilable with those of President Andrew Johnson, who tried unsuccessfully to withstand his force. Stevens engineered House approval for most of his own Reconstruction program and for impeachment of Johnson (whom the Senate failed to convict by one vote).

[12] Samuel S. Cox, *Union—Disunion—Reunion: Three Decades of Federal Legislation* (Reid, 1885), pp. 365-66.

[13] George S. Boutwell, *Reminiscences of Sixty Years in Public Affairs* (McClure, Phillips and Co., 1902), p. 10.

## MAJORITY LEADER OSCAR W. UNDERWOOD

In 1911 the Democrats elected Champ Clark as a relatively powerless Speaker and put the real power in the hands of their Majority Leader, Oscar W. Underwood of Alabama, who was also chairman of the Committee on Ways and Means and chairman of the newly constituted Committee on Committees, composed of the Democratic members of Ways and Means.[14] He held these positions from 1911 to 1915, when he went to the Senate. The Democrats, after sixteen years in the minority, were anxious for legislative achievement, especially after Woodrow Wilson became President and the Senate became Democratic in 1913.

Underwood developed a unique style of operation to attain success and was particularly interested in reducing the tariff. He placed principal reliance on the party caucus for gaining unity on controversial matters. After the Democratic members of a standing committee (meeting with Underwood and, after 1913, Wilson) had drafted a bill, Underwood would call the caucus to meet and debate it fully, often for a number of days or even weeks. Then the caucus would vote on a resolution stating the party position. According to caucus rules adopted in 1909, all Democrats were bound to support the party position adopted by two-thirds of the caucus, unless they felt the bill to be unconstitutional or unless they had made a prior pledge to their constituents or received instructions from their nominating authority. If a member felt that one of these exceptions applied to him, he had to announce his unwillingness to be bound to the caucus in person or, if not present, to Underwood in writing.[15] After the

[14] For accounts of Underwood's pre-1911 career in the House, see Burton Hendrick, "Oscar W. Underwood: A New Leader from the New South," *McClure's Magazine* (February 1912); and the sketch in O. O. Stealey, *130 Pen Pictures of Live Men* (n.p., 1910).

[15] For a good account of the caucus that adopted the rules, see the *Evening Star* (Washington), March 23, 1909. The rules governing the binding power of the caucus are as follows:

7. In deciding upon action in the House involving party policy or principle a two-thirds vote of those present and voting at a caucus meeting shall bind all members of the caucus; provided the said two-thirds vote is a majority of the full Democratic membership of the House, and, provided further, that no

caucus had taken its position, the bill then went quickly and routinely through the standing committee and to the floor, where another full debate was held, but with the outcome predetermined.

Underwood maintained strict control over the output of all standing committees in three additional ways. First, bills could be initially introduced in the caucus and considered in detail before being submitted to a committee. Second, the caucus could forbid, by resolution, bills on certain subjects or from other than specific committees. Third, the Rules Committee could not act contrary to the will of the caucus and Underwood in clearing bills for the floor.[16]

During the Sixty-second Congress (1911-13) Underwood could not hope to accomplish a great deal legislatively, since both the Senate and the President were still Republican. But he could accomplish much in terms of welding his party into an effective and unified majority, which he did with great skill. He began to use the caucus to assure success.

Early in the Sixty-second Congress, members of both parties were aware of what had happened to the distribution of power inside the Democratic party. As the Republican floor leader, James Mann, put it:

> . . . the gentleman from Alabama, Oscar Underwood, is not only the leader of the Democratic majority in the House, but he is the Democratic majority. He is not only the chairman of the Ways and Means Committee, but he is the Ways and Means Committee. In the old days they used to honor the Speaker of the House as being the Grand Chief Mogul, the man of power. The Speaker of the House today is the servant, not the master, of the gentleman from Alabama.[17]

member shall be bound upon questions involving a construction of the Constitution of the United States or upon which he made contrary pledges to his constituents prior to his election or received contrary instructions by resolutions or platforms from his nominating authority.

8. Whenever any member of the caucus shall determine by reason of either of the exceptions provided for in the above paragraph not to be bound by the action of the caucus on those questions, it shall be his duty, if present, so to advise the caucus before the adjournment of the meeting at which action is taken; or, if not present at the meeting, promptly to notify the Democratic leader in writing, so that the party may be advised before the matter comes to issue upon the floor of the House.

[16] Wilder H. Haines, "The Congressional Caucus of Today," *American Political Science Review*, Vol. 9 (November 1915), p. 699.

[17] *Congressional Record*, Vol. 47, Pt. 4, 62 Cong. 1 sess. (1911), p. 3562.

On matters on which the party did not choose to hold a binding caucus there were still large-scale defections.[18] Important caucuses were held during the Sixty-second Congress to discuss which committee should investigate the "money trust," and the question of reciprocity with Canada on tariffs.[19]

Thus when Wilson became President and the Senate became Democratic in 1913, Underwood was ready to supervise House passage of Democratic programs. When the Sixty-third Congress (1913-15) began, he was in control of his troops, now more numerous because of large numbers of new Democrats elected in the fall of 1912. As Underwood remembered the period:

> When the Sixty-third Congress met, there was a large and thoroughly organized Democratic majority prepared to do business for the nation. They were not raw recruits in legislative matters; they were veterans organized and trained in legislative work and procedure. They had not been in power long enough to become divided into cliques, or to be swayed by outside influences. They were primarily loyal to their party and its principles, and desirous of passing legislation that would be responsive to the needs of the country.[20]

The President was also extremely important in helping Underwood and other House Democratic leaders pass the major bills. The four outstanding accomplishments of these two years—the Underwood Tariff, the Federal Reserve Act, the Clayton Anti-Trust Act, and the Federal Trade Commission Act—all depended on an effective combination of Underwood, the caucus, and Wilson for success in the House.[21]

Even during the Sixty-third Congress, the Democrats were not completely unified. Underwood and Clark both felt compelled

[18] See, for example, the account of the effort needed to pass a campaign publicity law in the *Evening Star* (Washington) April 15, 1911.

[19] Lynn Haines, *Law-Making in America* (privately printed, 1921), pp. 11, 13.

[20] Oscar W. Underwood, *Drifting Sands of Party Politics* (Century, 1928), pp. 311-12.

[21] A lot has been written about the Sixty-third Congress. Unfortunately, however, no biography of Underwood exists. For material on the major legislative struggles of 1913-15, see Ray Stannard Baker, *Woodrow Wilson: Life and Letters* (Doubleday, Doran, 1931), Vol. 4; Carter Glass, *An Adventure in Constructive Finance* (Doubleday, Page, 1927); James Miller Leake, "Four Years of Congress," *American Political Science Review*, Vol. 11 (May 1917); Arthur S. Link, *Wilson: The New Freedom* (Princeton University Press, 1956); and Elston E. Roady, "Party Regularity in the Sixty-third Congress" (Ph.D. thesis, University of Illinois, 1951).

to disagree with Wilson over repealing the Panama Canal toll exemption for American coastwise shipping. Claude Kitchin of North Carolina, who became second ranking to Underwood on Ways and Means, and thus his successor as party leader, felt free to disagree on several major issues, including taxes on railway freight, Panama Canal tolls, and intervention in Mexico.[22]

Much of Underwood's success doubtless rested on his personal qualities. Much also rested on his institutional positions: Majority Leader, chairman of the most important legislative committee, and chairman of the committee that assigned all party members to their standing committee seats. Almost all Democrats were likely to have received something tangible from him. The binding caucus was a formidable psychological weapon in the quest for unity—few members cared to announce to their colleagues or write to their leader that they were unwilling to be "team players" on an important bill.

## LEADERSHIP BY A COLLEGIAL GROUP: THE REPUBLICAN STEERING COMMITTEE[23]

When the Republicans came back into the majority in 1919, they sought legislative success by expanding the number of Republican leaders and leadership posts in the party structure. Their first decision was to bypass the logical choice for Speaker, James Mann of Illinois, who had been Minority Leader for eight

[22] Alex M. Arnett, *Claude Kitchin and the Wislon War Policies* (Little, Brown and Co., 1937), p. 41. Kitchin was fortunate to become second ranking. When the Ways and Means Committee was first organized in April 1913, he was fourth—behind Underwood, Harrison of New York and Shackleford of Missouri. The other committees of the House were organized in June 1913, and the leadership decided, for some unknown reason, to punish Shackleford by removing him from Ways and Means and making him eighth ranking on Indian Affairs. Harrison resigned in September to become Governor General of the Philippines.

Kitchin had gone on the committee for the first time in 1911 only because the sitting North Carolina member on it was persuaded to leave after he had made a fight against free importation of lumber. See *Congressional Record*, Vol. 47, Pt. 4, 62 Cong. 1 sess. (1911), pp. 3571-72.

[23] For discussions of the Republican Steering Committee in the 1920's, see George R. Brown, *The Leadership of Congress* (Bobbs-Merrill, 1922), pp. 200-20; and Chang-wei Chiu, *The Speaker of the House of Representatives Since 1896* (Columbia University Press, 1928), pp. 329-35. The latter contains a list of the members of the Steering Committee from 1919 to 1927.

years. He had angered many Republicans by objecting to their private bills on the floor. An incident linking him to the meat packers, then being investigated, was at least a pretext for some opposition. He also bore the burden of being a close friend and protege of "Uncle Joe" Cannon. Many members suspected that he would try to recentralize power in his hands if elected Speaker.[24] Thus the Republican conference nominated Frederick Gillett, with the specific intention of having only a figurehead and fair presiding officer.

The Committee on Committees was Mann-dominated, however, and proceeded, over the vigorous protests of members with progressive leanings, to split the power among a number of his supporters. It elected Mann Majority Leader, but he refused this title. The power was split between the man who became Majority Leader (Frank Mondell of Wyoming), a five-man Steering Committee, the Republican members of the Rules Committee, and the Committee on Committees. Mann was particularly effective in influencing the work of the Committee on Committees.[25] This pattern of leadership, with some internal changes of personnel and form, continued until 1925.

The Majority Leader was chairman of the Steering Committee. The Committee on Committees chose the other members of it, and the conference ratified their selections. The Speaker and the chairman of the Rules Committee were formally barred from membership. The first members, chosen for the Sixty-sixth Congress (1919-21), were thought by many Republicans to represent too narrow a range of opinions. There was also some displeasure over the geographical distribution: Wyoming was the only state west of the Mississippi represented.

In the Sixty-seventh Congress (1921-23) the membership was increased to eight and the geographical representation was

[24] For material on Mann's loss of his race for the Speakership nomination see Brown, *Leadership*, pp. 191-92; and the *New York Times*, January 16, 19, 20, and 27, 1919; February 28, 1919.

[25] For material on how Mann retained power, even though losing the race for the Speakership, see Brown, *Leadership*, pp. 188-244; *The Searchlight*, Vol. 4 (May 1919), pp. 3-7; and the *New York Times*, February 28, 1919; and March 12, 1919. For a violent disagreement between Mann and Nicholas Longworth of Ohio over the course of the Republican party in the House in 1919 see the *New York Times*, March 17, 19, and 31, 1919.

broadened to include Minnesota and California. Although the official size of the Steering Committee remained at eight, it actually grew in size as the bars against party leaders meeting with the committee disappeared. In the Sixty-seventh Congress the chairman of Rules was invited to attend. Mondell also invited Speaker Gillett. In the Sixty-eighth Congress (1923-25) the Whip was added as a regular participant in Steering Committee meetings. The committee began meeting in the Speaker's room in the Capitol.

When Nicholas Longworth became Speaker in 1925, he chose to ignore the Steering Committee, which he felt had become too large. Instead, he relied on an informal "steering committee" of two or three close advisers. The Steering Committee had completed a four-stage process: creation, activity, enlargement, and loss of power.

In its active period from 1919 to 1925, the committee met almost daily to discuss party positions on the business of the House with chairmen and other Republican members of standing committees. The chairman of the Rules Committee, as soon as he began participating, discussed the role his committee should play and the timing of its actions. Speaker Gillett played no particularly important part.

Frank Mondell described the workings of the Steering Committee during his tenure as Majority Leader:

> The Republicans of the various committees of the House, after giving careful consideration to the matters that come before their committees, very frequently say to the Speaker, or to the chairman of the Steering Committee, or some members of it, "We have some matters with regard to which there is some difference of opinion as to the proper policy to follow . . . the members of our committee would like to take up with the Steering Committee and with the Speaker, and with other such members as you see fit to invite in, the general policy before our committee." We frequently have conferences thus suggested. We have done that with regard to every appropriation bill that has been presented to the House thus far.[26]

Occasionally the apparatus went awry. Once in the Sixty-seventh Congress, for example, the Steering Committee allowed the

[26] Mondell, quoted in Chiu, *Speaker,* pp. 331-32.

Rules Committee to report a rule for consideration of a resolution to investigate one of the Republican-controlled executive
departments. For the most part, though, the Steering Committee
carried out the wishes of the Republican leaders in the House,
even when these were not in accord with the Republican administration. For example, a bill in the Sixty-eighth Congress to increase civil service pensions was held up for an entire Congress,
and thus killed by an unfavorable Steering Committee decision
despite support for it from a unanimous House Civil Service
Committee, the Senate, and the administration.

The Republican membership was not united behind its lead-
ership in this period, even on matters of rules and organization.
Insurgency reached its peak in 1923 when, at the opening of the
Sixty-eighth Congress, a group of dissidents refused to vote for
Gillett as Speaker for several ballots. The party division in the
House was close enough that it prevented the Speaker's re-
election until Majority Leader Longworth agreed to some rules
changes demanded by the rebels.[27]

The House Republicans also opposed their leaders on some
important legislative questions. The Military Affairs Committee, for example, gave the leaders some anxious moments as it
worked on the universal military training portions of the National Defense Act of 1920.[28] Even on something as partisan as
the tariff, the Republicans were capable of splitting roughly in
half on a substantive issue.[29]

The Republican experiment with leadership by the Steering
Committee was unsuccessful. There were occasional lapses in
communications between the various leaders. Communications
with the White House were even more uncertain. The members,
including some committee chairmen, used the loose leadership
structure to pursue legislative ends other than those officially
sanctioned. These shortcomings led Longworth, once he became
Speaker, to re-centralize power in his own hands and those of a
few close associates.

[27] See Chiu, *Speaker*, pp. 32-34; and Howard Zinn, *LaGuardia in Congress* (Cor-
nell University Press, 1959), pp. 75-77.
[28] Lawrence H. Chamberlain, *The President, Congress and Legislation* (Columbia University Press, 1946), pp. 206-08.
[29] *Ibid.*, pp. 123-24.

When John McCormack became Speaker in 1962, he purposely created a collegial leadership situation in the Democratic party. Realizing that he could not immediately exercise Rayburn's power, he relied heavily and constantly on the advice and activity of his Majority Leader, Carl Albert, and his Whip, Hale Boggs. He saw to it that the Whip had adequate office space in the Capitol from which he could conduct the operations of his organization. All three leaders viewed the whip organization as important and all used it in seeking their legislative goals. The program for which the leaders labored was not of their own devising, but was substantially those parts of the Democratic President's program reported by the standing committees of the House.

Each element of the collegial leadership had its own importance, but the lack of cohesion that had troubled the Republicans in the early 1920's was not present in this arrangement. The functions were split between the various leaders, but there were numerous integrating meetings of the three principal leaders with committee chairmen and executive liaison officials. The unity of the Democrats was still far from perfect and some major bills were lost, especially in 1962 and 1963. But the Democrats cohered well enough in 1964, 1965, and 1966 to pass many major presidential proposals.

## Minority Party Patterns

The minority party since 1861 has used three patterns of leadership: (1) lack of purposeful leadership (disorganization), (2) leadership by the Minority Leader, and (3) leadership by a collegial group. Table X classifies the various periods of minority party leadership.

The classic goal of the minority party has been to thwart a

large portion of the legislative plans of the majority, although contemporary Republicans have been introducing and trying to pass their own alternative proposals. During most of the periods labeled "disorganized," the nominal leader was the Minority Leader, but he did so little to mobilize his party that it had slight impact on the legislative process. When minority parties have been effective, it is usually because they have relied largely on an active Minority Leader to provide the information and drive needed to win occasional victories. A new collegial pattern of leadership has emerged in the contemporary Republican party.

Table X shows that the minority party has lacked purposeful leadership about 40 percent of the time since 1861. The Democrats have been more susceptible to this state than the Republicans, who have generally opted for following an active Minority Leader. It is apparent that both parties have varied their leadership patterns with great regularity. Examples of each of the two minority party patterns other than disorganization are discussed below.

## LEADERSHIP BY MINORITY LEADER
## JOHN SHARP WILLIAMS[30]

After they became the minority party in the House in 1895, the Democrats had great difficulty in stopping any of the majority proposals. Their first leaders were, for a variety of reasons, inadequate. Then, in 1903, they chose John Sharp Williams of Mississippi as their leader. He remained in that post until 1908, when he stepped aside shortly before retiring from the House in order that Champ Clark, whom he favored, might be his successor.[31]

---

[30] In presenting this picture of Williams as minority leader, I have relied heavily on George C. Osborn, *John Sharp Williams* (Peter Smith, 1964), Chapter 7.

[31] In 1903, when he was first elected, Williams had competition from Champ Clark and David DeArmond, both of Missouri, and DeArmond would have liked to run against him for the Leadership position in both 1905 and 1907. DeArmond was also active in opposing some of Williams' substantive suggestions. One difference of opinion resulted in a fist-fight. Thus it was natural for Williams to prefer Clark to DeArmond as his successor and he timed his resignation to give every possible advantage to Clark. See Champ Clark, *My Quarter Century of American Politics* (Harper's, 1920), Vol. 2, p. 28.

## TABLE X
### *Patterns of Minority Party Leadership in the House, 1861–1967*

| Years | Pattern | Party | Chief Party Leaders in House and Positions[a] | Reason for End of Period |
|---|---|---|---|---|
| 1861–75 | Disorganization | D | — | Party became majority |
| 1875–81 | Minority Leader | R | Blaine & Garfield, M.L. | Party became majority |
| 1881–83 | Minority Leader | D | Randall, M.L. | Party became majority |
| 1883–89, 1891–95 | Minority Leader | R | Reed, M.L. | Party became majority |
| 1889–91 | Minority Leader | D | Carlisle & Crisp, M.L. | Party became majority |
| 1895–1903 | Disorganization | D | Crisp, Bailey, Richardson, M.L. | Retirement of Richardson; personality of Williams |
| 1903–11 | Minority Leader | D | Williams & Clark, M.L. | Party became majority |
| 1911–19 | Minority Leader | R | Mann, M.L. | Party became majority |
| 1919–31 | Disorganization | D | Clark, Kitchin, Garrett, Garner, M.L. | Party became majority |
| 1931–39 | Disorganization | R | Snell, M.L. | Retirement of Snell; personality of Martin |
| 1939–47, 1949–53, 1955–59 | Minority Leader | R | Martin, M.L. | Party became majority ('47, '53); defeat of Martin by Halleck |

[a] Abbreviations: M.L. (Minority Leader); Pol. Comm. (Chairman of Policy Committee); Conf. (Chairman of Conference); Research (Chairman of Research and Planning Committee).

TABLE X *(Continued)*

| Years | Pattern | Party | Chief Party Leaders in House and Positions[a] | Reason for End of Period |
|---|---|---|---|---|
| 1947–49, 1953–55 | Minority Leader | D | Rayburn, M.L.; McCormack, Whip | Party became majority |
| 1959–65 | Collegial | R | Halleck, M.L.; Arends, Whip; Byrnes, Pol. Comm.; Ford, Conf. | Defeat of Halleck by Ford |
| 1965– | Collegial | R | Ford, M.L.; Arends, Whip; Laird, Conf.; Goodell, Research | — |

SUMMARY (through 1966)
Pattern

| | Disorganized | | Minority Leader | | Collegial | |
|---|---|---|---|---|---|---|
| | No. | Years | No. | Years | No. | Years |
| Democrats | 3 | 34 | 4 | 16 | 0 | 0 |
| Republicans | 1 | 8 | 4 | 40 | 2 | 8 |
| Total | 4 | 42 | 8 | 56 | 2 | 8 |

In assuming the Minority Leadership, Williams was faced with what one observer called "a ploughing, snorting herd of Texas steers, suddenly released from all restraint." He immediately moved to create Democratic unity on a tariff issue that had previously left his party "as hopelessly irreconcilable as a crowd of street arabs disputing over a crap game."[32] After five days of exhortation from Williams, the Democrats emerged united, although the Republicans still passed the bill.

During the five years he was Minority Leader, Williams regularly consulted a small group on questions of party strategy. They were particularly anxious to have a united minority on questions that had previously split the Democrats: trade, imperialism, and currency.

Although he consulted with these lieutenants, Williams made the decisions and took the responsibility for them. At the begin-

[32] Thompson, *Party Leaders*, pp. 184-85, 187.

ning of the Fifty-ninth Congress (1905-07), he removed two Democrats from the Interstate and Foreign Commerce Committee because they had not supported the party's railroad rate bill in committee in the previous Congress. Although Cannon had granted him the power of assigning minority members to standing committees in hopes that this would aggravate internal Democratic dissension, Williams attempted to use this power to develop unity.

Williams also used the caucus to adopt minority programs, including demands for rules changes in the House. He then used the floor and the tactics open to him there to publicize Democratic positions and needle the Republicans for their actions. His tactics provoked Cannon and led to an increasing arbitrariness on the part of the Speaker. They also led to an increasingly united Democratic party and a growing split among Republicans.

The combination of consultation, personal control, and use of committee assignments, caucuses, and floor activity that Williams chose succeeded. The Democrats did not stop the major Republican legislative efforts between 1903 and 1908, but they helped create campaign issues that would elect more Democrats in the future. They also helped sow the seeds of dissension in the Republican party that led to the abridgement of Cannon's powers.

LEADERSHIP BY A COLLEGIAL GROUP:
THE POST-1959 REPUBLICANS[33]

In 1959 a majority of the House Republicans decided that, after being the minority party for twenty-four of the preceding

[33] In writing this section I have relied on interviews and on *Congressional Quarterly*, February 8, 1963, pp. 149-56; Charles O. Jones, *Party and Policy-Making* (Rutgers University Press, 1964); Robert L. Peabody, *The Ford-Halleck Minority Leadership Contest, 1965* (McGraw-Hill, 1966); Robert L. Peabody, "House Republican Leadership: Change and Consolidation in a Minority Party" (paper prepared for delivery at the 1966 meeting of the American Political Science Association); and Robert L. Peabody, "Party Leadership Change in the United States House of Representatives," *American Political Science Review*, Vol. 61 (September 1967).

twenty-eight years, it was time they tried a mode of leadership other than relying on a single Minority Leader to protect their interests and make their collective record. Since then the Republican leadership has been collegial, although the exact details of the pattern have been constantly changing.

As part of the agreement in 1959 through which Joe Martin was ousted as Minority Leader, the new Leader, Charles Halleck of Indiana, agreed to give more power to the rejuvenated Policy Committee, chaired by John Byrnes of Wisconsin. Gradually brought into this leadership circle were the chairman of the conference and several ranking committee members with claims to special respect in the most important legislative areas: taxation, spending, and defense.

When Byrnes became chairman of the Policy Committee, he immediately increased committee activity. It sponsored several special research projects in specific policy areas, such as defense and foreign policy, education, and employment. The main policy positions were taken after the bills had left the standing committee and were ready for floor action. Rarely was a conference called to discuss the Policy Committee decision or to instruct it.

By the Eighty-eighth Congress (1963-65) the Policy Committee had switched its attention from broad studies in policy areas to specific bills. The committee attempted to take positions on bills earlier, and to prepare written statements of the Republican reasons for supporting or opposing a given bill or amendment. These statements were useful to Republicans in floor debate.

The committee's main function was to discover Republican consensus and communicate information about it to the leaders and rank-and-file members. The committee also became heavily involved in internal Republican struggles over leadership positions. Where substantial disagreement existed, the committee either avoided the issue altogether or discussed it without issuing a statement. As a result, Republican voting on issues on which a definite stand had been taken revealed a high degree of cohesion.[34]

[34] Jones, *Party and Policy-Making*, pp. 87-90, lists nineteen bills in 1961 on which the Policy Committee took a specific position. On the average only 9 percent of Republican members opposed this position on the floor. In 1962, on nine

An exception to this normal pattern occurred in 1964 when the Policy Committee, over the earnest protestations of the second-ranking Republican on the Banking and Currency Committee, took a position against the administration's mass transit bill. When the bill reached the floor, thirty-nine Republicans (over 20 percent of the members of the party) voted with the Democrats despite the party position. At other times the Policy Committee hurt its own cause by taking a formal position and thus creating a highly partisan situation that made it more difficult to obtain conservative Democratic votes. The Republican sponsor of the campaign to require annual appropriations for all programs and prohibit direct borrowing from the Treasury made this complaint when the Policy Committee endorsed his efforts in 1963.

Minority Leader Halleck, although free to comment on substantive questions, limited his remarks in the Policy Committee largely to matters of political strategy and tactics. He both used and depended on the aid of the whip organization and the Policy Committee to defeat Democratic bills. His detractors within the party said that he would oppose anything merely for the sake of opposition.[35] He attempted to obtain party unity even on votes his party did not have a chance to win. His constant requests for unity irritated a large number of Republicans who felt that they must dissent from the party position some of the time in order to be re-elected.

Halleck also ran into opposition on certain of his policy positions. Some members were unhappy with his support of the Civil Rights bill in 1963 and 1964; others felt he was not active enough in supporting it. Some were also alienated by his stand

---

issues, only 6 percent of the Republicans voted against the Policy Committee positions on the floor. This compares with *Congressional Quarterly* party opposition scores of 16 in 1961 and 17 in 1962.

I have altered Jones' figures slightly (by treating absences differently) so that they are exactly comparable to the *Congressional Quarterly* scores, which are based on the percentage of the time an individual member voted against the majority of his party when it was opposed by the majority of the other party.

[35] Meg Greenfield, "Charles A. Halleck and the Restless Republicans," *The Reporter*, March 29, 1962, pp. 27-30.

late in 1963 against an arrangement whereby the United States could sell wheat to the Soviet Union.[36]

Such grievances, coupled with the loss of thirty-eight Republican seats in the 1964 election, led the party to oust Halleck as Minority Leader in early 1965 and replace him with Gerald Ford of Michigan. Ford's victory was based in part on another expansion of the number of Republicans who could call themselves leaders. After 1965, for example, no Republican could hold a leadership position and also be ranking member on a standing committee. The conference (and especially its chairman) moved into greater prominence, as the Policy Committee was downgraded.

In the Eighty-ninth Congress (1965-67) the Republicans deliberately sought to give their party a hierarchical chain of command. The leaders (the Minority Leader, the conference chairman, the Whip, the chairman of the Policy Committee, and the chairman of a new Research and Planning Committee) conceived of the minority role as one of constantly putting forth alternatives to majority proposals. On important issues they met with Republicans on the relevant standing committee and decided what course of action should be taken. If the standing committee delegation and the leaders agreed, and if time was short, no further action followed. If, however, time was ample, the matter was important, or there was some disagreement among Republicans on the standing committee, then a meeting of the Policy Committee was called to discuss the issue. If warranted, a second meeting of the Policy Committee was held to adopt a formal position. The process sometimes ended at this point. If there was time and if the matter was of such importance that the leaders felt party members should have another opportunity for discussion, a conference was called to allow debate.

The success of this experiment with collegial leadership in the minority has been quite limited. The Republicans have had a major impact on some important programs, but the majority party possesses the power to deny most of the credit due them.

[36] See the column by Rowland Evans and Robert Novak in the *Washington Post*, February 9, 1964.

Success at the polls, the ultimate aim of the leaders, has not been forthcoming. The individual leaders have not been able to entrench themselves in their positions.

## Origins and Consequences of Leadership Patterns

Changes in the pattern of leadership stem largely from conscious decisions by the leaders and members of a party. Both parties have maintained a willingness to experiment with their leadership pattern in order to gain legislative success.

Three important factors have most consistently influenced a party to change its leadership pattern. First, prolonged frustration with the way legislative matters are proceeding in the House often portends change. The tabular summary on the next page of ten patterns chosen as examples makes this point. In each of these examples, the party leaders and members were frustrated and dissatisfied with their legislative performance and willing to experiment with a new pattern to attain success.

Second, a change from minority to majority status often means that the new majority will use a pattern different from the last time it controlled the House. Five of the eight examples for the majority party involved new majorities. Four of these chose not to use the pattern of leadership they had used the last time they were in the majority. A new majority is especially anxious to accomplish great things, and is likely to feel the necessity for a new pattern of leadership to reach its goal.

Third, the personality of the principal leaders is a consistently important factor in explaining shifts in leadership patterns. In most cases, when a party changes its pattern to leadership by the Speaker, Majority Leader, or Minority Leader, it is because the new incumbent possesses the personal qualities that allow him the freedom to shape a new pattern. Carlisle, Reed, Cannon, Rayburn, Stevens, Underwood, and Williams could all establish new patterns of leadership because their personal qualities matched the expectations of the party members and gave them the confidence to lead forcefully. When a commanding personality is missing, or when many of the party members have reacted negatively to their leading figure, a party is likely to choose leadership by a collegial group or the President. If in the minority,

| Majority Party Pattern and Example | Main Sources of Frustrations at Beginning of Pattern |
|---|---|
| Speaker: Carlisle (1883–89) | In minority, 1881–83; lack of accomplishment in majority, 1875–81 |
| Speaker: Reed (1889–91, 1895–99) | Long minority status (1875–81; 1883–89; 1891–95); lack of accomplishment in majority, 1881–83 |
| Speaker: Cannon (1903–11) | In majority, but with an inept Speaker, 1899–1903 |
| Speaker: Rayburn (1940–47; 1949–53; 1955–61) | Preceded by inept or invalid Speakers (1933–40); North-South split in party; White House domination of Congress since 1933 |
| Majority Leader: Stevens (1861–68) | Southern domination of previous Congresses |
| Majority Leader: Underwood (1911–15) | Long minority status (1895–1911) |
| Collegial: 1919–25 Republican Steering Committee | Long minority status (1911–19) |
| Collegial: Post-1962 Democrats | Republican President (1953–61); success of conservative coalition (1937–61) |

| Minority Party Pattern and Example | Main Sources of Frustrations at Beginning of Pattern |
|---|---|
| Minority Leader: Williams (1903–08) | Impotence in long minority status (1895–1903) |
| Collegial: Post-1959 Republicans | Impotence in long minority status; general lack of success at the polls (1931–59) |

the party may go through a period of lack of purposeful leadership. The Republicans in 1919 chose a collegial pattern partly because of the reaction against Mann and the absence of any other commanding figure. In 1962 the Democrats chose a collegial pattern because their central figure for twenty-four years, Rayburn, was gone and no one could hope to take his place immediately. The Republican minority in 1959 established a collegial pattern because they had grown tired of their principal leader for twenty years, Joe Martin, and could find no single figure to whom they were willing to give all or most of the leadership power. President Wilson in 1915 and President Roosevelt in 1933 took over much of the internal leadership of the House, partly because of outside events (World War I and the Depression), but also because the Democratic leaders in the House had little support from their own members.

The legislative consequences of the various patterns are not wholly predictable. In the majority party, periods of legislative creativity and success have occurred under all four patterns of leadership. A tabular summary makes this point:

| *Years* | *Pattern* | *Party* | *Major Legislative Products* |
|---------|-----------|---------|------------------------------|
| 1865–69 | Majority Leader | R | Reconstruction legislation |
| 1889–91 1895–99 | Speaker | R | Thorough tariff revisions; Sherman Antitrust Act |
| 1905–07 | Speaker | R | Pure food; meat inspection; railroad regulation |
| 1913–15 | Majority Leader | D | Tariff; Federal Reserve; Clayton Antitrust Act; Federal Trade Commission |
| 1933–37 | President | D | New Deal |
| 1963–67 | Collegial | D | Education; conservation; medical care; tax revision; economic development |

The above table also indicates that centralization of power in one or only a few hands, regardless of pattern, is necessary for a period of great legislative success in the majority. Only one collegial pattern of majority leadership—that of the post-1962 Democrats—has resulted in outstanding legislative success, and in this case power was not distributed widely, but kept in the hands of the three principal leaders.

The same point can be made even more strongly in the case of the minority party. The only minority pattern that provides for centralized power is leadership by the Minority Leader. In all three periods (1875-81; 1883-89 and 1891-95; 1939-47, 1949-53, and 1955-59) during which the minority was largely successful in frustrating the majority, it relied on such leadership.[37]

The ten examples of leadership patterns used in this chapter underscore the point that a high degree of centralization is more likely to be related to legislative success than a low degree of centralization. Highly centralized power does not guarantee legislative success, but has been a prerequisite for it.

[37] Factors other than the personal qualities of the Minority Leader also aided the party in these three periods of success. For four of the six years between 1875 and 1881, the President and Senate were Republican. This helped the House Republicans, in a minority, in opposing a Democratic party divided on the major issue of the tariff. For eight of the ten years between 1883 and 1889 and 1891 and 1895, the Senate was Republican, and the Democrats were often divided on major issues. During the Fifty-third Congress (1893-95), when the President, Senate, and House were all Democratic, some Democratic Senators helped the Republican minority prevent the kind of tariff bill that most House Democrats desired. From 1939 to 1959 the Republicans, in a minority for sixteen of these twenty years, were aided in their attempts to block Democratic legislation by an informal coalition with conservative southern Democrats.

## ☆ 5 ☆

# Techniques of Contemporary Leaders

Most of the thousands of bills introduced into the House each year are ignored by the party leaders, who assume that the standing committees will do whatever is necessary. Sometimes, however, they must use all of their resources to achieve a favorable decision on a significant bill. This chapter examines the techniques available to the leaders as they struggle for legislative success.

Floor business is the principal preserve of the leaders. This is where they direct most of their attention and have their greatest impact. This is especially true of majority leadership, which is responsible for scheduling the business on the floor and developing efforts to enact it.

Leaders do not often attempt to influence committee business. Partisan influences on committees from the leaders, the administration, and some senior committee members are apparent in numerous case studies, but such studies emphasize that the parties are much more important on the floor than in committees.[1] A

---

[1] Studies of the Taft-Hartley Act, the Rent Control Act of 1949, and the Excess Profits Tax of 1950 all seem to point in this direction. See Stephen K. Bailey and Howard D. Samuel, *Congress at Work* (Holt, 1952), pp. 284-86, 346-51, and 429-30. Also, Bailey's study of the Employment Act of 1946, despite its conclusions that deny the presence of party influence and responsibility, makes clear that during the floor fight in the House, party leadership was an important factor. Ultimately, of course, the southern Democratic-conservative Republican alliance

study of the Landrum-Griffin Act of 1959, for example, indicates that the floor activity was almost all concerned with problems that tended to divide the two parties, although the Republicans desisted wherever they could in order to retain the Democratic allies essential to their success.[2] A study of the failure of the proposal for an Urban Affairs Department in 1961-62 shows how a clash between the House Republican Policy Committee and the Democratic President helped create a partisan tone in all of the ensuing debate.[3]

Clem Miller, in his remarkable series of letters to his constituents about the House, indicated the paramount importance of the floor, both for developing a feeling of party unity and as the place where the party leaders exercise the greatest influence.

> The House Floor is a great meeting place. . . . One gets a line on upcoming legislation or party strategy, and so on. . . .
> In recent weeks we have been talking about the locus of congressional power. Let us now relate it to the Floor of the House. Previously, we have seen that as an issue mounts in importance, ability to influence on the Floor of the House lessens.
> We have also seen that debate changes few votes. Now let us consider how votes *are* changed. Members do change the votes of other Members and Members do switch from vote to vote. This is done on a personal basis. . . .
> Voting lines are set by the committee chairmen (and by each committee's senior minority member) and hence by the Leadership; that generally is sufficient to carry the day; and finally . . . individuals may shift back and forth within this framework in response to personal appeals and deeply ingrained prejudices.[4]

To understand the contemporary leaders' techniques for influencing outcomes on the floor, they will be investigated in two ways. First, a catalog of eight techniques will be discussed, using specific examples. Second, the majority party leaders will be shown using a variety of techniques as they sought support for five different bills in the Eighty-eighth Congress (1963-65).

---

carried the day, but the maneuvering was largely partisan. See Stephen K. Bailey, *Congress Makes a Law* (Vintage, 1964), pp. 237-38, 173-78.

[2] Alan K. McAdams, *Power and Politics in Labor Legislation* (Columbia University Press, 1964), pp. 214, 226-27, 277-78.

[3] Judith Ann Heimlich, "The Urban Department Mr. Kennedy Did Not Get" (unpublished manuscript prepared for a Brookings Institution project).

[4] Clem Miller, *Member of the House* (Scribner's, 1962), pp. 4, 107, 109.

## A Catalog of Current Techniques

### DEVELOPING COMMITTEE UNANIMITY

Leaders of both parties can develop unanimous support for a particular position among their members on the standing committee handling the bill. With no defections among committee members in debate or in voting, the rest of the party members are more likely to follow.

Party members on a standing committee can take the lead in developing an alternative to the proposals of the other party or the administration. Under Presidents Kennedy and Johnson, some Republicans have made efforts to develop alternative positions by working through the party members on committees as well as the party leaders. In the Eighty-seventh and Eighty-eighth Congresses (1961-65), this usually involved a caucus and agreement on the part of committee Republicans before approaching Minority Leader Charles Halleck to ask for a meeting of the Policy Committee or the full conference. Only a few Republican committee delegations made such efforts; others felt that the opposition should merely oppose majority proposals.

In 1963, Republicans on the Ways and Means Committee met and worked out an alternative to the Democratic plan for a tax cut. They took their proposal to the Policy Committee, which in turn recommended a conference. The conference ratified the plan, and when it was embodied in the recommittal motion on the floor only one Republican voted with the majority against the motion and 173 Republicans voted for it, although the Democrats kept their own losses low enough to win.

Republicans on the Judiciary Committee met throughout 1963 to develop a united position on civil rights legislation. As a result, leading party members on the committee received much of the credit for passage of the bill with a high degree of Republican support.

In the Eighty-ninth Congress (1965-67), the Republican pattern of committee-leadership consultation changed. The new Minority Leader, Gerald Ford, encouraged all committee delegations to develop alternatives to almost all major Democratic proposals, including the Appalachia program (Public Works Committee), education (Education and Labor Committee), and Medicare (Ways and Means Committee). The Minority Leader and others in the leadership met with all Republicans on a standing committee to discuss various alternatives. After a unanimous position was reached, the Minority Leader sent a letter to all Republicans announcing the party position. Republican support for these proposals on the floor was high—although, given the small number of Republicans in the House, few victories were won.

SCHEDULING

The majority party alone has the power to manipulate the scheduling of floor business to suit its own ends. Generally, the majority leadership does not try to spring "surprises" in scheduling major bills: the usual tactic is to delay until the time is right for passage. This can mean delay of a day or two until attendance is more favorable, or it can mean a delay of many months to obtain needed support for a proposal.

The chronology of the bill providing subsidies for both growers and manufacturers of cotton, which the House passed on December 4, 1963, suggests the uses the majority party leaders can make of scheduling delays. A subcommittee of the House Agriculture Committee held hearings on the bill Feburary 5, and the full committee reported it June 6. On June 11, the Secretary of Agriculture wrote the chairman of the committee, Harold Cooley of North Carolina, that the administration strongly supported the bill. On the next day, however, the House killed a proposed extension and expansion of the area redevelopment program, with Cooley and many other southerners voting against the administration. One Democratic leader remarked immediately after this defeat, "Harold Cooley can forget the cotton bill."

Feeling against the southerners continued so high throughout the summer that the leaders and administration would not risk bringing the bill to the floor. In mid-August Cooley and other high-ranking southerners on the committee met with Majority

Leader Carl Albert, Majority Whip Hale Boggs, and Albert Rains of the Banking and Currency Committee to determine whether a trade could be arranged whereby southerners would support a new version of the area redevelopment bill in return for northern and liberal support for the cotton bill. No agreement could be reached.

By the week of October 21, Cooley had decided to schedule the cotton bill for the week after Veterans Day (November 11). The Speaker announced this decision, and on October 25, Albert and Boggs signed a letter to all Democrats outlining the objectives of the bill. On October 28 the whip organization began polling all Democrats on the question: "Will you vote for the 1963 cotton bill?" At a meeting on October 31, the Speaker reported that Democratic defections would require forty Republican votes to pass the bill. He rescheduled it for the week of November 18, giving the supporters an extra week to find the votes.

By November 8, on the basis of the whip poll results, the Speaker again decided to postpone the bill until the first week in December.

By chance, the cotton bill was the first major legislation before the House that was of primary importance to the new President, Lyndon Johnson. Just thirteen days after the assassination of President Kennedy, the House acted. During the week before the vote, the leaders used extensively (and almost exclusively) the argument that no Democrat should vote against the bill and help defeat the new President in his first test. With the Democratic leaders keeping all assistant whips on the floor to prevent members from straying, the House passed the bill on December 4. Even then forty-eight Democrats voted against it, but thirty-four Republican votes pulled the leadership and the new President through to success. The whip poll begun in October left at least seventy Democratic votes in doubt. Before the Speaker let the bill come to the floor, the poll was showing only twenty-five defectors, with another eight unsure. (Some of the forty-eight votes cast in opposition would probably have been changed if it were certain they were needed for a leadership and presidential victory.)

Two bills increasing the pay of federal employees, including congressmen, came to the House floor in 1964. The first version lost early in the session by a roll call vote of 222 to 184. After several months of work on recalcitrant Democrats, the leaders again brought it to the floor in June. This time it passed, 243 to 157. Before the Speaker had scheduled it the second time, he personally checked with enough members to know that it would win. Only then did he authorize the Majority Leader to announce that the bill would come to the floor in less than forty-eight hours.[5]

In dealing with the Appalachia bill in 1964, the Democratic leaders had a long fight—first with the Public Works Committee and then with the Rules Committee—before being able to schedule it for floor action. Continuing absences during September forced postponement, until finally Congress adjourned without action.[6] Early in the more heavily Democratic Eighty-ninth Congress, the administration won an easy victory despite the loss of fifty-six Democrats, a number that in 1964 would probably have defeated the bill.

## TAKING OFFICIAL PARTY POSITIONS

A technique available to the leaders of both parties is to state and disseminate official party positions on proposed legislation. Both information and some pressure accompany the dissemination.

Since 1962, the Democratic leaders customarily write all their members explaining the bill in question and asking for a certain kind of vote. For example, on the 1963 tax reduction bill, the Speaker, Majority Leader, Whip, and chairman of the Ways and Means Committee sent a short letter and digest of the bill to all Democrats twelve days before floor action was scheduled. They said simply, "The passage of this bill is essential to our national well-being. A motion to recommit, which would be highly de-

---

[5] *Washington Post,* June 14, 1964.

[6] The *Wall Street Journal,* September 3, 1964, indicates that the Appalachia bill was scheduled for floor action on Wednesday, September 2, but the number of Democratic absences on the preceding day forced the Speaker to postpone the bill. Had it come up, it is likely that the leadership and the President would have suffered a stinging defeat at the start of a national election campaign.

structive of the bill, will be made. We urge that you be present
for the debate, and that you vote to defeat the motion to recommit and for final passage of the bill."

The minority pattern in the Eighty-eighth Congress was for
the Policy Committee to take a position and then communicate
it to various regional and class groupings of Republicans
through their representatives on the committee. Sometimes John
Byrnes, chairman of the Policy Committee, would himself write
all Republicans. In the Eighty-ninth Congress, party positions
were taken either in the conference or simply in a letter from the
Minority Leader after consultation with members on a standing
committee.

PHONE CALLS AND PERSONAL CONTACTS

The leaders of both parties rely heavily on telephone and personal contacts (often on the floor) in trying to persuade members
to act in a certain way. Since 1962, for example, the Democratic
leaders meet a week or two before an important vote to decide
which members should be contacted and by whom. On the basis
of these discussions, the Speaker, Majority Leader, Whip, and
committee chairman involved each take a list of members to contact.

ARRANGING SPEAKERS FOR THE FLOOR

It is often important who speaks for or against a bill, not so
much for what he says as for who he is. The leaders of both parties are eager to get their most respected members to speak for
their position. This is particularly true of members who often
disagree with the leaders. Thus, Democratic leaders often seek
speeches from southern conservatives, while Republican leaders
seek speeches from northeastern liberals.

In the fight to defeat the Republican recommittal motion on
the 1963 tax bill, the Democratic leaders were able to persuade
George Mahon, then second-ranking on the Appropriations
Committee and a highly respected Texan with a moderately con-

servative voting record, to speak against the Republican motion. They also persuaded Omar Burleson, another conservative Texan of great seniority and reputation, to speak against the motion and for the bill. That Mahon and Burleson spoke and made effective arguments seems to have convinced a sufficient number of wavering Democrats to defeat the recommittal motion.

Persuading disliked members not to speak on their side is also something that the leadership must do. During the debate on the cotton bill in December 1963, the Speaker told two ranking southern Democrats on the Agriculture Committee not to speak for the bill because they would both lose votes. When another unpopular southerner did speak for it, the observation of one liberal westerner was, "There's another nail in the coffin."

MANAGING THE VOTING PATTERN[7]

There are three major aspects to leadership management of the voting pattern on the House floor. First, the leaders of both parties can try to make sure that key men vote the right way. This is obviously important on roll calls, where certain respected figures provide voting cues for a number of other members. It can also be true on teller votes, during which members on each side line up in the center aisle of the House and are counted by tellers appointed by the chairman of the Committee of the

[7] The analysis in this section is based in part on material found in Lewis A. Froman, Jr., and Randall B. Ripley, "Conditions for Party Leadership: The Case of the House Democrats," *American Political Science Review*, Vol. 59 (March 1965), pp. 59-61.

There are four types of voting in the House: (1) roll calls, in which each member votes individually and publicly when his name is called by the clerk; (2) teller votes, in which those voting aye first pass up the center aisle of the House, followed by those voting nay, and are counted by members appointed as tellers by the chair; (3) divisions, in which those voting aye, followed by those voting nay, stand and are counted by the chair; and (4) voice votes.

Pairs are used to record the position of absent members on a roll call. A regular legislative pair is an agreement to neutralize the votes of one absent member on each side of a question. A live pair results in a net gain of one vote for one side or the other because a member actually present is paired with an absent member. There are also "general pairs," which have no legislative value in that no position is announced for either of the absent members.

Whole. For example, during the House debate on the student loan provisions of the health professions assistance bill in 1963, a Republican offered an amendment that would have made segregated programs ineligible for funds. Had it passed, enough southerners would probably have voted against the bill on final passage (a roll call visible to their constituents) to defeat it. Yet it was difficult for northern supporters of the bill who came from pro-civil rights districts to vote against the anti-segregation amendment. Thus when the teller vote on the amendment was held, the Democratic leaders persuaded four of their five Negro members to vote against it, graphic proof to liberal Democrats that the amendment could be attacked as a sham.

Second, the leaders of both parties can ask probable opponents to be absent when a vote is cast. Rarely will more than two or three members of either party be persuaded to miss a final roll call deliberately. More were persuaded, however, on the second bill raising federal pay in 1964. An entire committee, made up largely of opponents, was convinced by the Democratic leaders to take a field trip the day of the vote. It is normal for five or more members of both parties to be missing by request on roll calls on recommittal motions and for ten or more to absent themselves during teller votes.

Third, the leaders have some leeway in manipulating the type of vote that is used on a particular matter. The minority is limited largely to supplying the people necessary to force a roll call vote (one-fifth of those present must concur in such a demand), or a teller vote (44 in the House and 20 in the Committee of the Whole must concur), instead of a voice vote. In addition to this, because of their control of the schedule, the majority leaders can adjourn the House if a series of teller votes looks as if it will result in too many unwanted amendments, postpone a roll call from one day to another, or force the House to stay in session and hold a roll call on a particular day rather than waiting until the next day.

The leaders of both parties generally have greater control over the behavior of their members on votes that have relatively low visibility to the voting public, the press, the political leaders at home, and other members of the House. Roll call voting on final passage of measures is the most visible. Roll calls on recommittal motions, which send a bill back to a standing committee, often with instructions to make specific changes and report the bill back to the floor, are somewhat less visible, especially if the motions do not include specific instructions, because the implications of such votes are more obscure to the electorate. Roll calls on specific amendments and procedural questions are even less visible.

Division and voice voting are often simply party votes because they happen so quickly, and because few members know the nature of the choice being made. As the members scurry from the cloak-rooms, many Democrats only want to know the position taken by the floor manager (usually the committee or subcommittee chairman); Republicans ask for the position of their contigent on the committee.

Teller voting, because it takes longer (and it is therefore easier to identify members as they line up to vote), and because members are notified by bells located in their offices and throughout the Capitol and House Office Buildings, is subject to more strenuous efforts by the leaders to keep members in tow. More members are likely to vote on teller votes than on divisions or voice votes, and a large number of voice and division votes are reversed because the leaders have time to call members to the floor. These exertions are rewarded by a substantial amount of party unity on most teller votes even by members who, if forced to a roll call, would vote against the leaders.

## WORKING ON POTENTIAL ALLIES IN THE OPPOSITION PARTY

Leaders of both parties can work on potential allies among the opposition. Formal collaboration between the leaders of the two parties occurs only rarely, such as in 1964 on the second bill authorizing a United States contribution to the International Development Association. The House defeated the first bill, although it was supported by all Democratic leaders and the Republican leaders on the committee. A number of factors contributed to the first defeat: the ineffectiveness and unpopularity of the committee chairman; careless, last-minute scheduling by the leaders; the lack of a meaningful Democratic whip poll; and the lack of lobbying by the Treasury (a partner in this venture with the Agency for International Development). In preparing for the second vote, Clarence Kilburn, the ranking Republican on the Banking and Currency Committee, and one of his assistants attended strategy sessions in the Speaker's office.[8] As a result of this, and more effective scheduling and persuasive activity by the Democratic leaders and executive officials, fifty-three members changed their votes to help defeat a recommittal motion.

The leaders of both parties favored the civil rights bill in 1963 and worked together to pass it, although there were still points of partisan friction. In the Judiciary Committee, for example, five Republicans (two southerners) joined with five southern Democrats and five uncompromising Democratic supporters of civil rights in voting for an exceptionally strong bill (the Republicans and southern Democrats hoping that it would fail on the floor). Ten Democrats, including two southerners, and nine Republicans were successful in substituting a more moderate bill.

Although supporters of the bill from both parties knew that they needed help from the other party, each organized its own floor effort: the Democratic Study Group led the way for the majority, and the Judiciary Committee Republicans took the leading minority role.[9] The formal party leadership was not in evidence much of the time, although McCormack, Albert, and Halleck all supported the bill. The parties continued to be suspicious of one another at the same time. When Majority Whip Hale Boggs of Louisiana spoke in support of an amendment to a major title of the bill, one of the leading Republicans, John Lindsay of New York, immediately asked if there was a Democratic "cave-in." The chairman of the Judiciary Committee as-

[8] This happens rarely. One observer of Democratic legislative politics in the House for eight years before this event said he could remember no other occasion on which party lines were crossed in a leadership meeting.

[9] See *Congressional Quarterly*, February 21, 1964, pp. 364-66.

sured his Republican allies that there was no cave-in, and the pro-civil rights coalition held together.[10]

On the mass transit bill in 1964, the second-ranking Republican on the Banking and Currency Committee, William Widnall of New Jersey, led in gathering support for the bill and used the promise of this support as a lever to force the Democratic leaders to move more quickly.[11] The committee voted it out in April 1963, but the Speaker felt that floor passage was unlikely at that time in the budget-cutting atmosphere surrounding the debate over a proposed $11 billion tax reduction. Accordingly, he asked the Rules Committee not to grant the bill a rule. In early March 1964, he announced that at least forty Republican votes would be needed for passage. He privately doubted that such support would be forthcoming; it took two and a half months for Widnall and a coordinated lobby with good Republican ties to convince him that the votes were indeed lined up.

Finally, the Speaker asked for a rule, and Rules acted on May 20. Again McCormack hesitated and in early June stated that he would not call up the bill until he was sure it would pass. His doubt was sustained by a whip poll showing that an extremely close vote was in prospect. Not until the Republican supporters were counted again did he announce that the bill would be brought to the floor on June 25, when it passed 202 to 189, with thirty-nine Republicans voting aye.

Another tactic, more open to the majority leaders, is to get some nationally known minority figure to urge at least some members of his party to support the majority proposal.

## MEETING DEMANDS FROM WITHIN THE PARTY

Sometimes the members of a party will make demands the leaders feel they must accept. The skill in using this technique

[10] *New Republic,* February 29, 1964, p. 19. See the *Congressional Record,* Vol. 110, Pt. 2, 88 Cong. 2 sess. (1964), pp. 2489-91.

[11] See Vincent J. Sheehan, "The Wandering Paths of a Transit Bill," *Reporter,* July 16, 1964, pp. 31-33; *Wall Street Journal,* June 25, 1964, and Royce Hanson, "Congress Catches the Subway: Urban Mass Transit Legislation, 1960-64" (unpublished manuscript prepared for a Brookings Institution project).

comes when accession can be transformed, at least partially, into manipulation. Early in 1964, for example, after the House had defeated the first bill raising federal employees' pay (including the pay of members of Congress), there was much disagreement about what the second bill should contain. California Democrats caucused three times and each time decided that they would demand that the full $10,000 increase for members be retained as the price for their support of the bill. The leaders knew that if the $10,000 provision were left unchanged, the bill would almost surely be defeated again. About a week before floor action, the leaders let it be known that floor consideration would be postponed unless the California Democrats (and some other liberals) would support a $7,500 raise for members. The President and the leaders asked Democratic members of the Senate Post Office and Civil Service Committee to promise to restore the $10,000 and stand by that position in conference. Thus the lure of possible success in conference was held out to liberal Democrats in exchange for their support, and the House passed the bill.[12]

In 1965 the administration farm bill called for an additional subsidy for wheat that would be financed by a tax on millers and bakers. The latter immediately made clear that they would pass the cost of the tax on to the consumer by raising the price of bread. This led numerous urban and suburban Democrats, usually staunchly loyal to the leaders, to protest forcefully to the Speaker. The Speaker in turn informed the White House and Department of Agriculture that the provision would have to be dropped or Democratic votes would defeat the bill; the administration capitulated.[13]

The overthrow of Minority Leader Halleck in 1965 came in part because the members felt that he had not acceded to enough of their legislative requests. Republicans on standing committee delegations striving to develop alternatives to Democratic proposals felt that he had not been willing to listen to them. For example, when Widnall sought to have the Republican Policy Committee resist its natural urge to oppose the mass transit bill

[12] See the *Washington Post,* June 14, 1964, for the best story covering some of these events.
[13] See the *Washington Post,* August 17 and 18, 1965.

because a number of Republicans favored it, the committee refused and asked for Republican unity in opposing the bill. When Republicans on the Education and Labor Committee sought to develop alternative education bills, they found Halleck unsympathetic. Younger members who had experienced this kind of reaction were among the leaders of the anti-Halleck group.

## *Majority Leaders in Action: Four Cases in the Eighty-eighth Congress*[14]

### THE HOUSE RAISES THE DEBT LIMIT, MAY 1963

In 1963, the House raised or extended the limit on the national debt three different times. The hardest and closest fight occurred in May, over a bill raising the limit in two stages—from $305 billion to $307 billion for about a month, and then to $309 billion for two more months. The Ways and Means Committee took over eight weeks to act on the Secretary of the Treasury's request. A straight party vote in the committee on May 2 favored the bill; the report was made to the House on Monday, May 6.

The leaders knew from the outset that this would be a close fight. Thus they immediately asked the Whip to take a poll to find whether Democratic members would favor the bill. An attendance check was also started to ascertain who would be in Washington and able to vote on Wednesday, May 15, and Thursday, May 16. The Speaker waited for the results of this before deciding definitely that the bill should be brought to the floor May 15.

Results of the poll on the question of the bill itself were given to the Speaker as they were recorded. On Tuesday, May 7, the Speaker telephoned seven Democrats reported as opposed or doubtful about the bill, persuading them to give commitments that they would vote for it. On the same Tuesday, the whip orga-

[14] For an excellent description of the passage of a bill in the Eighty-seventh Congress that also illustrates the leaders of both parties using a number of techniques, see Don F. Hadwiger and Ross B. Talbot, *Pressures and Protests* (Chandler, 1965), pp. 193-209, 233.

nization distributed to all Democrats a single sheet statement about the importance of raising the debt limit and the consequences of not raising it. This statement had been prepared by the Treasury but carried no identifying label.

The two principal lobbyists for the Treasury believed—as did Chairman Wilbur Mills of Ways and Means—that Minority Leader Halleck did not really want to defeat the bill, but only wanted to give the Democrats a scare. The rest of the leadership, however, felt that Halleck was intent on victory and proceeded on that assumption. The Treasury representatives also worked hard on Democratic members, starting with a list of forty-seven suggested by the Whip's office on May 6.

Chairman Mills played an active role as part of the leadership. On Wednesday, May 8, he sent all Democrats a letter from Secretary of the Treasury Douglas Dillon explaining the difficulties that might be posed if the bill failed. Mills also asked the Democratic members of Ways and Means to talk to all members they represented on the Committee on Committees and make a personal appeal for support of the bill. Dillon was successful in getting Robert Anderson, the last Secretary of the Treasury in the Eisenhower administration, to call Halleck and ask him not to create difficulties for Dillon by trying to defeat the bill. Anderson also called John Byrnes, ranking Republican on Ways and Means and chairman of the Policy Committee. These appeals made no apparent difference to Halleck or Byrnes, however.

On Friday, May 10, McCormack, Albert, John Moss (the deputy whip), and Mills met with Lawrence O'Brien, chief of White House congressional liaison, three O'Brien assistants, the administrative assistant to the Whip, and the Assistant Secretary of the Treasury for congressional liaison. Mills reviewed a list of all Democrats and announced their reported position on the bill. When a member was announced as doubtful or against the bill, the Speaker or Majority Leader called him immediately and urged him to support it. Likewise, when a member favoring the bill was reported as planning to be absent, the Speaker called him and asked him to stay. One member who was asked to cancel a trip abroad (which he did) used the occasion to arrange an appointment with O'Brien for himself and another Democrat to talk about a proposed veterans hospital consolidation in their districts.

Mills repeated his belief that Halleck really would not defeat the bill if the Republican recommittal motion failed. He said he would try to get the Parliamentarian to arrange a meeting between himself and Halleck to see if an agreement could be reached whereby enough Republicans would vote for final passage to guarantee success if the Republican motion was defeated. Mills also said he had discussed the bill with some Republicans who favored a tax cut and had made it clear to them that if the debt limit bill was defeated, there would be no tax cut bill.

The meeting ended with the general feeling that the vote on recommittal would be no particular problem. Conservative southern Democrats could vote against that motion because it also included a debt limit increase, although smaller than the administration measure. The consensus was that the vote on final passage would be extremely close, with the Democrats probably having enough votes to win by two or three even if no Republicans voted for the bill. Mills said that he needed an accurate head count the afternoon before the bill came to the floor so that it could be delayed if necessary.

On Monday, May 13, after the first quorum call, the whip organization called the offices of favorable members not answering the call to make sure they would be back by Wednesday. The House leaders, Mills, the Treasury, and the White House continued to contact the few remaining Democrats whose votes were in doubt. The final whip poll (completed by the morning of Tuesday, May 14) showed 203 Democrats present and voting aye, thirty-five Democrats present and voting nay, ten who would be absent, and eight whose position still could not be clearly ascertained. These results made the chances of success look shaky and so the leaders (principally the Speaker) proceeded to obtain commitments from thirteen Democrats opposed to the bill that they would vote for it if their votes were needed for victory. Thus the leaders felt that they could count on about 215 Democrats if they absolutely needed them, which would be enough to win without Republican help. Copies of a list of the thirteen pocket votes were distributed to McCormack, Albert, Boggs, Moss, and Mills, so that they could quickly spot these men on the floor. Last minute efforts on Wednesday were made to get the maximum attendance on the floor. Two members attended in wheel chairs.

All the preparations paid off. After the Republican recommittal motion had been defeated 222 to 195, the House passed the administration bill 213 to 204, with a lone Republican joining 212 Democrats. Only thirty-two Democrats defected. Three of the pocket votes were used, probably at the initiative of the member himself, rather than because of a specific request of the leaders.

In this single fight, then, the leaders used most of the techniques available to them. Mills was successful in producing Democratic unity in the committee; the schedule was timed to the benefit of the party position; letters and explanatory material were sent to all Democrats; there were numerous phone and personal contacts; and an effort (although abortive) was made to obtain some Republican votes.

THE HOUSE AUTHORIZES FOREIGN AID, AUGUST 1963

Support for foreign aid legislation had been constantly dwindling under President Kennedy. In an effort to rally public support, he appointed a committee headed by General Lucius Clay, a Republican, to investigate the program. The committee's report in the spring of 1963 had not been overly kind to the program. Thus the President and the leaders in the House knew that foreign aid bills in the House would face rough times.[15]

The Foreign Affairs Committee held two months of hearings and then spent another two months in executive session before reporting, on August 8, a bill authorizing about $4.1 billion, a cut of $438 million from the administration's request. All Democrats joined in the majority report. Only six Republicans dissented.

The leadership was relatively inactive until the bill actually came to the floor. Agency for International Development (AID)

[15] See Paul Duke, "The Foreign Aid Fiasco," *Reporter,* January 16, 1964, pp. 20-25, for a background discussion and also material on the equally fierce fight over the appropriation bill in 1963—a fight that helped keep Congress in session until Christmas.

and White House liaison personnel bore the brunt of the task of convincing the skeptical before the bill arrived on the floor on Tuesday, August 20.

By that day, however, the situation looked grim, and the House Democratic leadership held a large meeting to inspire an effort that would hold the line against Republican attempts to cut funds for the program and limit the administrative flexibility of the President. Present were McCormack, Albert, Boggs, Moss, Chairman Thomas Morgan of the Foreign Affairs Committee, AID Administrator David Bell, Under Secretary of State Averell Harriman, various liaison officials, and seventeen assistant whips. The meeting took the form of a briefing for the assistant whips. Harriman explained how aid was a valuable tool for exploiting Chinese-Russian differences. Morgan and Bell reviewed some of the expected Republican amendments (many of which had been defeated in committee) and explained why each of them should be defeated. Speaker McCormack stressed what he felt was the overly partisan nature of the Republican position on the bill. He pointed out that the Democrats had supported aid under Eisenhower and that Republicans should do the same thing under Kennedy. The assistant whips asked some questions, two of which resulted in memoranda given to all of them.

General debate, limited to five hours by the rule, took all of Tuesday and most of Wednesday, August 21. By late Wednesday the amending process began, and almost immediately the Republicans won two teller votes on relatively important amendments. Speaker McCormack took the floor to denounce the Republicans and plead for the bill. The Democrats narrowly defeated another amendment and the leaders hastily adjourned the House shortly before six p.m., rather than risk defeat on a whole series of amendments.[16] That evening they called fifteen of the eighteen assistant whips (all but the three whose devotion to the bill was questionable) and asked them to be on the floor throughout the following day with as many of their members as possible. The importance of setting a winning pattern in the initial teller votes was stressed. The White House also got General Clay to send a telegram supporting the bill to thirty Republican members.

[16] See the *Washington Post,* August 22, 1964.

The next day the House resumed the amending process and in a ten and a half hour session the leaders were more successful. The House adopted only two restrictive amendments opposed by the leaders, and no money was cut from the bill. Southern Democrats who had been voting with the Republicans in the teller lines the day before either went to the cafeteria or voted with their party. More Republicans, up to twenty, voted with the Democrats, whereas the day before only a handful had done so.[17] Just when the leaders thought they had won the day and were pressing for a final vote, a Republican demanded an engrossed copy (printed, with all amendments) of the bill, which deferred the vote until the following day.

When the House met at noon on Friday, August 23, its first action was a bitter defeat for the Democratic leadership. By a 222 to 188 vote, with sixty-six Democrats defecting, $585 million was cut from the bill. Thirty-five Republicans and twelve Democrats who had voted for the cut then voted for final passage, assuring a 224 to 186 victory for the reduced amount.

In this fight, then, the committee Democrats were united, although the Foreign Affairs Committee does not command a great deal of respect on the House floor. The leaders manipulated the schedule at one crucial spot to avoid defeats on teller votes. Phone and personal contacts were used, although as there was no whip poll perhaps some of the doubtful were overlooked. The White House got a prominent Republican to attempt to secure some Republican votes. Yet the nature of the issue was such that even with the use of a number of techniques, the opposition still won a significant victory.

TRADING IN THE HOUSE: FOOD STAMPS FOR
WHEAT-COTTON, APRIL 1964[18]

In June 1963, the Agriculture Committee held hearings on a bill to establish a food stamp program to guarantee the needy an adequate diet. Democratic Congresswoman Leonor Sullivan of

<hr>

[17] See the *Wall Street Journal,* August 26, 1963.

[18] For a fuller version of this story see Randall B. Ripley, "Bargaining in the House: The Food Stamp Act of 1964" (unpublished manuscript prepared for a Brookings Institution project).

Missouri had been sponsoring similar bills for almost a decade. The committee could not agree on a number of specific points and reached no agreement until early the following February when it tabled the bill eighteen to seventeen, with the aid of five defecting southern Democrats. The food stamp bill appeared to be dead.

Two developments occurred, however, that helped save the bill. First, liberals on the Rules Committee held up a tobacco bill that was supported by the anti-food stamp southerners on the Agriculture Committee. The liberals demanded a favorable report on the food stamp bill as the price for releasing the tobacco bill. The Agriculture Committee agreed to this demand on March 4.

Second, on March 6, the Senate added a wheat program to a cotton measure passed by the House the previous December, and the amended bill was returned to the House, where it almost immediately became linked to the food stamp bill. Both the administration and the Democratic members of the Agriculture Committee had a large stake in favorable House action on the wheat-cotton bill, but it was evident that there were a sizable number of potential nay votes among urban Democrats. These votes, with a solid Republican front against the bill, could defeat it.

Kenneth Birkhead, head of congressional liaison in the Agriculture Department, and the House Democratic leaders conceived the necessity of tying the wheat-cotton bill to some bill that would appeal to urban Democrats. They wanted to arrange a trade.

Until the House on March 12 defeated a pay raise for government employees, there had been talk that the pay raise and wheat-cotton might be linked, but after farm votes helped kill the pay raise, the urban Democratic anger grew. Gradually, during March, it became clear that the trade would involve the food stamp bill and the wheat-cotton bill. No formal announcement was made, nor was any formal meeting held to reach agreement between leaders of urban and rural blocs. Instead—typical of the operations of the House—the psychological climate had become favorable. The more individual members and the press discussed a possible trade of rural votes on food stamps for urban votes on wheat-cotton, the more firmly the idea took hold in the minds of the members. The trade was based on shared perceptions of a legislative situation, bolstered by individual lobbying efforts relying on the trade as a persuasive point.

During the weeks before Easter vacation, it became evident that the wheat-cotton bill was in much more danger of losing than was the food stamp bill. Thus most of the lobbying activity on the part of the executive and Democratic House leaders was aimed at passing wheat-cotton. The Speaker obtained pocket votes from nine northeastern Democrats as insurance.

The floor debate on April 7 and 8 was heated. All knew that the wheat-cotton bill was scheduled to follow the final action on food stamps, and there were many references to the upcoming—and more costly and controversial—legislation. The leaders asked for whip polls on both bills. They showed that 212 Democrats would vote for the food stamp bill, enough to win even without Republican help if there were the usual number of absentees. On the other hand, only 197 Democrats were likely to vote aye on the wheat-cotton bill—not enough if Republican lines held.

The House finished general debate on the food stamp bill and read the first section for amendment on Tuesday, April 7. On Wednesday, April 8, the House met an hour earlier than usual and resumed the amending process. During this process, the Republicans raised a civil rights question in an attempt to woo southern Democrats away from the program. They stressed that the pilot programs had, with a few exceptions, not been located in the South, and that Title VI of the pending civil rights bill would prevent much of the region from benefitting from the program.

Nevertheless, the Democratic ranks held during teller votes, and five Republican amendments objectionable to the leaders were defeated, including an amendment requiring matching state funds that the Agriculture Committee had adopted over the protests of its chairman.

In the midst of the amending process, the House recessed for two hours to pay respects to the late General Douglas MacArthur, whose body lay in state in the rotunda.

Chairman Cooley of the Agriculture Committee moved to cut off debate at six o'clock p.m. and the House passed this motion.

The Committee of the Whole rose; the Speaker resumed the chair and prepared to order a final roll call. A Republican demanded an engrossed copy of the bill. The Democrats were prepared for this possibility, and the printer was ready to accomplish the task within a few hours. The Speaker then let debate open on the rule for the wheat-cotton bill. Within a few minutes, liberal Democrats, including Mrs. Sullivan, realized that this might mean that the final vote on wheat-cotton would come before the final vote on food stamps. She quickly let the Speaker know that this would be unacceptable because the southerners, after voting aye on wheat-cotton, might either leave the chamber or vote nay on food stamps. Thus the Speaker interrupted the debate and declared a recess, acting under the agreement that had allowed the earlier recess to honor MacArthur.

The House reconvened at 9:05 p.m. and the Republicans protested vigorously that the recess agreement had been used to give the Speaker an unforeseen power. They offered a motion to adjourn and demanded a roll call, on which the motion was defeated. The minority then exercised its right of offering a recommittal motion, which provided that the amendment on state matching be restored to the bill. This was defeated 195 to 223. The House then passed the food stamp bill by a vote of 229 to 189.

To complete the day, an hour-long debate on the wheat-cotton bill was held, and the House passed it 211 to 203 before adjourning at 12:44 a.m.

An analysis of the last three roll calls indicates the degree of success of the trade of food stamps for wheat-cotton among Democrats. Twelve Democrats were absent for all three votes. Six more were absent for one or more of the three roll calls, but supported the administration when they voted. One hundred eighty Democrats supported the administration on all three roll calls and might best be labeled as "reliable traders." Twenty-six members were "hard-line liberals," voting with the administration twice on the food stamp bill and against the wheat-cotton bill. Twelve members were "hard-line conservatives," voting against the food stamp bill twice and for the wheat-cotton bill. Eight members were "half-hearted traders," voting with the administration on one food stamp roll call and against it on the other and for the wheat-cotton bill. Eight Democrats were against both programs on all three roll calls.

The trade was 82 percent successful in that only the hard-line liberals, hard-line conservatives, and half-hearted traders explicitly violated the terms of the bargain. Even if only the reliable traders are counted, the trade was 71 percent successful.

In this case the House leaders were successful partly because of the techniques they used: they managed the voting sequence and schedule so as to make the trade most effective; they made numerous phone and personal contacts; they helped channel demands from both the urban and rural segments of the party in such a way that all demands could be met and the administration could be satisfied at the same time.

### THE HOUSE SUPPORTS THE POVERTY BILL, AUGUST 1964

During the spring of 1964, a subcommittee of the Committee on Education and Labor held hearings on the proposed antipoverty program. From the outset, the Democrats made clear that they wanted the entire credit for this program in an election year. The Republicans did not know exactly how to react. Not until late April did they put forth their own alternative, which generated unanimous Democratic opposition and only partial Republican support. But at least they were sure they wanted to do nothing to help President Johnson and the Democratic leadership in the House. The Democrats sought unity by having a southerner, Phil Landrum of Georgia, steer the bill through the committee and on the floor.[19]

At the end of the subcommittee hearings, Democrats on the full Education and Labor Committee caucused for several weeks to discuss a number of changes and reach a unified position. By mid-May the committee was ready to begin executive sessions on the bill. After resolving a number of controversial issues—in-

[19] See the *Baltimore Sun*, April 20, 1964, for a good account of how some parts of this political fight developed.

cluding race and church-state relations—the committee on May 26 voted to report the bill by a straight party-line vote.

The bill went to the Rules Committee and the leadership expected swift action. On June 2, Carl Albert and Hale Boggs sent a letter to all Democrats urging them to support the bill. The Rules Committee, however, did not take up the bill until mid-June, and then Chairman Howard Smith, an opponent, indicated that he thought Republicans should have many witnesses testify at hearings. Finally, on July 28, by an eight to seven vote, Rules cleared the measure.

Floor debate began on Wednesday, August 5. A whip poll early in the summer showed that the vote would be very close, with a number of southern Democratic defections. Only minimal help could be expected from the Republicans.

On the morning of August 6, Sargent Shriver, the man who would head the poverty program if it came into being, had breakfast with three representatives from North Carolina to persuade them of its merits and solicit their votes. The North Carolinians asked him if Adam Yarmolinsky, a well-known liberal Democrat and official in the Defense Department, would be in the program and Shriver, in a moment of candor, said that Yarmolinsky would, indeed, be appointed to an important post. The North Carolinians reacted adversely. They thought Yarmolinsky radical and alerted the other members of their delegation. That afternoon, at a large meeting in the Speaker's office, the dean of the North Carolina delegation attacked Yarmolinsky vigorously and demanded a promise that he would not be in the program as the price for their support of the bill. Chairman Adam Clayton Powell of the committee and floor manager Landrum agreed. The Speaker and Shriver called the White House and got the needed guarantee from the President, and the North Carolinians then filed in to hear Shriver repeat the promise.[20]

After this affair, the whip poll on the morning before the day of the vote showed 200 Democrats in favor, five absent, and four

[20] On the sacrifice of Yarmolinsky see Rowland Evans and Robert Novak, "The Yarmolinsky Affair," *Esquire*, February 1965; and the story by Mary McGrory in the *Evening Star* (Washington), August 12, 1964.

doubtful. The 200, when increased by expected help from Republicans representing poverty-stricken areas, would be enough to pass the bill. To help insure Republican support, the administration encouraged a former Eisenhower Secretary of Health, Education and Welfare, Marion Folsom, to endorse the bill in telegrams to nine Republicans, including Halleck.

The final vote came on Saturday, August 8, and the House passed the bill 226 to 185. Seven of the nine North Carolina Democrats voted for it. Twenty-two Republicans joined 204 Democrats in supporting the bill.

In this case the key technique had been the development of committee unanimity among Democrats. The leaders miscalculated by assuming that capitulation to the North Carolina demand was essential to victory, but their use of other techniques was more skillful and helped produce the favorable outcome.

# ☆ 6 ☆

# Party Loyalty

Party loyalty in the House is interpreted by leaders and members alike as the willingness to follow the policy positions taken by the leaders. Roll call voting behavior has often been analyzed in terms of such loyalty, but the relationships between the individual member's perceptions of and feelings toward his party and its leaders, and his reactions to leadership requests for loyal behavior, have been largely unexplored. This chapter will discuss these relationships in an effort to explain more fully the leaders' use of psychological preferment to achieve a desired result.

## *The Impact of Party Position*

Comparable interviews were conducted with thirty-five Democrats and twenty-five Republicans who were members of the Eighty-eighth Congress (1963-65). The interviews ranged from thirty minutes to two hours in length and averaged about fifty minutes. They were focused on the role of party in the House and the member's own perceptions of the role of his party and its leadership. Each of the respondents was asked five questions in the same order. The initial response to each question was developed further through additional questions that varied according to the respondent and the situation. Many other general questions were also raised if time permitted.[1] The respondents were representative of their parties in terms of seniority, region, and voting loyalty.[2] They were also generally representative in other ways.[3]

Five questions were asked of them:[4]

1. How is a party position on legislation communicated to you?

2. Do you want to act in accord with party positions?

3. What legitimate reasons are there for you to act against party positions?

4. What kinds of appeals do party leaders make to you to achieve unity on legislation?

5. What can the leadership do to you if you do not support their position?

All but the third question proved productive, and even it was

[1] Interviews along the same lines were also conducted with about twenty other members of the House. In these, the five basic questions were worded differently and, in some instances, ordered differently or used only in part. The results of these less formal interviews confirm the findings and impressions stemming from the more formal interviews with the sample of sixty.

[2] Both parties were divided into thirds by seniority and by voting loyalty to party (as measured by the 1963 *Congressional Quarterly* party unity score), and an attempt was made to have one-third of the interviewees in each party come from each seniority grouping and each loyalty grouping. The Democrats were divided into three regional groups and the Republicans into four regional groups. An attempt was made to interview the same regional proportions contained in each of the whole party memberships. A small amount of error was introduced because of access problems in a few cases. The Democrats interviewed were almost perfectly representative of their party in terms of party loyalty (the *Congressional Quarterly* score used to stratify the sample), region, and seniority. The Republicans interviewed were slightly more liberal (that is, less loyal on the *Congressional Quarterly* score), and slightly less senior than all Republicans. Regional distribution was almost perfectly representative.

[3] See Appendix B.

[4] Six questions were originally planned. But a few pre-test interviews indicated that the first question (and several variations of it) was confusing to the respondent and usually caused a slow start to the interview. The question that was dropped (it would have come first) was: "How is a party position taken on legislation in your party?" This question was designed to find out if the member felt that his party did take positions. In order to allow room for a member to indicate that he did not think his party took positions, follow-up questions to the new question 1 ("How is a party position on legislation communicated to you?") were designed so as not to preclude the response: "There are no party positions; nothing is communicated."

significant in the sense that virtually all of the respondents mentioned constituency and conscience as equal reasons for opposing one's party. The responses to the first question will be analyzed in Chapter 7; the second, fourth, and fifth are of central concern here.

*Do you want to act in accord with party positions?* The answers to this question were placed in four categories: "yes-strong" if the member indicated that party position was generally his first consideration in making up his mind; "yes-weak" if he said party position was an important factor but not necessarily the first he considered; "not necessarily" if party rarely influenced his decision; "no" if he felt his party had deserted him and was wrong more than it was right.

Both parties responded similarly:

|  | *Democrats* (N = 35) | *Republicans* (N = 25) |
|---|---|---|
| Yes—Strong | *74%* | *72%* |
| Yes—Weak | *20* | *24* |
| Not Necessarily | *3* | *4* |
| No | *3* | *0* |

Among Democrats, the southerners were overrepresented in the *"yes-weak," "not necessarily,"* and *"no"* categories.[5] Northern and western Democrats were somewhat overrepresented in the *"yes-strong"* category and underrepresented in the other categories. It should also be noted, however, that the majority of southerners interviewed had feelings of party loyalty as strong as many of their northern and western colleagues, and stronger than some:

[5] The regions used throughout this chapter are the following: for the Democrats the South includes the eleven states of the Confederacy; the West includes all states west of the Mississippi except Texas, Louisiana, and Arkansas; and the North includes the rest. For the Republicans, the South and Border includes the eleven Confederate states plus Delaware, Maryland, West Virginia, Kentucky, Missouri, and Oklahoma; the Northeast includes New England, New York, New Jersey, and Pennsylvania; the West includes Montana, Wyoming, Colorado, New Mexico and everything west of that tier of states; and the Midwest includes the rest.

Different regions were used for the two parties because of differing regional traditions of loyalty and independence and hypotheses about variations by region.

| | South (N = 14) | North (N = 14) | West (N = 7) |
|---|---|---|---|
| Yes—Strong | 57% | 86% | 86% |
| Other Responses | 43 | 14 | 14 |

The party loyalty scores (based on roll call voting) for the respondents show that those who expressed the strongest party feelings were also the most loyal. The twenty-six Democrats in the *"yes-strong"* category had an average score of sixty-six; the seven in the *"yes-weak"* category had an average score of twenty-four.[6]

Among Republicans, the northeasterners were somewhat overrepresented among those in the *"yes-weak"* and *"not-necessarily"* categories. But again, their underrepresentation in the *"yes-strong"* category was not dramatic.

| | South and Border (N = 2) | Northeast (N = 9) | West (N = 4) | Midwest (N = 10) |
|---|---|---|---|---|
| Yes—Strong | 100% | 56% | 75% | 80% |
| Other Responses | 0 | 44 | 25 | 20 |

As with the Democrats, the conclusion can be drawn that Republicans from one particular region are less likely to have strong feelings of party loyalty than the bulk of their colleagues, but that as individuals many of them also feel strongly loyal to the party. Region is an important determinant of loyalty, but it does not absolutely divide the loyal from the disloyal. There are numerous staunchly loyal southern Democrats and northeastern Republicans.

The Republican average loyalty scores for the respondents show that those saying they are the most loyal actually vote that way. The eighteen Republicans in the *"yes-strong"* category had an average party loyalty score of sixty-two; the six in the *"yesweak"* category had a score of twenty-five.

---

[6] *Congressional Quarterly's* party unity score and party opposition score represent the percentage of the time a member voted for and against the majority of his party when the majorities of the two parties were opposing each other. The party loyalty score is the result of subtracting the party opposition score from the party unity score.

What the members said adds a dimension to the picture of the House that tabulations alone cannot provide. Their statements give some clues how members feel about their parties and the weight of the leaders' legislative positions.

Statements by two southern Democrats in the *"yes-strong"* category reveal some of the particular problems of remaining loyal while representing that region:

I go through great throes when I cannot go along with my party. It is not an easy choice to vote against your party.

―――

I try to find some way to be with the party. You like to be approved by the head of the family. You like to be remembered in the last will and testament.

Northern Democrats in the *"yes-strong"* category indicated the ease with which they could "go along." There were no expressions indicating that they were subjected to cross pressures:

I have a general conviction that my party is right.

―――

I cooperate 95 percent of the time with my party leaders. When I dissent it is only to let them know that I am around. Orneriness gets more results sometimes.

―――

I find that the party is right 99 percent of the time.

Western Democrats' comments reflected a similar lack of pressure, either real or imagined. Said one of them, "My policy is to accept everything Democratic unless it is terrible."

Southerners in the *"yes-weak"* category made evident their lesser commitment to the party and to the leaders, and their correspondingly greater commitment to the views of their constituency or to a more conservative view of government. But their comments also show a desire to please the party leaders when possible:

My first reaction on tough bills is, "Oh hell, another one of those damn things—this will be mean." I have some regrets at having to vote against the leaders so often. When I had to vote against my own chairman twice in a row on the floor I tried to avoid running into him.

―――

I will always try to be as much help as I can. I get no pleasure out of voting against the administration. You need to keep rapport with the leaders. It is much more comfortable when you are not a complete renegade on the outside looking in.

------

Personally, I am a loyal Democrat—although the party has strayed somewhat from the founder's principles. I like to support my leadership when I can. I would like to vote with the leadership on more things but I just can't. My constituency won't permit it.

A northerner in the *"yes-weak"* category indicated that he chooses his spots for loyalty with some care: "I want to help all I can—especially on the less visible issues where there is less passion in the district."

Even the one man in the *"no"* category—a southerner—began his answer with a vestige of party loyalty, although he rapidly showed his true feelings:

I want to help when I can, of course I do. But I consider my country first, my career second, and my party third. I am not much of a party man. Both of the parties have the country by the throat. There is not much difference between them. They are both spenders, wasters, and self-glorifiers. These parties need a good solid competitor to root them out. But there is no chance of that. Thus you have to stick with one party and have as much influence as you can.

Northeastern Republicans falling in the *"yes-strong"* category indicated that they had some problems in being loyal but that they wanted to be "party men":

I will vote against the party if it doesn't mean much. But I will go with them if the vote is close. I will also go along if I don't know much about the bill.    ------

There is a natural desire to go along. You also have some born mavericks. But very few consciously try to be mavericks. I may not change my mind on a record vote but I might give a live pair or go to the cafeteria.

A southern Republican tied party loyalty to electoral fortunes: "There is a desire to go along. We need a party record—and principles—as well as an individual record. The decline of the party image between 1962 and 1964 cost me 6 percent at the polls."

A western Republican was also concerned about image: "Yes,

I want to go along with the party. I am a team man. The leaders will explain to the public the reasons for a party position. A party image gets developed here. Then I can latch on to this. I can use this to explain my votes at home."

Midwesterners in the *"yes-strong"* category were extremely comfortable in their regularity:

I never dissent on major issues. We are regular in my state.

———

Sure I want to go along. It is easier to go with the party when in the minority. Ike wasn't conservative enough and I kicked over the traces a few times. But in the minority you are just looking for reasons to oppose what the majority supports. This is easier.

Republicans in the *"yes-weak"* category stressed district pressures, personal views, and even personal hostility to party leaders as reasons for their lack of total loyalty:

I don't feel any party line is mandatory. Anything for the good of my district and the good of the country I will support. Keeping one's independence is important. I don't feel that I have to vote for party positions. I do start off as a Republican with similar general premises —especially on fiscal responsibility.

———

There is always a reluctance to abandon the party position. Only if you think it is wrong can you do it. In 1963 on the vote on area redevelopment amendments I believed in the program, although it had been administered badly. But it had been working in my district and I stuck with it.

The one Republican in the *"not-necessarily"* category said: "I am a maverick. I like tangents. I don't want to feel coerced. But even we mavericks can show our responsibility and identity as Republicans on a few issues like debt limit and tax recommittal, although even on these I would change my vote to save the bill if necessary."

*What kinds of appeals do party leaders make to you to achieve unity on legislation?* The responses to this question fell in five categories. The first is "personal," indicating that the respondent felt that the typical appeal coming from a party leader would be: "We need you," "The President needs you," or "I need you, can't you help?" The second category, labeled "party," means that the member felt that an important number of appeals would be to loyalty to party, or loyalty to party program: "This is important to our party, can you help?" or "This bill is central to our program and we need to win it, please come along."

The third category is "merits." Here the member felt that significant appeals from party leaders were based on arguments about the substance of the bill itself. "Pressure" is the fourth category. This is a perception by the member of some explicit or implicit rewards or punishments that might be forthcoming as the result of certain courses of action or behavior. The fifth category, "no appeals," includes members whose own experiences led them to conclude that party leaders did not appeal to them in order to achieve unity on legislative matters.

Important differences between the parties are revealed by the responses:

|            | *Democrats* (N = 35) | *Republicans* (N = 25) |
|------------|-----------------------|-------------------------|
| Personal   | *86%*                 | *48%*                   |
| Party      | *46*                  | *44*                    |
| Merits     | *29*                  | *28*                    |
| Pressure   | *23*                  | *12*                    |
| No Appeals | *3*                   | *20*                    |

In the Eighty-eighth Congress the Democratic leadership chose to operate much more on the basis of personal appeals than the Republican leadership. This was in large part a conscious decision by Speaker McCormack and Majority Leader Albert, whose natural styles involve mainly personal appeals—flavored with a large degree of understanding for members who cannot go along on any given bill. Their styles were reinforced when Lyndon Johnson became President. He also put a heavy stress on personal appeals, although less on understanding dissent.

Both parties appeared to their own members to be about equally programmatic or party-oriented in appeal. The same holds true for the percentage of members feeling that the merits of legislation were a significant basis for appeals. Democrats felt that pressure was used in appeals on legislation more frequently than did Republicans, but the percentage of those mentioning pressure was not large. Only one Democrat out of thirty-five felt that party leaders made no appeals; five Republicans out of twenty-five were in this category. The difference is perhaps a reflection of the natural tendency of the majority party to work harder and more thoroughly on specific legislative proposals for which they will get the credit. It is also a reflection of McCormack's willingness to try to persuade even the most recalcitrant Democrats to go along with the party. Halleck, on the other hand, tended to dismiss certain liberal Republicans as being hopeless on most issues.

There were also significant regional variations in answering this question. Among the Democratic respondents a disproportionate number of those who saw pressure as a typical appeal were southerners, although it should be noted that only five of the fourteen southerners made this point. Most of those who felt an appeal to party program was regularly used were northerners.

| | South (N = 14) | North (N = 14) | West (N = 7) |
|---|---|---|---|
| Personal | *86%* | *93%* | *71%* |
| Party | *36* | *71* | *14* |
| Merits | *29* | *29* | *29* |
| Pressure | *36* | *21* | *0* |
| No Appeals | *0* | *0* | *14* |

The loyalty scores for Democratic respondents falling in the five categories reveal that the most loyal members feel programmatic appeals are used. The one who felt that no appeals were made on legislation was exceptionally loyal. Those who thought they saw pressure in the leaders' appeals were the least loyal, although not dramatically so.

The Republican regional figures show a pattern similar to the Democrats. The least loyal region, the Northeast, produced a high proportion of members seeing pressure, and the most loyal region, the Midwest, produced a high proportion of members feeling that no appeals were made. [The percentages for the South and Border and West are omitted in the following tabulation because of small numbers; the significant comparisons can be made only between the two regions producing the most Republicans.]

|  | *Northeast* (N = 9) | *Midwest* (N = 10) |
|---|---|---|
| Personal | *44%* | *50%* |
| Party | *44* | *40* |
| Merits | *33* | *10* |
| Pressure | *22* | *0* |
| No Appeals | *0* | *40* |

The loyalty scores show the most loyal Republicans to be those who saw either no appeal or appeals primarily to party and on the merits. Those who felt that personal appeals were regularly used were somewhat less loyal, and the few Republicans who felt pressure was regularly used were the least loyal.

Again, just as important as the tabulations based on the responses are the statements of the members as they reflected on the kinds of appeals made by the party leaders on legislation.

Democrats who saw primarily personal appeals usually illustrated their response with specific instances. They were approached on a personal basis and generalized from this that all Democrats were approached the same way:

On the tax bill in 1963 I told Mills [Ways and Means Chairman Wilbur Mills] he would get much help from us conservatives. Wilbur asked me to make a speech on it. I did, on the recommittal motion. President Kennedy called me on the tax bill. I told him I was for it. On the poverty bill the White House called and said, "Would you like to see the President?" I said no. Ten minutes later I got another call: "The President would like you to come see him." I went and got the treatment—and it was all put on a personal basis.

———

Under Kennedy the White House people called me on virtually every important piece of legislation. Once when seven or eight of us went to the White House to tell the President we couldn't support an important bill, he said, "That's all right—you go with us when you can. You help on taxes." Later he called me from Salt Lake City and thanked me for my work on taxes.

A southern Democrat expressed himself on persuasion: "Honest persuasion is used. It could play a much greater part. Joe

Fowler [Under Secretary of the Treasury Henry H. Fowler] took one and one-half hours to argue with me on the tax bill and he truly persuaded me. This is legitimate and welcome. Honest persuasion is not used enough."

A northern Democrat talked about the futility of pressure. "The attempts at pressure are few—and they are generally pretty crude. A Veterans Administration hospital in my district announced that they were going to be air-conditioned. The debt ceiling bill was pending. The VA called me and reminded me that if the House failed to pass the bill it would have to cancel the air-conditioning contract for want of money."

Republicans minimized the use of personal appeals. They did not feel this was the style of their leaders. Said one of them, "Personal appeals are effective only on a piecemeal basis. Zonal or regional opposition requires the use of other chips."

Republicans also felt that an appeal to party could be used most effectively if a victory were possible. They seemed somewhat more resentful of specific instances of pressure than Democrats.

Both an extremely loyal Republican and one of the least loyal indicate that they received no appeals at all from the party leaders:

> The party leaders make no appeals or practically none to me. They write me off. There is little or no pressure. There were more appeals in the Eighty-third Congress when we had the responsibility of the majority and of the government.

> ———

> I have a high record of party regularity. I have never been asked to change a vote in four years and one month. I am very high in party unity. They just don't bother me.

*What can the leadership do to you if you do not support their position?* Members had four basic responses to this question. Only the first category of "nothing" is exclusive: members falling here felt that their leaders had no leverage over them if they refused to go along on legislation. Respondents in the other three categories could answer in any combination. "Isolation" indicates that the psychological pressure of not being an accepted member of the group is a substantial weapon in the hands of the leaders. Members answering in the third category, "projects," felt that the leaders could use their control over specific legislation that might involve funds for the district, private bills, or small pieces of general legislation to reward the loyal and punish the disloyal. The final category, "committee assignments," includes respondents who felt that loyal members get the best assignments to standing, special, and select committees.

Significant differences between the parties are revealed by the tabulation of responses:

|  | *Democrats*<br>(N = 35) | *Republicans*<br>(N = 25) |
|---|---|---|
| Nothing | *34%* | *36%* |
| Isolation | *43* | *28* |
| Projects | *26* | *8* |
| Committee Assignments | *26* | *56* |

A little over a third of both parties felt that the leaders had no leverage. Democrats felt isolation to be more significant than Republicans. Majority status may help to explain this difference in perception. Or perhaps the more personal style of the Democratic leaders, revealed in the analysis of the preceding question, also made the pressure of not being acceptable to the leaders more salient to the individual Democratic member.

Many more Democrats than Republicans felt that projects dear to the heart of a maverick member could be aborted by the leadership. Obviously the White House has a significant influence in the allocation of projects. Also, given the power of the Speaker over minor legislation being pushed by only one or a few members, it is not surprising that leadership control of projects was more important to Democrats than to Republicans.

Over twice as many Republicans as Democrats felt that their leaders used committee assignments to reward the faithful and punish the obstinate. This is a natural consequence of the committee assignment systems used by the two parties.[7]

Again regional variations appear. Southern Democrats felt iso-

[7] See Nicholas Masters, "Committee Assignments in the House of Representatives," *American Political Science Review*, Vol. 55 (June 1961), pp. 345-57; and Chapter 3, above.

lation and the control over projects (including legislation) were the two weapons most used by the leadership. Westerners were also impressed by the use of isolation in greater proportion than their numbers in the sample would warrant. Northerners were disproportionately represented among those who said that the leadership could do nothing to a member if he did not support them.

|  | South (N = 14) | North (N = 14) | West (N = 7) |
|---|---|---|---|
| Nothing | 21% | 50% | 29% |
| Isolation | 57 | 21 | 57 |
| Projects | 43 | 14 | 14 |
| Committee Assignments | 29 | 29 | 14 |

The loyalty scores for Democrats show no significant differences between men who perceived the situation quite differently.

Among Republicans the most important overrepresentation occurred among midwesterners, who felt that the party leadership could do nothing to dissenters, and among northeasterners, who felt that committee assignments were used as rewards and punishments by the leaders. [The percentages for the South and Border and West are omitted in the following tabulation because of small numbers.]

|  | Northeast (N = 9) | Midwest (N = 10) |
|---|---|---|
| Nothing | 22% | 60% |
| Isolation | 44 | 10 |
| Projects | 11 | 0 |
| Committee Assignments | 67 | 40 |

Those feeling the leadership could do nothing were the most loyal; those worried about isolation were the least loyal.

The responses of the members to this question of what the leadership can do to enforce its wishes deserve quotation. Some Democrats were insistent that isolation is an effective form of pressure. As one of these men put it:

When you vote against the leadership it gets sticky over there in the chamber. As a personal matter you hate teller votes more than roll

calls. The pressure on teller votes is meaner: the Speaker, Majority
Leader, and Whip stand in the aisle where you've got to walk by
them. That's mean. There's lots of pressure from that stare. And diminished numbers on divisions and teller votes make each vote more
important. This is the psychology of the group. You don't really get
chewed out. They are polite to me. When the Speaker or Carl Albert
say, "Can't you help us out?" this is worse than if they were nasty. It is
tough to refuse.

A few southern Democrats stressed the importance of projects.
Apparently the leaders use their tangible resources more with
the southerners than with the other members of the Democratic
party:

Every member needs the help of the Speaker. The Speaker must be
on your side to get recognition, to have a bill called up, to get a bill
scheduled, to see to it that a bill gets assigned to the proper committee, to get an appointment to the Interparliamentary Union, to get a
good committee assignment, to help you in the Rules Committee.
These are the areas in which you need the Speaker's friendship to further your career.        ———

The leadership has always been reasonable to me. Although there
are some things that are well timed. For example, the environmental
health center for my state was announced just after the vote on the
poverty bill and the tie between the two things was made clear to me
before the vote.

Other Democrats stressed the importance of committee assignments and felt constrained to be loyal because of the influence
that the leaders could wield in this area. One of their number
said:

Committee assignments are a terrifically important stick in the
hands of the leadership. A member can make two choices if he wants
some independence—fight the leaders from the beginning of his career or fight them after getting the committee of his choice. I made
the second choice. I am on Appropriations and now am getting more
and more effective each year. Subcommittee assignments are also important. For example, on the anti-Nasser amendment there was conflict between my feelings and practicality. In my heart I felt this
should be a presidential determination. But at home I have a large
Jewish population. Also this was my Committee's bill. There is a
strong tradition of supporting your own committee and chairman.
I stuck with Mahon [George Mahon, chairman of the Appropriations

Committee] and Johnson. Also the vote came up one day before Subcommittee assignments. This was a consideration. Mahon said he appreciated my vote and that is important.

Some Republicans indicated that the leadership could do nothing to enforce its legislative wishes, although a few were unhappy with this apathetic approach. Many Republicans disagreed, however, and pointed to isolation and committee assignments as weapons that their leaders could and did use:

They can use committee assignments against you. Select committees count too. I have a whole folder of requests to Halleck for the last six years. I never got anywhere. In 1964 I even got 60 members to sign a petition to support me for a vacancy on a Commission. I didn't get it. Psychological pressure is disturbing too. You get ridiculed in the cloakroom or you get the silent treatment. Six members would not talk to me in 1964.      _____

If you don't go along, you are made to feel like an illegitimate child at a family dinner.      _____

Party loyalty and position are considered by the Republican Committee on Committees in making assignments. This is perfectly proper. I have not felt discriminated against because I have not asked for a change. Also there is psychological pressure. There will be a groan on the floor when a non-Republican vote is cast by a Republican member on a close issue. Then you are immediately cornered by Halleck or Arends and the relations are pretty strained.

_____

The Appropriations Committee Republicans are not inclined to be left-wingers. The same is true of Ways and Means and Rules. Another important sanction is just the feeling of not being part of the ingroup. This is not exactly ostracism but may be a disciplining factor.

## Membership Response to Leadership Appeals

What difference do leadership appeals make? How are feelings of loyalty (or disloyalty) to party evidenced? Comments in the interviews indicate that the range of responses is wide. Many in both parties said that they would stretch a point to be loyal to their leaders on an issue about which they did not know much or about which they did not particularly care. Members of both parties were also acutely aware that roll call voting on the floor was not the only action that would help or harm the leadership. They talked about the multiplicity of locations and occasions for helping or hindering programs—in committee and on teller votes especially.

Several members of both parties said that they would vote against the party now and then just to show their anger over some specific matter or so that they would not be taken for granted. This type of member also made it clear that he would not advertise a defection prior to the actual vote.

The most prominent theme in the comments was that members respond to appeals by the leaders by bargaining on the basis of a generalized trading of credits. Democratic comments in particular show a sophisticated view of the bargaining process:

You try to get administration support for some of your own smaller legislative projects. You have to play heads up ball. There is a whole range of things a member can do to help the administration and play heads up ball. There is a lot of bargaining to engage in and I will bargain with anybody. ———

When you do things for the administration or leadership it is like putting money in the bank. You build up a reservoir of good feeling and friendship. Eventually you will need some favors from them.

———

There are very few direct trades of votes for favors. What you are doing is building up an account to draw on. For example, when the *Congressional Quarterly* rating showed me as extremely loyal I wrote a letter to the President calling it to his attention.

———

The poverty bill was not destined to be popular in my district. I was reluctant to say yes. For one thing I was having trouble getting through to Jenkins [Walter Jenkins, Special Assistant to the President] at the White House. I said no to the Whip. Then people began coming around. Sarge Shriver [Sargent Shriver, Director of the Office of Economic Opportunity] and I had a chat. I told him I would go along if I could. Then I voted yes—I had always intended to. There are never just straight trades. People help because they like you and want to help you build up credits.

———

The one-for-one bargain is very rare. And most members would resent it. There are more subtle things.

Roll call votes on the floor are not the only occasion when the response to party leaders' wishes can be significant, but they are the only occasion when the responses can be measured reliably. Thus, in order to say more about the responses to party leadership in the Eighty-eighth Congress, roll call votes have been used as the basis for analyzing which kinds of members of both parties are the most likely to be loyal to the party. Most of the statistical work on which the following general statements are based is omitted for reasons of clarity, although the tables which produced the most unexpected results are included in Appendix C.[8]

Regional differences in loyalty were the first consideration. They were so significant in both parties that loyalty in relation to the other variables was analyzed both in aggregate terms and for regional groupings within each party.

| *Democrats* | | *Party Loyalty Score* |
|---|---|---|
| South (N = 95) | | 27 |
| North (N = 103) | | 77 |
| West (N = 58) | | 71 |
| | | — |
| | Average | 57 |
| *Republicans* | | |
| South and Border (N = 19) | | 68 |
| Northeast (N = 54) | | 34 |
| West (N = 29) | | 60 |
| Midwest (N = 76) | | 69 |
| | | — |
| | Average | 57 |

Loyalty varied according to the urban, suburban, or rural nature of the district. In the case of the Democrats, the rank order of most loyal to least loyal was suburban (party loyalty score, hereafter abbreviated PL = 76), urban (PL = 72), and rural (PL = 41). When analyzed regionally, Democratic patterns of loyalty remained roughly the same in rank order, but the rural

---

[8] The tables in Appendix C present figures on variations in loyalty related to (1) the urban, suburban, or rural nature of the congressional districts, (2) seniority of the members, (3) median income in the congressional districts, and (4) percent owner-occupied dwellings in the congressional districts.

members were much closer to the urban and suburban members in degree of loyalty except in the South.

Among Republicans, rural members were the most loyal (PL = 64). The urban members were the next most loyal (PL = 52), and the suburban members were the least loyal (PL = 41). The ideological stances of these three groups tended to be the same within both parties: suburban members the most liberal (hence the most loyal Democrats and the least loyal Republicans) and rural members the most conservative (least loyal Democrats and most loyal Republicans). The Republicans also have striking regional differences. In the southern and border states, urban members (from conservative cities like St. Petersburg, Dallas, and Roanoke) were the most loyal and the rural members were the least loyal. In the Northeast, the urban members were much less loyal than even the suburban members. The westerners and midwesterners conformed to the aggregate pattern.

The effect of seniority was not completely clear. Among Democrats, the less senior members tended to be the most loyal. The same general pattern held throughout the regions except in the West, where members of middle-level seniority were the least loyal. In the Republican party the pattern was even less clear, although roughly the same: the less senior men were more loyal. In the South and West, however, the most senior men were the most loyal. The interviews help indicate why the junior men tend to be more loyal: they feel that the party leaders have rewards at their command, particularly in the form of committee assignments. Members with greater seniority feel that this power of the leaders can no longer affect them personally.

Margin of electoral victory in 1962, when the members of the Eighty-eighth Congress gained their seats, showed no persistent relationship to loyalty in either party.

Figures on loyalty to party in voting were also examined to see if there was any consistent relationship between electoral margin in the immediately forthcoming election (1964) and loyalty to party. Among Democrats who ran and won in 1964, the overall pattern and two of the three regional patterns (the exception was the North) were identical: those who eventually won by the narrowest margins were less loyal than those with slightly larger winning margins, who in turn were more loyal than those with the largest winning margins. Those who had just cause to fear for their seats were somewhat less loyal to party, probably hedging against Republican tendencies in their districts. Those who had the least cause to fear for their seats felt independent because they did not need party help. Those Democrats who were defeated in primaries and in the general election were less loyal in general than any of the categories for those reelected.

Among the Republicans who won reelection in the more conservative regions of the South and Midwest, those with both the narrowest and largest margins of victory were the most loyal. In the other two regions, and in general, the pattern was for those with the lowest winning margins to be the most loyal (and most conservative). This could be expected, given the general Democratic sweep in the 1964 elections. The defeated Republicans were generally the most loyal and most conservative.

Party loyalty was also examined in relation to four socio-economic variables. In the Democratic party as a whole, increasing median income in the district was associated with increasing loyalty by the member in the House. This is contrary to what might be expected since the electoral success of the Democratic party is supposedly based on an appeal to the lower income groups. The regional breakdowns in the North and West are less clear than those for the South, but in general, except for the very poorest districts in the North and West, the same pattern of increasing income accompanying increasing loyalty is present. The poorer districts also tend to be more rural, which helps explain this pattern.

The Republican case shows no clear pattern. Some of the poorest districts produce representatives just as loyal as those coming from the wealthiest districts. This, coupled with the Democratic pattern, suggests that median income *alone* is not a reliable predictive variable for how members of either party will behave *inside* Congress.

A more careful analysis of the relation of percent of urban population in the district to loyalty inside the House confirms the finding based on *Congressional Quarterly's* three classifications. The Democratic pattern is somewhat mixed, although there is a tendency for more heavily urbanized districts to have more loyal Democrats representing them. In the Republican party the pattern is reversed. Members coming from more urbanized districts tended to be less loyal, although this pattern did not hold for the South and Border and the Midwest, where conservative cities produced some of the most loyal Republicans in districts more than 90 percent urban.

Percentage of Negro population was also considered in relation to loyalty. Region is the important factor in the Democratic case—the most loyal southern Democrats in the House came from the districts with the fewest Negroes; the most loyal northern Democrats came from the districts with the most Negroes. So few Republican districts have over 10 percent Negro population that no meaningful statements can be made about the relations here.

Percentage of owner-occupied dwellings has been used by others as a predictive device for election returns.[9] When this characteristic of congressional districts was related to voting loyalty in the House, no particular pattern resulted for either party.

In summary, socio-economic factors in a member's district tend to be much less predictive of his party loyalty than broadly political factors—particularly region, urban nature of the constituency, and even seniority within the House. Election returns are not closely and consistently related to loyal or disloyal behavior. Negro population has a regional impact among Democrats. Median income and percentage of owner-occupied dwellings were not reliable predictors of loyalty in the Eighty-eighth Congress.

## Psychological Preferment

There are competing loyalties that a member weighs before voting or acting. Often these loyalties do not clash directly. Members can also re-enforce their own predilections by choosing what they hear. Most members, however, think of party before they think of anything else, particularly at the stage of voting on the floor. Even if a member often votes against his party, he is still concerned with retaining the good will of the leaders and mem-

[9] See, for example, Lewis A. Froman, Jr., *Congressmen and Their Constituencies* (Rand McNally, 1963).

bers. His friends are likely to be in his own party, and he knows that he can jeopardize his standing with some of them unless he is willing to stretch a point and occasionally help the party, even though he may feel somewhat differently about the issue. Only a handful act almost independently of party. Their friends are few —usually other mavericks.

For most members of the House, the life of an habitual maverick would be intolerable. Acting against the party involves a substantial amount of personal discomfort, which can even be expressed physically. The only Republican to vote against his party's recommittal motion on a major administration bill in 1963 answered the roll call while crouching behind the rail on the Democratic side of the House chamber. He explained: "It's 190 degrees over there (pointing to the Republican side)." Another Republican, after voting with the Democrats on the Area Redevelopment Act amendments in 1963, said that he simply refused to go into the Republican cloakroom any more. He indicated that he could no longer talk to his party colleagues: "Those old men don't ever want to do anything."

The job of a party leader is to call on feelings of loyalty to party at the crucial moments. The same people cannot be approached every day, but by mixing the content of the appeal and choosing a slightly different roster in each crisis, the leader can usually rally enough of his troops to make a good showing, presumably to win a victory if in the majority party.

The leaders are aware of the mix of personalities, beliefs, and district characteristics represented by their members. They consider whether a man is habitually brave in the face of what he thinks his district would want, or whether he is over-sensitive to the real or imagined demands of the district. They know whether he is happy conforming to the wishes of the leadership or whether there is something in his make-up that demands an occasional show of independence. They have an idea of the general political views that may sway his behavior. What the leaders do, in a variety of ways, is to appeal both to the sense of solidarity that the member is likely to feel with his party and to the fear of possible ostracism, which means the immediate loss of psychological preferment and a possible future loss of tangible preferment.

# ☆ 7 ☆

# Competition for Leadership

The influence of the party leaders is largely determined by how effectively they meet competition for the loyalty of the members. The individual congressman is under constant pressure from a variety of other sources: constituents, interest groups, the bureaucracy, the White House, committee members and chairmen, state party delegations, various groups within the House, and individual members. When these pressures conflict with party position, the leaders must find ways of communicating with the members more persuasively than the competitors.

Competitors outside the House can certainly have an impact on the members' legislative behavior. Knowledge of this phenomenon is relatively extensive.[1] But knowledge of competition within the House is less extensive. This chapter first will discuss the three major competing power centers in the House. Then it

[1] On the impact of constituents see Warren E. Miller and Donald E. Stokes, *Representation in the American Congress* (Prentice-Hall, forthcoming); Lewis A. Dexter, "The Representative and His District," *Human Organization,* Vol. 16 (Spring 1957), pp. 2-13; and Dexter, "What Do Congressmen Hear: The Mail," *Public Opinion Quarterly,* Vol. 20 (Spring 1956), pp. 16-27. On the impact of interest groups see Lester W. Milbrath, *The Washington Lobbyists,* (Rand McNally, 1963). On the impact of the executive branch see G. Russell Pipe, "Congressional Liaison: The Executive Branch Consolidates Its Relations with Congress," *Public Administration Review,* Vol. 26 (March 1966), pp. 14-24; Meg Greenfield, "Why Are You Calling Me, Son?" *Reporter,* August 16, 1962, pp. 29-31; and "Lyndon's Lobbyists: How They Get What He Wants," *Nation's Business,* April 1965.

will turn to the resource the leaders often use to meet this competition—their dominance of the communications process.

## Competing Power Centers

Inside the House the leaders face three leading potential competitors for the attention and loyalty of the membership: the standing committee delegations (including specialized experts on these delegations); the state and regional delegations of each party; and various groups (principally the Democratic Study Group, the [conservative Democratic] Boll Weevils, and the [Republican] Wednesday Club in the last few Congresses).

The leaders' fundamental strategy for dealing with actual or potential competition is to seek harmony rather than to allow divisive conflict to develop. When ideological strife appears in the party, the leaders seek to reconcile the competing groups. The leaders may be intense partisans, but they are not usually intense ideologues. If they were, they would automatically lose some of their support and probably some of their effectiveness.

To achieve harmony, or at least the appearance of harmony, the leaders have three basic alternatives. First, they can appear to ignore the competition, while quietly combating it. This alternative is generally chosen only when the competing group is small in size, such as the Wednesday Club, the Boll Weevils, or small state delegations in either party.

Second, the leaders can adopt the position of a potential competitor as their own. This is often done when the standing committees report bills. The majority party leaders will often support committee decisions, without offering any criticism, and urge members to accept them. If the committee minority dissents, the leaders of that party will often urge their members to do likewise.

Third, the leaders can meet the competition by negotiating a compromise. Such negotiations often take place between the leaders of both parties and committees (or the party contingents on them), state delegations (especially from large states or regions with a large number of members), and groups (especially the Democratic Study Group in recent years).

## STANDING COMMITTEES

Not all standing committees automatically compete or cooperate with the leaders; party considerations have various impacts on different committees. Some conduct their work almost without regard to party labels. Thus they often report bills that have bipartisan support and cannot easily be rejected by the leader of either party. Armed Services, Interstate and Foreign Commerce, Science and Astronautics, and Appropriations seem to work this way most of the time. The important Appropriations Committee has a long tradition of nonpartisanship. A House member, writing about the committee in the 1920's, said: "When its great bills come into the House, the ranking member is likely to make a critical speech for political effect, but within the committee room there has been no factitious opposition. On the contrary, all have worked together for economy."[2]

Deliberate defiance of the leaders is not always allowed, however. Members are expected to be "responsive to party expectations," which are generally voiced by the leaders.[3] For example, after Chairman Clarence Cannon died in May 1964, the new chairman, George Mahon, was quick to assert his own authority and that of the President and the leaders over the most troublesome of his subcommittee chairmen, Otto Passman of the Foreign Operations Subcommittee. Mahon won a substantive victory in the subcommittee and committee and on the floor in the summer of 1964, and cemented the triumph by reconstituting the subcommittee early in 1965 so as to put Passman's anti-foreign aid position in a minority.[4]

[2] Robert Luce, *Legislative Procedure* (Houghton Mifflin, 1922), p. 118.

[3] Richard F. Fenno, Jr., *The Power of the Purse* (Little, Brown, and Co., 1966), p. 28. This volume contains much evidence that the situation in the 1920's has not changed. See also Fenno, "The House Appropriations Committee as a Political System: The Problem of Integration," *American Political Science Review,* Vol. 56 (June 1962), pp. 310-24.

[4] Richard Bolling, *House Out of Order* (Dutton, 1965), p. 93; *Evening Star* (Washington), January 28, 1965.

Other committees tend to operate on nonpartisan lines, but can be changed into partisan groups by the introduction of a specific issue. On these issues the party leaders and the committee contingent are likely to reach agreement on a common substantive position. The Committee on Interior and Insular Affairs is a good example. Its normal operations have little to do with party considerations, but when public power is at issue, the committee divides along partisan lines. The Judiciary Committee is another example. As one member said, when asked to characterize the degree of partisanship in the committee, "That depends. Sometimes it works for months and months [on a nonpartisan basis] and then it blows up all of a sudden. Sometimes when it blows up, it blows up over an executive proposition, rather than something that the chairman and the majority have undertaken on their own hook."

Ways and Means used to be the most partisan of committees; the majority wrote bills in meetings to which they did not invite the minority. It was not until 1934 that the committee allowed the minority members to participate in its deliberations on a tariff bill.[5] But in recent years this committee has operated far differently: members from both parties work on bills to produce acceptable compromises; only on the final vote to report the legislation, and during floor debate, do party lines appear and remain solid.[6]

Three contemporary committees often mentioned by members as consistently dividing along party lines are Education and Labor, Public Works, and Agriculture.[7] In committees of this

---

[5] In the mid-1920's, Paul Hasbrouck characterized the committees of the House as "non-partisan agencies of reference," with two exceptions: Ways and Means and Rules. Hasbrouck, *Party Government in the House of Representatives* (Macmillan, 1927), pp. 60-63.

[6] John F. Manley, "The House Committee on Ways and Means: Conflict Management in a Congressional Committee," *American Political Science Review*, Vol. 59 (December 1965), pp. 927-39.

[7] On Education and Labor see Frank J. Munger and Richard F. Fenno, Jr., *National Politics and Federal Aid to Education* (Syracuse University Press, 1962). On Public Works see Frank Smith, *Congressman from Mississippi* (Pantheon, 1964), pp. 182-83, 195-98. On Agriculture see Charles O. Jones, "Representation in Congress: The Case of the House Agriculture Committee," *American Political Science Review*, Vol. 55 (June 1961), p. 367; and Jones, "The Role

nature the committee leaders and their central party leaders are likely to work together closely.

The extent of the party leaders' involvement varies from committee to committee. Summarizing the views of members of the Brookings Round Tables in 1959, Charles Clapp said,

> There is agreement that the intervention of House leadership in the committee process tends to be minimal. It seldom is evident with respect to minor legislation and occurs less frequently than might be expected when major bills are being considered. Leaders expect to be informed of the progress of legislation within committees and of the problems involved, and may make routine checks of this nature. But seldom is their role one of harnessing committee members to the party will; where the chairman is strong and reliable, that function is ordinarily left to him.
>
> Leadership activity varies with the particular committee and personalities involved as well as with the importance of the legislation.[8]

In interviews with members of several committees, the variation in activity and in perceptions of the leaders' role became quite clear. Strong committees, which rarely have trouble getting their bills passed on the floor without amendments, do not look to the leaders for help or guidance. Instead the chairmen (if in basic agreement with the administration's programs) tend to look on themselves as leaders and shapers of party positions. Rank-and-file members also look on these chairmen as part of the House leadership on bills coming from their committees and even on other matters. On the other hand, weak committees, which often lose bills or pass them only with unwanted amendments, look to the leaders for assistance in developing support. Majority members of the Post Office and Civil Service Committee or the Agriculture Committee, for example, are grateful for leadership aid in winning pay raise and farm bill votes.

In the Eighty-eighth Congress, the Democratic Speaker and Majority Leader maintained close relations with the committee chairmen. On important bills, the chairman was often considered part of the leadership. A few chairmen denied that they played such a role and made it clear that they preferred not to

---

of the Congressional Subcommittee," *Midwest Journal of Political Science,* Vol. 6 (November 1962), pp. 342-43.

[8] Charles L. Clapp, *The Congressman* (Brookings Institution, 1963), pp. 270-71.

get entangled with the leadership, even though their preferences on the legislation were the same. As one chairman put it, "There aren't any strategy sessions when one of my bills is ready for the floor. I just tell the leadership how much time I want and what trouble, if any, they can expect on it." When a chairman was unsympathetic to the leadership point of view even after a bill had been reported from his committee, the leadership then drafted a ranking Democrat or subcommittee chairman to act as part of the leadership until that particular bill had cleared the floor. For example, James Morrison of Louisiana was the committee leader on the 1964 pay bill instead of the chairman of Post Office and Civil Service, Thomas Murray of Tennessee.

Party contingents on committees often initiate policy development and even strategy development. In late 1964, for example, the majority staff of the Banking and Currency Committee conducted its own poll on the prospects of a bill combining an extension of funds for area redevelopment and accelerated public works. They presented their estimates to the leadership and to the relevant executive agencies in an effort to force action.

Since 1959 the Republicans have placed the heart of their policy development process in the party delegations on the standing committees. Unanimity here is usually necessary before the leaders are willing to announce a "party position." Disunity discourages development of such a position, as indicated by a letter from Minority Leader Gerald Ford to all Republicans on February 9, 1965:

On Thursday, February 4th, the House Republican Leadership met with the Republican members of the Committee on Banking and Currency to discuss H.R. 3818, a bill to eliminate the requirement that Federal Reserve banks maintain certain reserves in gold certificates against deposit liabilities.

At this conference eight (8) of the Republicans on the Committee on Banking and Currency indicated they were supporting the legislation although all agreed the bill was not a permanent solution to this critical problem. They furthermore indicated it would be pointed out by them in the debate that the Administration had not taken the necessary corrective action to improve the U.S. balance of payment problem which of course is the cause of our current difficulty.

It was also determined at the conference with the leadership that three (3) of the Republicans on the Committee on Banking and Currency were opposed to the bill or had voted against reporting the legislation. Because of the time factor and other reasons no minority report was filed.

Because of the above circumstances the Leadership determined there would be no House Republican Party position taken on H.R. 3818.

A special relationship exists between the party leaders (particularly those in the majority) and the members of the Rules Committee. Before 1937, the Rules Committee was the faithful servant of the majority leadership.[9] From 1937 to 1961, it often thwarted the Democratic majority. The Republican Rules Committee did a better job for its leadership in 1947-48 and 1953-54. Even after the enlargement of the committee in 1961, it still embarrassed the Democratic administration by killing major bills. Howard Smith of Virginia, chairman from 1955 through 1966, used the committee to delay or kill bills he personally disliked.[10]

In 1964 the administration and leadership sought to make sure their wishes would prevail. A few weeks after the committee had killed the transportation bill (with the ten Democratic members split evenly), President Johnson asked the Democrats on the committee to an off-the-record meeting. All came but two anti-administration Democrats and one pro-administration member involved in a hard primary campaign. The President asked for special help in getting the poverty bill, the medicare bill, foreign aid authorization, federal pay increases, the Appalachia bill, mass transit, area redevelopment, and a new housing program to the floor.[11]

In the committee the leadership works through two or three chief lieutenants, one of whom characterized his role:

Frankly, we are delegated to carry certain bills. This is the Speaker's decision. I am sure he consults with others as to the most ideal man for it. I am sure that the Speaker consults with people who may have a direct interest and with the committee people and then you

[9] See James A. Robinson, *The House Rules Committee* (Bobbs-Merrill, 1963); Christopher Van Hollen, "The House Committee on Rules: Agent of Party and Agent of Opposition" (Ph.D. thesis, Johns Hopkins University, 1951); and Lewis J. Lapham, "Party Leadership and the House Committee on Rules" (Ph.D. thesis, Harvard University, 1954).

[10] For an example of Smith's views of the committee's role, see the *Congressional Record*, Vol. 109, Pt. 10, 88 Cong. 1 sess. (1963), p. 13341.

[11] *New York Times*, May 14, 1964; *Washington Post*, May 15, 1964.

finally wind up by trying to get [the bill]. You can only go to the well so often. Members sometimes say to the Speaker, "I don't want to carry the ball on that. Will you please ask X or Y to carry it?" A little negotiation takes place.

The Republican minority members of the Rules Committee in the last ten years have developed a different relationship with their leaders. The senior Republican on the committee until his death in August 1965, Clarence Brown of Ohio, was a leader in his own right. The five Republicans tend to vote as a unit, usually for the most conservative position. They take their own policy stand, consulting with the Minority Leader but not necessarily agreeing with him.

The growth of "administration bills" and "the program of the President" in this century both increased and decreased the independence of the committees from the House leaders. A commentator in the mid-1920's wrote that "Political parties to all appearances consent to stand aloof [from committees], for the very discreet reason that they can find no solid leverage for pressure upon the committees." He also noted that because of the growth of "administration bills" there was greater committee domination of the House calendars and greater committee success on the House floor.[12] But, as scattered "administration bills" developed into a readily identifiable program of the President, the leadership was also afforded more opportunities for inquiring into committee progress and the shaping of legislation.[13] The voting public now had a measure for looking at congressional performance: Is Congress enacting what the President wants? The public did not need to realize that committees in large part made this determination. Naturally, the results would not always work to the majority party leadership's advantage, but an air of "let's get some legislation passed" began to pervade the House more than it had in previous decades.

The President and his administrators also began to work directly with and on their party delegations on the committees. This had evident results, for even a strong chairman of a fiercely

[12] Hasbrouck, *Party Government,* pp. 63, 75.

[13] See Richard Neustadt, "Presidency and Legislation," *American Political Science Review,* Vol. 48 (September 1954), pp. 641-71, and Vol. 49 (December 1955), pp. 980-1021.

independent committee can be overcome by pressure and activity from the White House.[14]

President Kennedy in 1963, for example, had each committee chairman in the House come to the White House for a private session on legislative plans for the coming year. Kennedy did not attempt to dictate to them, but the organizing and motivating effect of a private conversation with the President was likely to work to the advantage of the President's program.

Departments and agencies are in constant contact with committee members of the President's party, and their efforts result in tangible gains for the legislative program. For example, to get the chairman of the Committee on Interstate and Foreign Commerce to report the community health centers bill in 1963, personnel from the National Institute of Mental Health, after canvassing the members, provided assurances that over half of the House was committed to support the bill.

The President's wishes are not always passed along formally. The Majority Leader might, for example, say to the chairman of the Armed Services Committee: "I saw the President yesterday and he is thinking that two more atomic aircraft carriers should be authorized this year." This is no command or threat, but just the informal suggestion that the President has some ideas about a problem facing the committee.

In passing their opinions to other members of their party, committee delegations behave differently. Among the Democrats, some prepare outlines of the majority positions on legislation that translate technical language into words that can be understood by all members. Other committees rely on letters from the Speaker and Majority Leader, or communications from the executive branch, to carry their case to their colleagues before the bill reaches the floor. Other committees do not communicate with their colleagues individually except through their formal reports and in debates on the floor.

Some Republican committee delegations do not bother to take positions. Others are active in asking the leaders to call a conference for discussion of a party position initiated by the committee delegation.

[14] See, for example, Raymond Bauer, Ithiel de Sola Pool, and Lewis A. Dexter, *American Business and Public Policy* (Atherton, 1963), p. 33.

Republican members indicate that the views of an individual Republican on a committee are often circulated, perhaps with leadership cooperation, some with considerable impact. Said one Republican:

We frequently receive letters from colleagues, giving us information concerning a specific bill and urging us to vote for or against it. In my own experience, some of the most effective bits of communication I have seen are such letters. I refer particularly to letters from a party colleague serving on the committee which is handling a specific bill, the letter containing his brief summary of the bill and his reasons for urging Republican support or opposition.

The views of individual Democrats on committees are not circulated as formally. But individual Democrats are also influential because once they gain reputations as "specialized experts" on some subject or some bill, a number of their colleagues will regularly look to them, through informal conversations, to provide the reasons for support or opposition.

## STATE PARTY DELEGATIONS

State delegations also take positions that influence legislative results. Each delegation is in part unique; although there are also common elements in groups of delegations. Some compete directly and often with the party leaders. Some support the leaders. Some take few positions on legislation affecting more than their state or region. The leaders in both parties must know when they need to counteract the positions of certain state or regional delegations and they must know what help they can expect from these sources.

Roll call analysis has shown state delegations to be most influential on two sorts of issues: "tough questions, controversial both within the party and within the House" and "matters of trivial or purely local importance." The impact of state delegations on the voting behavior of individual members was greater than the impact of party contingents on standing committees, apparently because of the bipartisan associations on the latter.[15]

More qualitative analysis has suggested that the characteristics

[15] David B. Truman, *The Congressional Party* (Wiley, 1959), pp. 261, 275, 277.

of individual state delegations develop through the years and are more than a composite of the personal characteristics of the members of a delegation at any given time.[16] This gives the leaders an element of predictability in fashioning their relations with delegations.

An important factor that helps determine the impact of state delegations is the frequency and type of meetings held. The delegations in both parties vary greatly. Data on several aspects of state delegation meetings in the Eighty-eighth Congress were collected in interviews. Members were asked about the frequency of meetings, subject matter of the meetings (broad legislative proposals or purely local problems), and whether delegation unity on issues was consciously sought in the meetings. The following patterns emerged:

| *Type of Delegation* | *Democrats* | | *Republicans* | |
|---|---|---|---|---|
| | *No. of Delegations* | *No. of Members* | *No. of Delegations* | *No. of Members* |
| Type 1 (rarely met, discussed only local issues, did not seek unity) | 4 | 53 | 5 | 59 |
| Type 2 (rarely met, discussed national issues, sought unity) | 4 | 42 | 0 | 0 |
| Type 3 (met often, discussed national issues, sought unity) | 5 | 57 | 8 | 79 |
| Type 4 (met often, discussed national issues, did not seek unity) | 3 | 32 | 0 | 0 |

This sample suggests that about half of the delegations (containing about half the members) meet regularly and consciously

[16] See Alan Fiellin, "The Functions of Informal Groups in Legislative Institutions," *Journal of Politics*, Vol. 24 (February 1962), pp. 72-91; John H. Kessel, "The Washington Congressional Delegation," *Midwest Journal of Political Science*, Vol. 8 (February 1964), pp. 1-21; and Leo M. Snowiss, "Congressional Recruitment and Representation," *American Political Science Review*, Vol. 60 (September 1966), pp. 627-39.

seek unified positions. These are the delegations with which the leaders must most often negotiate in order to prevent direct competition for the support of a number of members.

The interviewees suggested some of the reasons for the various patterns in the delegations. The typical reason given by Democrats in explaining why their state or regional delegation did not meet was splits of one kind or another, usually personal or ideological. A man from a small northern state said:

Neither my state nor my region has been welded together in a firmly knit unit. It could be. But right now the metropolitan area boys have arrived at an agreement with the southern bloc. They don't have public opinion to face at home. Our meetings are just *ad hoc* and sporadic. We could use more meetings. I would like to make demands—get the promise of help for our railroads if we support aid to Appalachia, for example. But we are stupid.

Members from small western states had not met in the past on any regular basis but planned such meetings for the Eighty-ninth Congress. Said one, in explaining the reasons for these meetings:

We need this to get leverage. We didn't meet before because Rayburn didn't want us to. He said he had enough blocs to contend with. But now we are getting organization. We will consider Western problems but we also want broader discussions.

A southern delegation met in the past, but in recent years has given up the attempt because of growing splits in the delegation. Said two of its members:

We seldom get together. We are split all over the lot. There is little point in meeting; we could never arrive at a consensus on anything.

---

We get together only occasionally. But the state is really split apart. One district has, for example, been overwhelmingly loyal to the Democratic ticket. My district went for Thurmond in '48, Republicans the next three times, and we got a 1200 vote majority for Johnson only because he called the publisher of the largest newspaper in the district and got his support.

Another southern delegation experienced a different trend. They had not met for a variety of reasons in the past, but in the Eighty-ninth Congress they made plans to meet regularly and to seek unity on important issues. Two members of the delegation indicated some of the important considerations:

Until this year we practically never met. This year we will meet once a week on legislation. Our dean for many years preferred to announce his views rather than to talk about it. He did not believe in a delegation caucus. We may not adopt solid positions on everything but having meetings will certainly promote unity. We can learn a lot from each other.          ——

We have not caucused in the past on legislation. But our delegation is changing. We have lost a lot of seniority. I am dean now and have not been here long. When I came, everyone else from the state was an old man with long service. Now the South is beginning to meld with the rest of the nation. We as leaders must take responsibility for helping guide this change. For example, on the Appalachia bill one damn fool in our delegation is against it. But we will educate him in our delegation meetings. We will bring him around.

Another variant of the delegation that does not meet often is one northern state that is almost 100 percent behind the party position. Said two members:

We usually support the party position. I sometimes check with our dean on my own. But meetings are not necessary.

——

Meetings for us would serve no purpose. We vote alike anyhow. We could build up leverage this way but have chosen not to do so.

Some delegations meet regularly but have a definite understanding that unity will not be sought openly. Three members talked about a large southern delegation:

We meet every Wednesday for lunch and alternate between open meetings with guests and closed meetings with just the members. These are completely informal and non-binding. There is no agenda. We fight shy of trying to stick together as a formal thing. But we do try to stick together when we can.

——

At our Wednesday meetings there is a very restrained and respectful attitude. No lobbying attempt will be tolerated at these meetings.

——

Our regular meetings are supplemented: the present dean will invite us over to his office for coffee, or the Speaker will come to our table in the dining room, where we eat almost every day, and let his position be known.

Comments from members in delegations that meet regularly

on legislative topics as well as on local topics indicate how unity may be sought. A westerner:

We meet informally every ten days or so. We know the probable position of everyone. We never bind ourselves. But we do have lots of personal conversation. And there are informal efforts to get unity.

A southerner:

We usually meet on controversial matters. The purpose of the meetings is to get a better understanding of the issues from a member of the committee or from our dean. There are various alliances in the delegation. But we still maintain good relations. We learn much at these meetings and do want to stay together when we can. On one important bill in 1962 we swung the whole vote for the administration.

A member from a big city in the North:

On the big stuff we meet in our dean's office. We usually meet only when there is some dissatisfaction with the leadership position. When they see us meeting, they worry about it. But we usually get back the dissenters. One man left the group on the cotton bill, but we got him back when the wheat-cotton bill came to the floor. In our city the best position is to be a solid group. The newspapers try to divide us; nationalistic situations can divide us. But we need to be solid.

A Democrat from another southern state indicated that delegation meetings work for unity even if the dean is not active in the meetings. "We have a lunch—mostly social—every Wednesday. Sometimes we will discuss legislation. Our dean rarely comes to the lunch. We can bring guests. There are no formal attempts to gain unanimity. The members from our state are independent; yet these discussions tend to produce more unity."

Republican members made similar comments, although there seemed to be less urgency attached to delegation meetings because of minority status.

Some delegations did not meet because there was underlying unity. Said one midwesterner: "There are only a few of us and we think alike anyhow and see each other daily, so why hold delegation meetings?" But the more typical pattern was for a delegation not to meet because of splits. A western Republican stated, "Our delegation is not too important in developing unity on legislation. We meet only on call, and usually on problems of our state alone. We are too split on broader questions to get anywhere." Three members of a large eastern delegation indicated the same thing:

We are going to try to meet more now than we have in the past. But this will fall through. We just don't have enough in common in our districts.          ———

We tried to have meetings before. There is talk now of meeting once or twice a month to take state delegation positions. But we are not likely to do so. It is almost impossible to develop a position for our state.          ———

Our delegation is probably the worst about not meeting. In the past we had very old members who couldn't conceive of using a state delegation for policy. Now we would be more effective—except there is one man who is keeping us ineffective. Unfortunately, he is the dean of the delegation.

The members of active Republican delegations displayed a variety of motivations. Some of these groups met precisely because they already thought alike. Others met to work out differences and arrive at a common position. A midwesterner offered this testimony: "I am something of a renegade on labor issues, but in general our informal meetings—which we hold a couple of times a month—encourage unity. The attitude is: 'Let's stick together if we can. If there is no strong reason to the contrary, vote with the state party group.'" Another man from the same state took a little different view: "We are the closest-knit Republican delegation in the House. Mostly we vote as a unit. We meet three or four times a month and our feeling is that it is smart to stick together."

An eastern Republican indicated that his delegation tries to get unity in the face of difficulties: "We have lunch two Wednesdays a month. We discuss legislation coming from each of the committees on which we sit and other broad matters as well as local matters. We have tried to get unitary voting, but all of us are extremely independent." A member from another eastern state with similar problems indicated a similar method of operating:

We meet every second Tuesday and discuss legislation—both that coming to the floor and that in committee. We have stuck together on organizational matters in the party and we saved Arends [Leslie Arends, challenged for Whip in 1965] in the recent fight. Our governor will call now and then and try to keep us united.

A member of a large midwestern Republican delegation indicated that delegation activity can enhance a natural feeling of unity:

Our delegation meets every second Wednesday and talks about general legislation. We try to see how the legislation will help or hurt our state, the nation, and Republican principles. We certainly try to have unity in our delegation. We feel we are the best delegation in Congress and unity helps us. We attempt to reason with possible dissenters. We try to get them to go along. Our dean chairs these meetings. The great respect for him breeds influence on his part.

Even small delegations meet to encourage unity:

We meet irregularly, but get together often on the floor. Our meetings have a spirit of "stick together if you can."
In the summer of 1961 the Republicans from our state started meeting every Tuesday at noon. We discuss the legislation coming up on Tuesday, Wednesday, and Thursday. Most of us work closely together—we will huddle constantly on the floor and in the cloak room. We always want to explore the possibilities of all going the same way.

### BLOCS, GROUPS, AND CLUBS

Formally organized voting blocs that function as units separate from state delegations have become less important in recent years in the House. The best known and most effective of these was the farm bloc in the 1920's, which generated support in both houses for legislation to aid the farmers.[17] Occasionally, remnants of this bloc reappear.[18]

[17] See Arthur Capper, *The Agricultural Bloc* (Harcourt, Brace, 1922), pp. 9-12, for a discussion of the origins of the farm bloc. See also John D. Black, "The McNary-Haugen Movement," *American Economic Review*, Vol. 18 (1928) pp. 405-27.

[18] For example, in February 1958, after a special House election in Minnesota that the Republicans won by an abnormally small margin, there was a caucus of Republican members from farm districts. Two of their leaders saw the Secretary of Agriculture and after the meeting one of the leaders said that the Secretary's policies would cause the loss of twenty-five Republican seats in the November 1958 elections. Walter Rosenbaum, *The Burning of the Farm Population Estimates* (Bobbs-Merrill, 1965), p. 14.

Since World War II, there have been three ideologically based groups that have been important enough to take, or threaten to take, positions unsatisfactory to the party leaders. The most important in the internal workings of the party is the Democratic Study Group (DSG), formally organized and relatively visible.[19] It began as a loose alliance of liberal Democrats formed in 1957, under the leadership of Representative Eugene McCarthy of Minnesota. The group immediately established a whip organization, which functioned sporadically in 1957 and 1958. In 1959, both the DSG and its whip organization were formally established. The DSG prepares position papers and holds meetings on upcoming legislation. It also attempts to get maximum attendance of its members on the floor during the amending process, so that the teller votes may be won for the liberal position.

In the Eighty-eighth Congress the DSG had 126 of the 257 Democrats as members. In the Eighty-ninth Congress it claimed 180 of the 295 Democrats. The membership list was not public. The leaders and members of the organization are liberals, although some of those from the big cities are more loyal to their political organizations than to ideology. The DSG contains almost no southern members.

In interviews, members of the DSG indicated that all members are not equally active or devoted. Some thought the informational services valuable and attended meetings regularly. Others thought the group a failure and indicated that they were not even sure whether they had paid their dues .

In the 1964 campaign the DSG moved into a preserve formerly left to the party as a whole when it gave financial aid to the campaigns of 105 liberal Democratic candidates, seventy-nine of whom were elected. Each individual chosen to receive help got beween $250 and $1,250; the total spent was $38,250.[20]

---

[19] Bolling, *House*, pp. 54-58; Kenneth Kofmehl, "The Institutionalization of a Voting Bloc," *Western Political Quarterly*, Vol. 17 (June 1964), pp. 256-72; and Mark Ferber, "The Democratic Study Group: A Study of Intra-Party Organization in the House of Representatives" (Ph.D. thesis, University of California, Los Angeles, 1964).

[20] By comparison, the Democratic Congressional Campaign Committee, an arm of the leadership chaired by Michael Kirwan of Ohio, in 1964 distributed $306,330 to Democratic candidates of all ideological hues. See the *Evening Star* (Washington), February 3, 1965.

The relations between the party leaders and DSG leaders have been generally good. Any antagonism is based on personalities, not on programs. The DSG is made up of men loyal to the programs supported by the leaders and the administration. DSG members vote with the party and the leaders consider them a positive influence. The leaders also welcome DSG activity in working for floor attendance by liberals on teller votes on amendments that can drastically alter the nature of a bill.

Typically, DSG leaders approach the central leaders to discuss a problem (either legislative or organizational) before taking any public position. Negotiation that takes place in these meetings has been so successful that there have been no major splits between the leadership and the DSG. For example, after the 1964 election they arrived at a common position on needed rules changes and on the punishment for the two Democrats who had supported a Republican for President.[21] The implicit threat of DSG defection if the leaders thwart them on a major issue increases the leaders' willingness to compromise. At the same time the DSG leaders realize that open opposition to the Speaker would soon backfire: non-DSG members would frown on such disloyalty; many big city DSG members would, in a showdown, support the Speaker; and the Speaker could use his many powers to make life unpleasant for the leaders of an open rebellion.

Another Democratic group active in legislative matters (although less so than the DSG) has no official name, but has been dubbed by the press the Boll Weevils. This group, of fluctuating and uncertain membership, is composed primarily of conservative southern Democrats. In the Eighty-eighth Congress about thirty to thirty-five members attended the Weevils' sessions.

The Weevils have been gathering since the end of World War II. Howard Smith of Virginia and William Colmer of Mississippi acted as the first two chairmen. During the Eighty-eighth Congress and a few years prior to it, the chairman was Omar Burleson of Texas. The group meets at the call of the chairman to decide conservative positions and strategy on major issues. It does not meet with Republicans, although its members occasionally

[21] See Roger H. Davidson, David M. Kovenock, and Michael K. O'Leary, *Congress in Crisis: Politics and Congressional Reform* (Wadsworth, 1966), pp. 125-44.

get together informally with the conservative Republican leaders.

Usually, in the Eighty-eighth Congress, the Boll Weevils sought to defeat or amend legislation sponsored by the administration and the Democratic leadership. But on at least one notable occasion the Weevils decided to support the administration. This was when the most conservative Democratic member of the Ways and Means Committee met with the Weevils and convinced them that the Republican recommittal motion on the tax bill in 1963 was a phony attempt at economy. Not all of the conservative group voted against the Republican motion, but enough did so to ensure an administration and leadership victory.

The Democratic leaders have usually ignored the Weevils, feeling that direct competition would be more productive than abortive attempts at compromise. When the number of conservative Republicans is great enough, the Weevils have had some success on the floor; they have had no success in changing the position of the leaders. Only rarely have the leaders met with success in attempts to change the Weevils' position.

The third group of some current importance is the Republican Wednesday Club. It was formed in the Eighty-eighth Congress and had a membership of fourteen, later expanded to twenty-one. The members are more liberal than most Republicans. The club meets weekly to discuss the status of major bills in various committees and encourage the development of responsible Republican alternatives to Democratic proposals. Minority Leader Halleck largely ignored the Wednesday Club; as a result, most of its members were active in the movement that led to the ouster of Halleck in early 1965.[22] The individual members of the Wednesday Club were closer to Minority Leader Ford, who considered some of their views.

In addition to the Wednesday Club, several other Republican clubs help transmit information. These clubs are based on a mixture of congeniality, geography, committee assignment, and year of entry into the House. There is no evidence to suggest,

[22] See Robert L. Peabody, *The Ford-Halleck Minority Leadership Contest, 1965* (McGraw-Hill, 1966).

however, that these largely social clubs have enough ideological weight to force the leaders to compete or compromise with them.[23]

## Dominance of the Communications Process

To win the competition with both internal and external competitors, the party leaders must maximize their dominant position in relation to the communications process. They strive to condition the members to look to them first for persuasive communications. This they can do by earning a reputation for providing accurate information about not only substantive facts, but also about the intentions of others. They can also improve their standing with the members by receiving communications from them about their preferences and wishes and, through subsequent action, by giving them the impression that these desires make a difference.

To find out how successfully the leaders communicate their position on bills to the members, interviews were opened with the question: "How is a party position on legislation communicated to you?"[24] This was followed with specific questions about the various organs of communication, committee contingents, state delegations, and any clubs or intra-party groups to which the members belonged.

Interviews showed that members knew their party's general position on bills, but felt dissatisfied with the amount and content of information the leaders communicated to them. The following table summarizes the organs of communication named in response to the question. Members usually mentioned several.

[23] In the last few years the major Republican clubs have been the Chowder and Marching Society (organized in the Eightieth Congress), the S.O.S. (Eighty-third Congress), and the Acorns (Eighty-fifth Congress). There are also clubs of members coming as freshmen to different Congresses. See Charles O. Jones, *Party and Policy-Making* (Rutgers University Press, 1964), pp. 28, 153. See also Neil MacNeil, *Forge of Democracy* (McKay, 1963), pp. 295-96.

[24] See the opening pages of Chapter 6 and Appendix B for information on the interviews.

The percentages refer to the percent of all interviewees (thirty-five Democrats, twenty-five Republicans):

| Organ of Communication | Number (multiple replies) | Percent of Respondents |
|---|---|---|
| Democratic Members (N = 35) | | |
| No communications | 2 | 6% |
| General knowledge (press) | 15 | 43 |
| President | 20 | 57 |
| Speaker | 20 | 57 |
| Majority Leader | 20 | 57 |
| Majority Whip (and whip organization) | 16 | 46 |
| Committee members | 10 | 29 |
| Republican Members (N = 25) | | |
| No communications | 2 | 8 |
| General knowledge (press) | 4 | 16 |
| Policy Committee | 23 | 92 |
| Conference | 3 | 12 |
| Minority Leader | 10 | 40 |
| Minority Whip (and whip organization) | 4 | 16 |
| Committee members | 16 | 64 |

Almost every member indicated that his party leaders communicated positions on legislation to him. Only four said there were no such communications, and three of these admitted in further questioning that their party did, in fact, take legislative positions about which they found out. Only one Republican indicated that there was often no way for him to know the party position on a bill. In general, then, when members vote against party positions they are aware of what they are doing.

Fifty-seven percent of the Democrats (although not all the same men) relied on the President, Speaker, and Majority Leader for communicating party positions to them. Forty-three percent (including some of the group above) looked to the press for such information. The President, Speaker, and Majority Leader, as well as press reports about them, were, of course, all saying the same thing. Thus virtually all Democrats received the same message informing them of the party position. Only six of thirty-five Democrats mentioned neither the President nor the press as purveyors of party positions. Since press coverage of the President far overshadows press coverage of the Speaker or any other House officials, this meant that, in effect, over 80 percent of all Democrats assumed the party position to be the position of the President. Only six claimed that they listened exclusively to internal House sources for statements of Democratic legislative positions.

The central leaders of the majority played a more important role in communicating party positions than did the central leaders of the minority. This is not surprising, given the great number of Republican leaders in the Eighty-eighth Congress and the small number (three) of Democratic leaders.

The tabulation underscores the importance of the Republican Policy Committee in communicating party positions; it clearly was the primary focus of collegial leadership in the eyes of individual party members.

Committee chairmen and senior members of committees were not regarded by most Democrats as major sources of information on party positions. Only one man (himself a chairman) said that he relied solely on the communications of the chairmen and senior members for his understanding of party legislative positions. All other Democrats, even those who received some communications from chairmen and senior committee members, looked either to the President (or press reports of his positions) or to the central leaders. Individuals still might follow committee chairmen, rather than the President or Speaker, but they understood that the party position was stated by the President or Speaker, not by the committee chairmen.

In the minority party, senior committee members were much more important in communicating party positions. This group of Republicans, rather than the Minority Leader, was perceived as the second most communicative component of the collegial leadership.

Some of the members pointed up various aspects of the communications process within the House. Democratic responses in-

dicate the great range of the meaning of party position and the
different sources to which they look for the "official" statement
of party positions.

A northerner:

On the great issues party position is a matter of public knowledge.
Any Congressman just knows the party position.

Another northerner:

There is a general lack of information around here. The pages
know more than I do. They don't inform me. We don't know about
changes being made in bills.

A southerner:

No fixed people speak for the party. You get the position more or
less by a process of osmosis. The party position is enunciated by the
Speaker and Majority Leader and those whom he calls in on strategy
sessions. More fundamental—the party position is established first at
the White House. Communications come from a number of springs.

Another southerner, elaborating on the thesis of his colleague:

I am not so sure party positions are communicated. Members merely conclude that the leadership determines party positions. And there
is a tendency on the part of the leadership to accept what the standing
committees do. Most administration-sponsored legislation is consistent with party pledges. When the President speaks, this is enough—
plus debate on the floor. There is no attempt to communicate the
party position based on the platform. You don't need a constant re-
minder. Your district and environment and inheritance let you know
which way to go. By not communicating more firmly, the leadership
probably gets more support. There are a variety of ways of communicating. You pretty well know the national party position. The leadership lays it on the line with certain members—the centrally nominated city boys. Down my way there are more challenges. There is no
planned or prescribed method of communication. You are well aware
on most legislation. You are not aware on other legislation—then the
leadership or committee leadership will let you know.

A liberal westerner, who was happy with uncertain communications because he could then look for direction where he
wanted to look anyway:

In defining a party position we have no meetings for discussion. We
liberals get our position from our backgrounds and philosophy and

people in the liberal community. I read *Harpers,* the *Atlantic,* the *Washington Post,* the *New York Times,* ADA [the Americans for Democratic Action] publications, and listen to Rauh, Schlesinger, and Morgenthau [Joseph Rauh, Arthur Schlesinger, Jr., and Hans Morgenthau, nationally known liberal intellectuals].

Other Democrats saw more clearly that specific organs could and did speak or at least pretend to speak for the party. As one northern Democrat put it: "When the Speaker, Majority Leader, or Whip speak on the floor it is a party position. When committee chairmen speak you take this with a grain of salt." A southerner saw something of the same phenomenon but was unhappy about it: "This morning I got a letter from the three House leaders on Medicare. They urged a rubber-stamping of the President. The party didn't establish this policy. Only rarely does the party establish policy. The President simply states what he wants. The 'yes man' type of member is more prevalent now than when I came here."

The Republicans were almost unanimous in agreeing that in the Eighty-eighth Congress the Policy Committee spoke officially for the party. But as they looked into the Eighty-ninth Congress they saw a confused situation.

A northeastern member:

We are in a state of flux right now with our communications. We are operating under a difficult situation—a small minority and a determined President. There is a pretty haphazard process of making policy in 1965. We find out either from the newspapers or through letters from Ford. There is also the usual ear-on-the-ground grapevine, on the floor or at lunch with someone. The Wednesday Club is especially valuable because there is a real discussion of pending legislation. I also learn from the Acorns [a largely social club of House Republicans] and from my committee work.

A southerner:

To find out what is going on, an individual can seek out the ranking members of a committee or members of the leadership. You also develop a network of individuals who know different areas—not necessarily ranking men. I do this.

Another northeasterner:

Nobody can speak for the party. Not the minority leader nor the committee members. It is extremely difficult to take party positions. On very few things are we unanimous. There is an official party position but not a factual one. There has to be near-unanimity before there is a real party position.

A midwestern Republican indicated that in addition to the Policy Committee just the chance of floor dispute will pull the party together and, in effect, communicate a position to all members:

Then the situation develops on the floor. Here you sort of sense the party position. There is communication by voice there. For example, on the anti-Nasser amendment the Minority Leader and Bow, ranking Republican on the Appropriations Committee, took positions. Then emotion developed. Mahon made some tasteless statements. This helped us to consolidate the Republicans as one.

A party leader from the midwest also saw the great problems of communicating within the party:

Communications is the toughest job of the leadership. Those who complain the most don't have their office organized to receive communications. There are terrible difficulties in communicating. The whip organization is a chief communicator. Communications is the reason for its existence. A party position rises in the committee system —which produces expertise in basic fields. Other members look to committee members for leadership. Then the position is modified in order to get a consensus of the whole party. Everyone has his own network of people he seeks advice from. There is not a blind following of committees. Outsiders may become more expert too.

In the Eighty-eighth Congress, then, both parties in the House had established communications patterns that were perceived by a majority of their members in much the same way. Among Democrats the President, aided especially by the Speaker and Majority Leader, was the commanding figure. Both he and the central House leaders overshadowed the committee chairmen as sources of party positions. The communications pattern within the majority party seemed relatively centralized, and the leaders were in a strong position.

In the minority, virtually all members looked to the Policy Committee for statements of party positions. But since the Policy Committee was primarily a spokesman for senior Republicans on the standing committees rather than an organ of the leaders, this pattern of communications was not as centralized as it might appear. The importance of the senior committee members in their own right also suggests a decentralized pattern. Minority members in the Eighty-eighth Congress may have known where to look for an authoritative statement of party position, but its content depended almost wholly on which standing committee handled the bill in question. The decreased visibility of the Policy Committee in the Eighty-ninth Congress gave even more weight to communications from the senior members on standing committees. In such a situation, the influence of the leaders is restricted.

# ☆ 8 ☆

# Party Leaders in the House Today

The place and tasks of the party leaders in the House have, in some respects, been almost constant since 1861 and seem likely to remain so. One major unchanged element is the central position of the leaders in legislative work. Standing committees determine the content of a bill, but the party leaders, often working with the committee chairmen, are the grand strategists and practical tacticians who decide the timing of the committee report, the compromise amendments that need to be adopted as the price of passage, the timing of floor action, the general flow of floor debate, and the sequence of votes. Other major elements of relative stability are certain differences of outlook and operations between the majority and minority parties, and between Democrats and Republicans.

In other respects, the place and tasks of party leaders have changed over time, and are likely to continue to change. The most important changes have concerned bureaucratization of the parties, patterns of leadership, allocation of functions, and use of the four major leadership resources. The thrust of some changes (for example, reduced resources, greater committee autonomy, and the growing power of seniority) has weakened the leaders' legislative hold on party members. The thrust of other changes (the use of increasingly sophisticated techniques, the growing organizational complexity of the parties, and more organized aid from the White House) has strengthened the hand of the leaders.

The following discussion of these elements of stability and change provides a summary assessment of the growth and development, present state, and future prospects of party leadership in the House.

## *Elements of Stability*

### CENTRALITY AND IMPACT OF THE LEADERS

Parties in the House are highly organized; they are also focal points for the loyalty of the members. The leaders call upon both organization and loyalty to influence legislative outcomes. The members face competing loyalties and organizations, particularly in the standing committees, but on the floor the wishes of the leaders tend to predominate.

The impact of the leaders is reflected in the whole range of legislative activity and behavior in which the average member engages. When he decides whether or not to be present for a given action on the floor, it is likely that he has considered the wishes and needs of the leaders. When he decides to speak or not to speak on the floor, especially on an important bill, he probably will weigh the desires of the leaders. Even in his committee work he is likely to give considerable attention to what is good for the party, as well as what is good for his district or for specific national or local interest groups.

Not only is this true of contemporary members, it has been true since the late 1880's. The frame of reference has been constant: what do the party leaders want? Variations have occurred because party leaders at some periods had more resources with which to cajole or punish reluctant or recalcitrant members. At other times the personalities of the leaders have allowed them to discipline straying members. Active Presidents have played a large part in helping the leaders of their party line up the members in the House, on the floor, and in committee.

But even during periods when the effective use of cajolery and punishment was difficult, when leaders were hesitant about demanding unity too frequently, and when the President was unwilling to venture into active legislative combat, the parties have remained the major realities and symbols to which the rank-and-file member could attach himself. Party leaders have been the principal agents for using the real aspects of party and for activating its symbolic aspects by appealing to the members for specific results. The party leaders are less likely to define the desired results by themselves than they were in the nineteenth century, but this change has not altered their basic task: to produce the right number of votes, speakers, bodies or absences, or committee members when the occasion demands.

The great impact of party leaders on legislative results and on the daily life of the members stems in part from physical facts. It is the party leaders who set many of the terms of debate and then attempt to manage the result. They encourage the individual member to be on the floor at critical moments. They supply him with routine information about the schedule. They generally facilitate his obtaining a committee assignment that will be important to his district, satisfying to him, and helpful in his campaigns for reelection.

But the leaders also have a more important and far-reaching impact. In supplying a member with substantive information they can teach him something new and broaden his horizons in regard to legislation that is national in scope. The individual member could probably obtain this information himself if he took the trouble, but he rarely has time to request or digest it. The material supplied by the leaders helps him overcome these limitations. Various party committees give him additional aid in understanding the legislative matters on which he must vote.

The leaders also help make the individual member more important and effective. As leaders perform the function of persuasion, they give the member an opportunity to make demands of his own. If he can build up enough credits in the bargaining process, he may succeed in focusing attention on a valuable legislative idea that would otherwise be ignored.

The leaders of both parties, especially the party with the President, also give the individual member a feeling of closeness to the White House. As they perform the liaison function they can take his messages to officials in the White House and give him insights into the thinking of the President or important administration officials. This has a psychological effect on the individual member, encouraging him to feel that he has an important role in the government. It has the more tangible effect of giving him helpful information.

The leaders, particularly those of the majority, also help increase the quantity of legislation that the House considers and passes. External factors create the conditions necessitating legislation, but leadership guidance is necessary to maintain an orderly legislative process. In their direction of this process, the leaders no longer have time to be much concerned with the details or quality of the proposals for which they labor. They take the word of the President, the bureaucracy, and the standing committees of the House that the measures are good and meet an objective need.

## MAJORITY-MINORITY DIFFERENCES

Many of the most fundamental differences between the parties are not so much distinctions between Democrats and Republicans as between the majority and the minority, whose basic legislative objectives usually conflict.

The legislative task of the majority party, if it also controls the White House, has come to be supporting the President's program. The House leaders do not have a program of their own, but work with what the President recommends. If it does not have the President behind it, the majority party in the House is restricted in what it can accomplish, and its goals are less clear—the Speaker and other leaders can support alternatives developed by standing committees, but the prospects of success are dimmer.

The legislative role of the minority party is not as clearly defined. Its leaders can act on the legislative proposals of the majority in several different ways. They can simply seek to obstruct and block the proposals of the majority, without offering alternatives or tempering amendments. They can oppose the majority position by offering alternatives. They can promote bipartisan compromise, offering alternatives and changes and expecting to reach compromises with the majority on some of them. They can also promote bipartisan cooperation, supporting much of the majority program without attempting to offer alternatives or compromises.

Being in the minority, particularly for a long period of time, is frustrating. The leaders become frustrated when they cannot produce victories in legislative fights. Followers also become frustrated by lack of victories and by a suspicion that their leaders are not doing all they could to topple the majority. Furthermore, the rank-and-file are frustrated by the lack of many advantages that the majority members take for granted, such as knowing the schedule well in advance, adequate staff, and ready access to the executive branch for information and assistance. Leadership in the minority tends to proliferate and decision-making becomes more difficult. It thus becomes almost impossible to win legislative victories of any consequence. Leaders are more likely to leave the House to seek other avenues of self-expression.

The majority member is also under severe strain, but he can operate with the ease and freedom that the possession of power brings. He can help control legislative decisions both in committee and on the floor. His chances of obtaining staff help from a committee or from the bureaucracy are relatively good. He may even appoint some members of a committee staff.

When a majority is well established, members tend to be content with their lot. Their leaders are also content and do not leave the House for outside political or financial opportunities. Leadership tends to be compact, with only one or a few men directing the major legislative work.

### DEMOCRAT-REPUBLICAN DIFFERENCES

There are two major differences between the post-1910 Democratic and Republican parties, regardless of whether they are in the majority or minority.

First, Republicans are more inclined to govern themselves by committee. The major experiments in widely based collegial rule have been by the Republicans: the Steering Committee from 1919 to 1925 and the shifting mixture of Policy Committee and conference after 1959. Within the party the principles of hierarchy and centralized leadership are constantly in conflict with the principle of democracy. Thus the Republicans have had major internal crises that resulted in the establishment of collegial government. In 1919 they chose a figurehead Speaker, placing a Steering Committee in power. After 1925, Nicholas Longworth succeeded in transforming committee government into government by the Speaker. For twenty years before 1959, Joseph Martin was the key figure in a centralized leadership pattern. Since then, the party has been radically decentralized following internal fights in which Martin, Charles Hoeven, and Charles Halleck were replaced as party leaders and an attempt to replace a fourth leader, Leslie Arends, narrowly failed.

Furthermore, Republicans have been the innovators in developing large-scale party organs, which the Democrats have later copied. The Republicans preceded the Democrats in appointing a formal Whip, establishing an extensive whip organization, and creating a meaningful Steering Committee.

The Democrats, despite their liberal members who want committee government, have been content with more centralized rule. Even when in the minority and dissatisfied with specific leaders, they have never attempted to replace them by a committee or a group. On the few occasions that the Democrats have established a committee that was, in theory, to function as part of the leadership, it never developed much influence. Such was the fate of the various attempts to have an operating and influential steering committee. The Democratic whip organization has become important, but is clearly subordinate to the central leaders. Throughout the twentieth century, either one principal leader (for example, Williams, President Wilson [1915-19], President Roosevelt [1933-37], Rayburn) or a small group of leaders (for example, Underwood and Wilson; McCormack, Albert, and Boggs) has made the command decisions. There have been no leadership revolts inside the party to parallel the Republican revolts.

The second persistent difference between the parties in the House is the greater devotion of the Republicans to ideological unity. For example, through the years they have used committee assignments more consistently than Democrats to reward the faithful and punish the less than faithful. Since 1925 the progressives in the Republican ranks have been few in number, and have usually been made to feel unwelcome. In the same period, dissenting Democrats have been more numerous and less discriminated against within the party.

These two differences are related to one another. Rank-and-file Republican members are more concerned with internal democracy because they realize that party leaders exercise considerable power over their careers and futures in the House. Thus they constantly seek a greater voice in internal party decisions as a means of self-protection. When a leader stands in their way, as Charles Halleck did in 1965, they replace him with a more malleable man. Democrats on the other hand are willing to give their leaders more security (and the power that stems from security) because these leaders exercise less immediate power over their careers. Democratic leadership is centralized, but more willing to tolerate dissent. Part of the price for centralization is the tacit understanding that the leaders will not punish individuals except in extreme cases, but will instead be tolerant with all members calling themselves Democrats.

## Elements of Change

### BUREAUCRATIZATION OF THE PARTIES AND PATTERNS OF LEADERSHIP

The developmental process analyzed in Chapter 2 produced the main attributes of the contemporary House and the contemporary parties, in three main stages: centralization of power (essentially completed by about 1895), institutionalization of the House (completed by about 1919), and the bureaucratization of the parties. The third stage is not yet completed; both parties remain willing to experiment with organizational forms. Contemporary Republicans are particularly active in arranging and rearranging the various components of the party's hierarchy. The Democrats are less active in this regard, but still willing to make changes.

Related to the process of bureaucratization is the specific pattern of leadership chosen by each of the parties at any given time.

Since 1861, both parties have chosen almost all of the possible majority and minority patterns. There is every reason to expect that they will continue to alternate among the various patterns; they may even invent new patterns if the need arises.

## THE ALLOCATION OF LEADERSHIP FUNCTIONS

Increasing bureaucratization and experimentation with leadership patterns means that the six leadership functions are likely to be reallocated from time to time. Such reallocations have taken place in the past. The Democratic caucus from 1911 to 1915, for example, was important in organization, scheduling, informing, and persuading. It now performs only an organizational function. The Republican Steering Committee helped schedule the business of the House and persuade Republicans to support the party from 1919 to 1925, when it surrendered these tasks to the Speaker. Before the whip organizations were created, the function of promoting attendance was not handled systematically; thus turnout on important votes on the floor was often low. But since this function has been performed systematically, attendance on important votes has increased. The Speaker from 1911 to 1925 played a minor role in persuading party members to stick together, but for the last four decades he has generally been the chief persuader for his party.

## LEADERS' RESOURCES

Throughout the post-1861 period the leaders have had four primary resources upon which they could draw in their attempt to perform functions and use techniques to influence legislative outcomes: use of rules, influence on tangible rewards or preferment for individual members, influence on psychological rewards or preferment, and dominance of the communications process. These resources are mutually reinforcing, which further enhances the influence of a skillful leader.

Specific events outside the House, such as the growth of the President as a legislator, can increase or decrease the ability of the leaders to use their resources. Likewise, events inside the

House, such as the removal of the Speaker's committee appointment power in 1911 or the restoration of a 21-day rule in 1965, can either limit or enhance the resources available to the leaders.

Each leader can also use his own skills to increase the legislative impact of available resources. Some leaders choose to let resources lie idle; others seek to exploit every possibility. For example, before 1909-11 the Speaker had greater opportunities to use the rules and offer tangible rewards than he has had since. But skillful post-1911 Speakers have been able to use the rules to promote legislative results they desire and have been able to insinuate themselves into the committee assignment process at critical spots.

The two resources most open to growth or shrinkage because of the capabilities of individual leaders are influence over psychological preferment and dominance of the communications process.

Party is the primary symbol of loyalty for the individual member. It is also the primary measure of "normal" or acceptable behavior with reference to legislation. For most members loyalty is instinctive; they feel uncomfortable when acting contrary to the wishes of fellow party members and leaders.

The potential psychological hold of the party leaders over most of their members is great. They have been chosen by a majority of the members. They have some tangible resources that increase their power and prestige. They are also in a favorable location for approving or disapproving the behavior of the party's members. The need for approval is great in most men, especially in politicians; thus most members of the House behave in ways they think pleasing to the leaders. Part of this behavior will include aiding the passage or defeat of legislation in accord with the leaders' wishes. The individual member who feels the necessity of preserving his freedom to maneuver and stray occasionally from the party position has an alternative to outright and uncompromising dissent: he can bargain with the leaders.

The leaders are at the center of the communications network in the House and can use this position to influence legislative results. If they gain a reputation for supplying a constant flow of useful and reliable information to their members and if they give evidence of respecting the opinions that members communicate to them, their influence grows. They do not have the field to themselves, and they can never be assured of the full attention of all the members. But they have inbuilt advantages over other actual or potential competing communicators. Their largest advantage is that they have many opportunities to establish a relationship of trust and mutual respect.

*   *   *   *   *   *

During the past century, party leaders in the House have developed systematic and effective patterns for influencing the legislative behavior of the membership. Their activities have a two-fold impact on the degree to which the House contributes to the resolution of basic social conflicts, providing both order and efficiency in the legislative process. Thus each year the House is able to consider a large number of bills, many of which deal with the most controversial issues facing the nation. Congressional consideration can provide at least partial answers to these problems and can channel potentially disruptive disputes into a formal process that holds the promise of relief for all contestants.

On balance, the parties and their leaders have performed their tasks well. They have demonstrated a great capacity for change in response to internal and external conditions that threaten order and efficiency in the legislative process.

The public, however, has a right to demand an accounting for the quality of congressional action. The leaders can account for the quantity and efficiency of action, but their primary job is to help pass or defeat proposals originated and developed by others. Thus the performance of Congress and the quality of its response in legislating to meet the tangible needs of the country cannot be judged by studying congressional leadership alone. The role of other participants, especially the President, other executive officials, and the members of standing committees must be analyzed before the responsiveness and responsibility of congressional performance can accurately be judged.

# Analysis of Party Leadership

Materials on Congress published before 1967 contain only fragmentary information on the place and impact of party leadership in the House. The purpose of this appendix is to summarize what is available to individuals interested in the subject. In Chapter 1 the thrust of previous scholarly writing is summarized in five generalizations. This appendix indicates the extent, content, and degree of agreement in existing literature relevant to each of the generalizations in the hope of saving time and repetitive effort for those wishing to explore the topic further.

I. *Intraparty friendships are stronger than interparty friendships and this helps produce a feeling of party unity that can have legislative consequences.*

The literature on this point is not extensive, but it is virtually unanimous. Throughout the history of Congress, members have expressed the need for party government and party loyalty, and they have also identified one of the prime forces leading to a feeling of party loyalty: friendship and association with one's fellow members. Congressmen who participated in the Brookings Institution Round Tables in 1959 agreed that "it is much easier to become acquainted with party colleagues than political opponents." A Republican explained that "the system seems to prevent one's forming strong friendships on the other side of the aisle." A Democrat said, "I don't know more than a very few Republicans by sight."[1] Another Democratic member of the House testifies to the same effect: ". . . interparty friendships seldom become close ones. . . ."[2] Working knowledge

[1] Charles L. Clapp, *The Congressman* (Brookings Institution, 1963), p. 14.
[2] Frank Smith, *Congressman from Mississippi* (Pantheon. 1964), p. 146.

of the legislative needs and wants of colleagues is likely to be limited to one's own party. Requests from fellow party members are likely to have more weight for this reason. Some interparty friendships can also have important legislative consequences, however.[3]

II. *Action on the House floor can involve psychological pressures that push an individual member to act in accord with the majority of his party.*

The literature supporting this proposition is slim, but the degree of agreement is high. Perceptive members of the House have been more aware of this phenomenon than outsiders. The late Clem Miller, a Democratic member from California from 1959 to 1962, described vividly how the force of party loyalty develops on important floor votes. In one specific example he used, members who differed with most of the party on the merits of a bill were, in effect, "stared down" by their colleagues.

Another interesting series of votes occurred on the second housing bill. The Republicans proposed a series of limiting amendments. The southerners bounced up about forty strong to vote with the Republicans for the first amendment on a teller, pass-through count. The hostility on the part of other Democrats to this action was as visible as an unsheathed knife. Then, as each amendment came along fewer southerners arose with the Republicans, till at last there were only five left, conspicuously self-conscious.[4]

George Norris of Nebraska, a Republican member of the House from 1903 to 1913, observed the same phenomenon in the early part of this century.[5]

A study based on close observation of floor action suggested that party considerations are uppermost in many members' minds when important legislation reaches the floor. Members are anxious to go along with the party if possible, and their natural desires are heightened by leadership activity.[6] An intensive study of a decade of trade legislation reaches a related conclusion: that members do not con-

---

[3] See, for example, John F. Manley, "The House Committee on Ways and Means: Conflict Management in a Congressional Committee," *American Political Science Review*, Vol. 59 (December 1965), pp. 937-38, on the friendship and cooperation between Chairman Wilbur Mills of the Ways and Means Committee and John Byrnes, ranking Republican member on the same committee.

[4] Clem Miller, *Member of the House* (Scribner's, 1962), p. 111.

[5] George Norris, *Fighting Liberal* (Collier, 1961), pp. 105, 134-35.

[6] Lewis A. Froman, Jr., and Randall B. Ripley, "Conditions for Party Leadership: The Case of the House Democrats," *American Political Science Review*, Vol. 59 (March 1965), pp. 52-63.

sciously express "party interest" as the criterion for their policy stands, but that they prefer "to act in ways helpful to the party" when possible.[7]

The leaders increase the pressure on their members during floor consideration of bills by making more specific requests at this stage than in committee, where success is usually harder to attain.[8]

**III.** *There are other loyalties in addition to party that motivate members, the most important of which is loyalty to the constituency.*

The literature on this point is relatively extensive. The findings cover a number of important aspects of the relations between the constituency and the member, although they are far from exhaustive.

Members are never solely party-oriented. Interest or ethnic groups in the individual's constituency, the local party as distinguished from the national or congressional party, friends and associates in state and local government or in the federal executive branch, and some more or less abstract principles, all impinge on the member and are potential competitors for part of his loyalty.[9]

The most consistently important competitor is constituency: the wishes, real or imagined, of the individual member's district. Knowledge about the member's voting record or policy positions is not usually widespread in his district, but since "the Congressman is a dealer in increments and margins," the politically active constituents are in a position to influence him.[10]

The relationship between constituency, constituency party, and congressional party is unclear. One study concluded that "the public's contribution to party irregularity in Congress is not so much a matter of encouraging or requiring its representatives to deviate from their parties as it is of the public having so little information that the irregularity of Congressmen and the ineffectiveness of the congressional parties have scant impact at the polls."[11] This statement ig-

[7] Raymond A. Bauer, Ithiel de Sola Pool, and Lewis A. Dexter, *American Business and Public Policy* (Atherton, 1963), p. 449. See also pp. 421-23.

[8] See, for example, Holbert N. Carroll, *The House of Representatives and Foreign Affairs* (University of Pittsburgh Press, 1958), pp. 32-34, 262-69.

[9] Duncan MacRae, Jr., *Dimensions of Congressional Voting* (University of California Press, 1958), pp. 278-80.

[10] Warren E. Miller and Donald E. Stokes, "Constituency Influence in Congress," *American Political Science Review*, Vol. 57 (March 1963), p. 55. See also Donald E. Stokes and Warren E. Miller, "Party Government and the Saliency of Congress," *Public Opinion Quarterly*, Vol. 26 (Winter 1962), pp. 531-47.

[11] Stokes and Miller, "Party Government." p. 546.

nores an important alternative: ignorance and apathy on the part of
the voters can also allow individual members of Congress to be *more*
loyal to the party than actual feelings in the constituency would dictate. A study of state legislatures points out that local parties are not
much interested in communicating their policy positions to elected
representatives. One of the conclusions reached in this study seems to
apply to the House: "While organization pressure may produce party
responsibility, it is not a necessary condition for cohesion in legislative parties."[12]

Furthermore, the individual congressman must judge which views
are representative of his whole constituency. He often tends to choose
those views that reinforce his own preferences.[13]

Both intensive and extensive roll call analysis show party to be su-
perior to apparent district interests. For example, party has a greater
impact on roll call voting than urban-rural, foreign-native, or north-
south differences.[14]

Despite competition, party commands the loyalty of most members
much of the time. This is not necessarily because it can outcompete
other objects of loyalty in a direct confrontation. Instead, party is
often most effective in mobilizing its members as a reasonably solid
unit when the competitors are silent. Huitt suggests how the party
becomes especially important to the individual members in these situations:

> In the pressure of technical and complicated legislation the individual
> member is greatly in need of cues which will help him decide what to
> do. On most issues . . . there is no clearly discernible constituency in-
> terest. On many there will not even be a position which seems the ap-
> propriate one for a politician with his bundle of commitments. The
> party in this situation provides invaluable assistance when it suggests a
> party position. Beyond that, the party usually has an emotional appeal
> for its members which is reinforced by the sharing of common hazards
> under its banner at election time. There are very practical selfish reasons

[12] Thomas A. Flinn, "Party Responsibility in the States: Some Causal Factors,"
*American Political Science Review*, Vol. 58 (March 1964), p. 61.

[13] See Bauer, Pool and Dexter, *American Business*, Chap. 32; and Lewis A. Dexter,
"The Representative and His District," in Nelson W. Polsby, Robert A. Dentler and
Paul A. Smith (eds.), *Politics and Social Life* (Houghton Mifflin, 1963), pp. 495-512.

[14] Julius Turner, *Party and Constituency: Pressures on Congress* (Johns Hopkins
Press, 1951). For additional extensive analysis see David R. Mayhew, *Party Loyalty
Among Congressmen* (Harvard University Press, 1966). For examples of intensive roll
call analysis that make the same general point see Roland J. Pennock, "Party and
Constituency in Postwar Agricultural Price-Support Legislation," *Journal of Politics*,
Vol. 18 (May 1956), pp. 167-210; and Randall B. Ripley, "Congress Considers Federal
Aid to Airports," and "Bargaining in the House: the Food Stamp Act of 1964." (un-
published manuscripts prepared for a Brookings Institution project).

for maintaining the party tie, too; Congress is organized on party lines and in the hands of the leaders are many small and a few large resources for strengthening the hand of the loyal partisan.[15]

Members, of course, are not mere adding machines who calculate the various pressures on them and respond with an appropriate pattern of behavior. They have their own policy preferences. Thus two men from the same party coming from the same district in two successive Congresses can vote differently on the same issues.[16]

IV. *Party leaders seem to be especially important in influencing the roll call behavior of their members.*

The extensive literature based on roll call analysis is unanimous in reaching this conclusion. There have been few qualitative studies to explore the implications of the quantitative work, however.

Judged by roll call votes, party is the most important single factor in the internal operations of the House and in influencing the behavior of individual members. Truman has said that "the persistent reality of party in the functioning of the [House] chamber is unmistakable."[17] "The party label is clearly the single most reliable indicator of congressional voting behavior" although "it is admittedly somewhat less than perfect."[18] Turner made the same point when he said, "Party pressure seems to be more effective than any other pressure on congressional voting."[19] Other students of Congress have accepted this evidence and have repeated these statements in a number of forms.[20]

The impact of party on voting appears to be different when the House is dealing with foreign affairs from when it is dealing with domestic policies and programs. There has not been general agreement,

[15] Ralph K. Huitt, "Congressional Organization and Operations in the Field of Money and Credit," in Commission on Money and Credit, *Fiscal and Debt Management Policies* (Prentice-Hall, 1963), p. 419.

[16] Lewis A. Froman, Jr., "The Importance of Individuality in Voting in Congress," *Journal of Politics*, Vol. 25 (May 1963), pp. 324-32; and Lee F. Anderson, "Individuality in Voting in Congress: A Research Note," *Midwest Journal of Political Science*, Vol. 8 (November 1964), pp. 425-29.

[17] David B. Truman, "The State Delegations and the Structure of Party Voting in the U.S. House of Representatives," *American Political Science Review*, Vol. 50 (December 1956), p. 1045.

[18] *Ibid.*, p. 1023. See also David B. Truman, *The Congressional Party* (Wiley, 1959), pp. vi, vii.

[19] Turner, *Party and Constituency*, p. 23.

[20] See, for example, V. O. Key, Jr., *Politics, Parties and Pressure Groups* (Crowell, 1964, 5th ed.), p. 678.

however, on the nature of this difference. An early study concluded that party is reflected more strongly in voting on foreign affairs than is region.[21] More recent studies have indicated that increasing isolationist voting is the result of region and not party, especially among southern Democrats and, to some extent, mountain state Democrats and midwestern Republicans.[22] There is also some dispute over whether cohesiveness on foreign problems is directly related to party leadership. One well known study by Dahl found a direct relationship.[23] A later study by Westerfield suggested that party plays a somewhat more limited role in foreign affairs.[24]

The structure of roll call voting leaves room for significant leadership activity. One study analyzed the stability of voting coalitions in the House and concluded that "The exact membership and relative strength and position of blocs change over time. The crucial features of the change seem to be the content of issues and *perhaps the skill and strategy of leaders.*"[25]

Truman argues that roll call voting in the House in both parties shows a "structural stability." But within some limits there is a good deal of looseness about the coalitions and combinations making up the majority within each party on a variety of votes. There were no permanent voting blocs that could be clearly identified by the regional or demographic characteristics of constituencies. This leaves large areas in which the influence of the party leaders can be brought to bear. The explanation of the voting behavior of individual members of the House

> . . . lies in peculiarities of the power structure in their constituencies, in special features of the attitudes and values of the individual representatives, and in the characteristics of their associations within the legislature. The last two of these three point to discretionary features of the voting choice. The factors of individual attitude and intralegislative

[21] George Grassmuck, *Sectional Biases in Congress on Foreign Policy* (Johns Hopkins Press, 1951).

[22] See Malcolm E. Jewell, "Evaluating the Decline of Southern Internationalism through Senatorial Roll Call Votes," *The Journal of Politics*, Vol. 21 (November 1959), pp. 624-46; Leroy N. Rieselbach, "The Demography of the Congressional Vote on Foreign Aid, 1939-58," *American Political Science Review*, Vol. 58 (September 1964), pp. 577-88; and Bruce L. R. Smith, "Isolationist Voting in the U.S. House of Representatives," *Public Policy*, Vol. 12 (1963), pp. 337-70.

[23] Robert A. Dahl, *Congress and Foreign Policy* (Harcourt, Brace, 1950).

[24] H. Bradford Westerfield, *Foreign Policy and Party Politics* (Yale University Press, 1955).

[25] William Riker and Donald Niemi, "Stability of Coalitions on Roll Calls in the House of Representatives," *American Political Science Review*, Vol. 56 (March 1962), p. 65. Italics added.

relations, moreover, may be subject to influence from within the legislative party, perhaps especially from the party leader. . . .[26]

Truman suggests that the floor leaders can make a difference in voting behavior. Their votes and activity on important roll calls can give the cue to most of their party's members.[27] They are not alone as cue-givers on the House floor. State delegations, senior members from similar constituencies, and party colleagues on committees can all influence individual members of the House in their voting on the floor. But, if the voting preferences of the elected leaders clash with the preferences of the other cue-givers there is some evidence that, on roll call votes, the wishes of the elected leaders will prevail with the majority of the members of the party. This occurs, for example, when the wishes of the leaders and committee chairmen clash directly.[28]

In short, no other single influence seems to be as predictive as the position of the floor leaders. State delegations vary radically in their degree of cohesion.[29] Furthermore, the party contingents on standing committees do not seem to be a consistently important influence on the roll call voting behavior of individual members.[30] The program of the President, which is also the program of the President's party in Congress, had a "centripetal effect." This "gave coherence to . . . leadership structures and meaning to the roles of the leaders, especially those in the principal 'elective' positions."[31] Likewise, it gave to the member of the majority party something substantive to which he could point, and something for him to accomplish. By extension, alternative minority proposals perform the same function for both leaders and members of the minority party.

The most provocative published study to date that suggests *why* the leaders are such effective cue-givers deals with the Connecticut House of Representatives. Individual members have predispositions and perceptions that work in favor of the party. These enhance the impact of the leaders: *"Pressure is not experienced, it is anticipated."* Pressure is not necessary for effective party leadership. The leaders can establish patterns of loyal behavior among most of the membership without using pressure or even possessing resources that would allow the development of pressure. The automatic competitive aspects of legislative life also help to generate loyalty to party.

[26] Truman, *The Congressional Party*, pp. 190-91.
[27] *Ibid.*, pp. 245-46.
[28] *Ibid.*, pp. 140, 242.
[29] *Ibid.*, p. 268.
[30] *Ibid.*, p. 275.
[31] *Ibid.*, pp. 289-90.

This analysis of the situation in Connecticut is suggestive for what might be found in the national House of Representatives. "These party-favoring perceptions—strong in some cases, weak in others—are the raw materials the party leader has to work with. He does not have to create anew the sense of loyalty, the community feeling, or the combative team spirit within the party. What he must do, however, is to translate party feeling into willingness to take *his* instructions."[32]

## V. *Party machinery has an impact in persuading members to support the party leaders.*

What little literature there is on this point supports the proposition strongly. The present Democratic whip organization is controlled by the leaders and helps them obtain the maximum number of favorable votes for parts of the President's program.[33] The Republican Policy Committee in recent years has given limited, but important, help to Republican leaders in their attempts to develop unanimous opposition to Democratic proposals and support for Republican alternatives.[34]

[32] James D. Barber, "Leadership Strategies for Legislative Party Cohesion," *The Journal of Politics*, Vol. 28 (May 1966), pp. 347-67. Quotations from pp. 352 and 358. Italics in the original.

[33] Randall B. Ripley, "The Party Whip Organizations in the United States House of Representatives," *American Political Science Review*, Vol. 58 (September 1964), pp. 561-76.

[34] Charles O. Jones, *Party and Policy Making: The House Republican Policy Committee* (Rutgers University Press, 1964).

# APPENDIX B

# Nature of the Interview Sample, Eighty-eighth Congress

In footnote 2 of Chapter 6 the method for selecting House members for interviewing was explained. In order to check the representative-ness of the interview sample on grounds other than those used to stra-tify it at the outset, nine further tests were applied to the sample after the interviews were completed. The Democrats interviewed were slightly less loyal to the party (on two tests other than the one used for stratification) than all Democrats. They were almost perfectly rep-resentative of all party members in terms of the nature of their dis-trict: urban, suburban, or rural (as defined by *Congressional Quarter-ly*). The Democratic respondents were also quite representative on the basis of the 1962 election results. The spread on the basis of the 1964 election results was less representative, with no Democratic vic-tor by close margins (under 52 percent) included in the sample. The interviewees were generally representative of socio-economic spread in Democratic districts, judged by median income, percent urban (using the census definition), percent Negro, and percent owner-occupied dwellings. Several minor overrepresentations indicate that the respondents came from slightly more well-to-do districts than the average Democrat.

The Republicans interviewed also tended to be slightly less loyal to the party (on the two additional tests) than all Republicans. On the basis of urban, suburban, or rural character of the district the Repub-lican sample approximated the actual situation for all Republicans in the Eighty-eighth Congress. The sample is skewed slightly toward safer seats in the 1962 election but is almost perfectly representative of the electoral margin of those Republicans re-elected in 1964. The socio-economic spread of the districts represented by the interviewees is generally good, but slightly weighted toward those of higher socio-economic status than the average.

The following two tables are presented as fair samples of the nine tests.

TABLE B-1

## Margin of Electoral Victory, Median Income of District, and Percentage of Urban Population in District for All Democrats, Eighty-eighth Congress, and the Interview Sample of Thirty-five Democrats

| Characteristics | Percent of All Democrats (N = 256) | Percent of Respondents (N = 35) |
|---|---|---|
| *1962 Margin of Electoral Victory* *(Percent of Vote)* | | |
| 50–51.99 | 6 | 11 |
| 52–54.99 | 10 | 9 |
| 55–59.99 | 20 | 17 |
| 60 and over | 64 | 63 |
| Total | 100[a] | 100 |
| *Median Income of District* | | |
| $1,000–$3,999 | 25 | 17 |
| 4,000– 4,999 | 18 | 20 |
| 5,000– 5,999 | 27 | 31 |
| 6,000– 7,999 | 31 | 31 |
| Total | 107[b] | 99[b] |
| *Percentage of Urban Population in District*[c] | | |
| 0–39.9 | 18 | 20 |
| 40–59.9 | 24 | 20 |
| 60–89.9 | 24 | 23 |
| 90 and over | 34 | 37 |
| Total | 100 | 100 |

[a] Because of peculiarities in the electoral situation in Alabama in 1962 the eight Alabama Democrats in the Eighty-eighth Congress are omitted from this calculation.

[b] Percentages do not always total 100 because of rounding.

[c] This is based on the census definition of urban population.

TABLE B-2

## Margin of Electoral Victory, Median Income of District, and Percentage of Urban Population in District for All Republicans, Eighty-eighth Congress, and the Interview Sample of Twenty-five Republicans

| Characteristics | | Percent of All Republicans (N = 178) | Percent of Respondents (N = 25) |
|---|---|---|---|
| *1962 Margin of Electoral Victory* | | | |
| *(Percent of Vote)* | | | |
| *50–51.99* | | 6 | 0 |
| *52–54.99* | | 16 | 12 |
| *55–59.99* | | 29 | 28 |
| *60 and over* | | 49 | 60 |
| | Total | 100 | 100 |
| *Median Income of District* | | | |
| $2,000–$4,999 | | 21 | 16 |
| 5,000– 5,999 | | 34 | 36 |
| 6,000– 6,999 | | 25 | 20 |
| 7,000– 7,999 | | 21 | 28 |
| | Total | 101[a] | 100 |
| *Percentage of Urban Population in District*[b] | | | |
| *0–49.9* | | 26 | 20 |
| *50–69.9* | | 33 | 32 |
| *70–89.9* | | 20 | 28 |
| *90 and over* | | 20 | 20 |
| | Total | 99[a] | 100 |

[a] Percentages do not always total 100 because of rounding.
[b] This is based on the census definition of urban population.

# APPENDIX C

# Analysis of Party Loyalty Scores, Eighty-eighth Congress

The following four tables present the statistical material on which the most unexpected findings of the last section of Chapter 6 were based.

The party loyalty score is derived by subtracting *Congressional Quarterly's* party opposition score from its party unity score. These two scores represent the percentage of the time that each member voted for or against the majority of his party when more than 50 percent of each party voted against one another.

TABLE C-1

## Party Loyalty Scores by Party, Region, and Urban-Suburban-Rural Nature of District, Eighty-eighth Congress[a]

| Democrats | Number of Members | Party Loyalty Score |
|---|---|---|
| Urban—all Democrats | 95 | 72 |
| South | 18 | 48 |
| North | 55 | 79 |
| West | 22 | 73 |
| | | |
| Suburban—all Democrats | 31 | 76 |
| South | 4 | 62 |
| North | 19 | 80 |
| West | 8 | 74 |
| | | |
| Rural—all Democrats | 125 | 41 |
| South | 72 | 20 |
| North | 27 | 71 |
| West | 26 | 68 |
| | | |
| *Republicans* | | |
| Urban—all Republicans | 35 | 52 |
| South and Border | 5 | 77 |
| Northeast | 7 | 6 |
| West | 11 | 54 |
| Midwest | 12 | 67 |
| | | |
| Suburban—all Republicans | 37 | 41 |
| South and Border | 2 | 70 |
| Northeast | 22 | 25 |
| West | 5 | 67 |
| Midwest | 8 | 61 |
| | | |
| Rural—all Republicans | 103 | 64 |
| South and Border | 11 | 64 |
| Northeast | 25 | 49 |
| West | 12 | 62 |
| Midwest | 55 | 70 |

[a] Classification of districts as urban, suburban, or rural is based on the study in *Congressional Quarterly Almanac* (1963), pp. 1170–84.

TABLE C-2

## Party Loyalty Scores by Party, Region, and Seniority, Eighty-eighth Congress

| Democrats | Number of Members | Party Loyalty Score |
|---|---|---|
| 1–3 Terms—all Democrats | 94 | 67 |
|     South | 23 | 34 |
|     North | 41 | 78 |
|     West | 30 | 75 |
| 4–7 Terms—all Democrats | 72 | 54 |
|     South | 27 | 23 |
|     North | 31 | 77 |
|     West | 14 | 62 |
| 8 Terms and over—all Democrats | 85 | 48 |
|     South | 44 | 25 |
|     North | 29 | 75 |
|     West | 12 | 69 |
| *Republicans* | | |
| 1–2 Terms—all Republicans | 64 | 62 |
|     South and Border | 9 | 67 |
|     Northeast | 16 | 37 |
|     West | 10 | 63 |
|     Midwest | 29 | 75 |
| 3–6 Terms—all Republicans | 66 | 53 |
|     South and Border | 7 | 67 |
|     Northeast | 21 | 30 |
|     West | 15 | 58 |
|     Midwest | 23 | 65 |
| 7 Terms and over—all Republicans | 45 | 54 |
|     South and Border | 2 | 76 |
|     Northeast | 17 | 36 |
|     West | 3 | 57 |
|     Midwest | 23 | 65 |

## TABLE C-3
### Party Loyalty Scores by Party, Region, and Median Income of District, Eighty-eighth Congress[a]

| | Democrats | | | | | | | |
|---|---|---|---|---|---|---|---|---|
| Median Income | All | | South | | North | | West | |
| | N[b] | PL[c] | N | PL | N | PL | N | PL |
| $1,000–1,999 | 1 | −27 | 1 | −27 | — | — | — | — |
| 2,000–2,999 | 12 | 24 | 10 | 13 | 1 | 79 | 1 | 84 |
| 3,000–3,999 | 50 | 27 | 41 | 20 | 6 | 63 | 3 | 47 |
| 4,000–4,999 | 46 | 45 | 25 | 29 | 13 | 72 | 6 | 58 |
| 5,000–5,999 | 67 | 71 | 5 | 56 | 29 | 78 | 23 | 73 |
| 6,000–6,999 | 62 | 75 | 2 | 20 | 44 | 78 | 16 | 73 |
| 7,000–7,999 | 14 | 81 | — | — | 8 | 84 | 6 | 77 |
| 8,000–8,999 | 1 | 88 | — | — | — | — | 1 | 88 |

| | Republicans | | | | | | | | | |
|---|---|---|---|---|---|---|---|---|---|---|
| Median Income | All | | So. & Border | | Northeast | | West | | Midwest | |
| | N | PL | N | PL | N | PL | N | PL | N | PL |
| $1,000–1,999 | — | — | — | — | — | — | — | — | — | — |
| 2,000–2,999 | 1 | 53 | 1 | 53 | — | — | — | — | — | — |
| 3,000–3,999 | 5 | 69 | 2 | 81 | — | — | — | — | 3 | 60 |
| 4,000–4,999 | 29 | 68 | 6 | 71 | 5 | 35 | — | — | 18 | 76 |
| 5,000–5,999 | 59 | 73 | 5 | 74 | 16 | 50 | 11 | 62 | 27 | 69 |
| 6,000–6,999 | 44 | 52 | 1 | 75 | 17 | 30 | 8 | 65 | 18 | 67 |
| 7,000–7,999 | 26 | 36 | 2 | 35 | 11 | 15 | 7 | 52 | 6 | 55 |
| 8,000–8,999 | 9 | 47 | 1 | 66 | 4 | 26 | 2 | 51 | 2 | 74 |
| 9,000–9,999 | 2 | 71 | — | — | 1 | 62 | — | — | 1 | 81 |

[a] Data on median income are taken from the *Congressional District Data Book* for the Eighty-eighth Congress, item 138.

[b] N stands for number of members.

[c] PL stands for party loyalty score. The rank order correlation coefficient for the party loyalty score of all Democrats is 1.0, which means that there is a probability of less than 1 percent that this pattern occurred by chance. The rank order correlation coefficient for the party loyalty score of all Republicans is −0.19, which means that a meaningful pattern is not present.

TABLE C-4

## Party Loyalty Scores by Party, Region, and Percentage of Owner-Occupied Dwellings in District, Eighty-eighth Congress[a]

| | Democrats | | | | | | | |
|---|---|---|---|---|---|---|---|---|
| Percentage of Owner-Occupied Dwellings | All | | South | | North | | West | |
| | N[b] | PL[c] | N | PL | N | PL | N | PL |
| *Under 30* | 21 | 77 | — | — | 20 | 77 | 1 | 81 |
| *30–34.9* | 3 | 89 | — | — | 3 | 89 | — | — |
| *35–39.9* | 3 | 80 | — | — | 1 | 82 | 2 | 85 |
| *40–44.9* | 9 | 69 | 1 | −27 | 6 | 82 | 2 | 78 |
| *45–49.9* | 12 | 56 | 5 | 23 | 3 | 83 | 4 | 77 |
| *50–54.9* | 20 | 54 | 11 | 35 | 5 | 75 | 4 | 80 |
| *55–59.9* | 35 | 46 | 19 | 23 | 11 | 75 | 5 | 65 |
| *60–64.9* | 50 | 51 | 26 | 29 | 15 | 78 | 9 | 72 |
| *65–69.9* | 52 | 49 | 23 | 21 | 12 | 76 | 17 | 69 |
| *70 and over* | 46 | 65 | 9 | 41 | 25 | 74 | 12 | 66 |

| | Republicans | | | | | | | | | |
|---|---|---|---|---|---|---|---|---|---|---|
| Percentage of Owner-Occupied Dwellings | All | | So. & Border | | Northeast | | West | | Midwest | |
| | N | PL | N | PL | N | PL | N | PL | N | PL |
| *Under 30* | 1 | −5 | — | — | 1 | −5 | — | — | — | — |
| *30–34.9* | 1 | −1 | — | — | 1 | −1 | — | — | — | — |
| *35–39.9* | — | — | — | — | — | — | — | — | — | — |
| *40–44.9* | — | — | — | — | — | — | — | — | — | — |
| *45–49.9* | 3 | 48 | — | — | 2 | 36 | — | — | 1 | 71 |
| *50–54.9* | 5 | 39 | — | — | 1 | 7 | 4 | 47 | — | — |
| *55–59.9* | 9 | 46 | 1 | 66 | — | — | 4 | 57 | 2 | 71 |
| *60–64.9* | 23 | 58 | 5 | 71 | 7 | 19 | 6 | 72 | 5 | 74 |
| *65–69.9* | 59 | 57 | 7 | 59 | 20 | 38 | 9 | 60 | 23 | 73 |
| *70 and over* | 74 | 60 | 5 | 78 | 20 | 44 | 5 | 57 | 44 | 66 |

[a] Data on percentage of owner-occupied dwellings are taken from the *Congressional District Data Book* for the Eighty-eighth Congress, item 193.

[b] N stands for number of members.

[c] PL stands for party loyalty score. The rank order correlation coefficient for the party loyalty score of all Democrats in the last six categories is −0.03, which means that a meaningful pattern is not present. The rank order correlation coefficient for the party loyalty score of all Republicans in the last six categories is 0.77, which means that there is more than a 5 percent probability that this pattern occurred by chance. (At the 5 percent significance level the value of the coefficient with an N of 6 must be .886 or higher.)

# Bibliography

The footnotes throughout this volume indicate the literature that has been directly useful. This short bibliography contains those items that someone interested in pursuing this subject further should turn to first.

For a more complete bibliography on this and closely related subjects see Charles O. Jones and Randall B. Ripley, *The Study of Party in Congress: A Bibliography and Research Guide* (University of Arizona Institute of Government Research, 1966).

Alexander, DeAlva S., *History and Procedure of the House of Representatives*. Boston and New York: Houghton Mifflin, 1916.

Atkinson, C. R., and Charles A. Beard, "The Syndication of the Speakership," *Political Science Quarterly*, Vol. 26, September 1911, pp. 381-414.

Bailey, Stephen K., and Howard D. Samuel, *Congress at Work*. New York: Holt, 1952.

Barnes, James A., *John G. Carlisle*. New York: Dodd Mead, 1931.

Berdahl, Clarence A., "Some Notes on Party Membership in Congress," *American Political Science Review*, Vol. 43, 1949, pp. 309-21, 492-508, 721-34.

Binkley, Wilfred E., *President and Congress* (3rd ed.). New York: Vintage, 1962.

Blaine, James G., *Twenty Years of Congress: From Lincoln to Garfield*. 2 Vols. Norwich, Conn.: Henry Bill Publishing Co., 1884-86.

Bolling, Richard, *House Out of Order*. New York: Dutton, 1965.

Brown, George R., *The Leadership of Congress*. Indianapolis: Bobbs-Merrill, 1922.

Busbey, L. White, *Uncle Joe Cannon*. New York: Holt, 1927.

Chiu, Chang-wei, *The Speaker of the House of Representatives Since 1896*. New York: Columbia University Press, 1928.

Clapp, Charles L., *The Congressman: His Work as He Sees It*. Washington: The Brookings Institution, 1963.

Clark, Champ, *My Quarter Century of American Politics*. 2 Vols. New York: Harpers, 1920.

Dunn, Arthur Wallace, *From Harrison to Harding*. 2 Vols. New York: Putnam's, 1922.

Follett, Mary P., *The Speaker of the House of Representatives*. New York: Longmans, Green and Co., 1896.

Galloway, George, *History of the United States House of Representatives*. New York: Crowell, 1962.

Gwinn, William R., *Uncle Joe Cannon, Archfoe of Insurgency*. New York: Bookman, 1957.

Hasbrouck, Paul D., *Party Government in the House of Representatives*. New York: Macmillan, 1927.

Hechler, Kenneth, *Insurgency*. New York: Columbia University Press, 1941.

Jones, Charles O., *Party and Policy-Making: The House Republican Policy Committee*. New Brunswick: Rutgers University Press, 1964.

Korngold, Ralph, *Thaddeus Stevens*. New York: Harcourt, Brace, 1955.

Lindsey, David, *Sunset Cox, Irrepressible Democrat*. Detroit: Wayne State University Press, 1959.

Lowell, A. Lawrence, "The Influence of Party Upon Legislation in England and America," in *Annual Report of the American Historical Association*, Vol. 1, H. Doc. 702, 86 Cong. 1 sess. Washington: Government Printing Office, 1902.

Luce, Robert, *Legislative Procedure*. Boston: Houghton Mifflin, 1922.

McCown, Ada C., *The Congressional Conference Committee*. New York: Columbia University Press, 1927.

MacNeil, Neil, *Forge of Democracy*. New York: McKay, 1963.

MacRae, Duncan, Jr., *Dimensions of Congressional Voting*. Berkeley and Los Angeles: University of California Press, 1958.

Martin, Joe, *My First Fifty Years in Politics*. New York: McGraw-Hill, 1960.

Miller, Clem, *Member of the House*. New York: Scribner's, 1962.

Peabody, Robert L., and Nelson W. Polsby, eds., *New Perspectives on the House of Representatives*. Chicago: Rand-McNally, 1963.

Robinson, William, *Thomas B. Reed*. New York: Dodd Mead, 1930.

Summers, Festus P., *William L. Wilson and Tariff Reform*. New Brunswick: Rutgers University Press, 1953.

Timmons, Bascom N., *Garner of Texas: A Personal History*. New York: Harper, 1948.

Truman, David B., ed., *The Congress and America's Future*. Englewood Cliffs, N.J.: Prentice-Hall, 1965.

Truman, David B., *The Congressional Party*. New York: Wiley, 1959.

Turner, Julius, *Party and Constituency: Pressures on Congress*. Baltimore: Johns Hopkins Press, 1951.

Watson, James E., *As I Knew Them*. Indianapolis: Bobbs-Merrill, 1936.

# Index